FIXED

Revised and updated

Cheating, doping, rape
and murder . . . The inside track
on Australia's racing industry

MATTHEW BENNS

EBURY
PRESS

As the title suggests, this book makes a number of serious allegations concerning the racing industry in Australia. However, it should not be assumed that any person named or referred to in this book is involved in any unlawful activity: many individuals' names are mentioned by way of background and context to these stories, and care must be taken to read all relevant material in this book concerning any person named or identified.

An Ebury Press book
Published by Random House Australia Pty Ltd
Level 3, 100 Pacific Highway, North Sydney NSW 2060
www.randomhouse.com.au

First published by Ebury Press in 2012

This revised edition published in 2013

Addresses for companies within the Random House Group can be found at
www.randomhouse.com.au/offices

National Library of Australia
Cataloguing-in-Publication entry

Benns, Matthew
Fixed: cheating, doping, rape and murder: the inside track
on Australia's racing industry / Matthew Benns

ISBN 978 085798 326 8 (pbk)

Horse racing–Australia
Horse racing–Australia–Corrupt practices
Doping in horse racing–Australia
Gambling–Australia

364.163

Cover design by Adam Yazxhi, Maxco
Cover photograph courtesy of iStock
Typeset in Minion Pro 12.5 on 17pt by Midland Typesetters, Australia
Printed in Australia by Griffin Press, an Accredited ISO AS/NZS 14001:2004
Environmental Management System printer

Random House Australia uses papers that are natural, renewable and recyclable products and made from wood grown in sustainable forests. The logging and manufacturing processes are expected to conform to the environmental regulations of the country of origin.

'Some people show evil as a great racehorse shows breeding.'

Ernest Hemingway, *A Moveable Feast*

This book is dedicated to the 509 jockeys and countless horses who have died on racecourses in Australia.

INTRODUCTION

Black Caviar cruised out of the barrier for the $500,000 Goodwood Stakes at Morphettville in Adelaide in front of a record crowd of 30,000 on 9 May 2012. Almost every one of them had turned up to see the world's greatest racehorse clock up a record twenty-first victory from twenty-one starts. The bookies said that $1.04 was over the odds; Betstar boss Alan Eskander said that, even at that price, he was giving away 'some more free money'.[1]

And the mighty mare did not disappoint. Jockey Luke Nolen, his familiar salmon silks fluttering in the breeze, barely moved in the saddle as Black Caviar's eight rivals, hopelessly outclassed, pushed themselves to the limit, whips flailing, in her wake. When she effortlessly reached the post, she was a length and a quarter ahead of local sprinter We're Gonna Rock.

Nolen described it as 'just a working gallop', adding that 'she was never out of second gear'.[2] 'I'm not a punter,' Nolen said. 'I don't worry about margins. As long as she bloody wins, I don't care.'[3] Trainer Peter Moody was delighted with the relaxed pace. 'I told Luke that if he hit her I would hit him,' he joked.[4] 'No one's ever given us any more for winning by big spaces.'[5]

This was Australian horseracing at its finest. Black Caviar would soon fly to England to represent the nation against the best the world could produce at Royal Ascot. The English media was already sending out television crews to film her in training; Australia Post had released a commemorative stamp pack showing the first twenty wins by the world's highest-ranked sprinter. 'We cannot believe the amount of inquiries we are getting from here and overseas to do things with her,' said owner Neil Werrett.[6]

Surely it couldn't get any better? Black Caviar is a legendary horse, up there with the likes of Tulloch, Kingston Town and Phar Lap, and she is the face of Australian racing. It is an industry that earns millions of dollars, employs 50,000 people and delivers $5 billion in gross domestic product to the Australian economy. When equine influenza affected racing, the government handed over $235 million in compensation packages to keep the industry afloat. Race days in Australia attract thousands, ambassadors such as Jesinta Campbell and Laura Dundovic set the benchmark for high fashion, while marquee tents sponsored by Tooheys set the tone for alcoholic enjoyment.

But by the end of these days many women are staggering from the track, heels in hand, and appear in the newspapers spreadeagled and vomiting in the gutter. Black Caviar struggled at Royal Ascot. Jockey Luke Nolen took a pasting from the armchair critics who said he let her idle on the home stretch. The mighty mare won by a nose and it turned out she was carrying an injury. Like many things in racing, there were problems beneath the surface.

Racing has an ugly side. It is a place where horses are hit, doped and mistreated. Where jockeys' lives are put on the line for a pittance. Where trainers are placed under impossible pressure to win, or are bribed, threatened and cajoled into losing. Where bookies look for the fix and crooked punters come to launder money.

Away from the winning world of Black Caviar, there is another side to racing. This book tells you how the industry is fixed.

RACE 1
MURDER

'I have to meet a bloke,' said the dapper trainer and owner Les Samba. His killer.

Samba had flown to Melbourne from Adelaide for a weekend at the Inglis Yearling Horse Sale. He'd checked in at the Crown Metropol in Southbank on the evening of Saturday 26 February 2011, and the next morning had taken his hired silver Hyundai i45 sedan out to Tullamarine to look at yearlings at Oaklands Junction. It was cold and wet – Samba borrowed Inglis director Peter Heagney's waterproof jacket – but he hadn't allowed the weather to dampen his spirits. There had not been a hint of trouble. The sixty-year-old grandfather, regularly described with the euphemism 'racing identity', had no clue that he was just a few hours away from bleeding his life out on a seafront street.

Back at the Crown Metropol, Samba bumped into jockey Brent 'Babe' Thomson in the casino lobby bar. Thomson, who has won the Cox Plate four times in his career, asked if he fancied sharing a glass. 'I have to meet a bloke,' said Samba, declining.[1]

'He didn't look like he was too worried about anything,' Thomson said later. 'He wasn't edgy or stressed in the slightest. In fact, he looked pretty relaxed.' Thomson suggested they meet for dinner with a group of friends from the racing industry at upmarket Italian restaurant Giuseppe Arnaldo & Sons. But Samba was a man on a mission. 'He loved good wine and nice food, and the racing company,' said Thomson, 'so to knock that back he must have had a solid commitment.'[2]

Samba had less than two hours to live.

The grey-haired horseman drove to Port Melbourne and went for a drink at the Cricketer's Arms in Cruikshank Street. The pub was owned by Samba's former son-in-law, jockey Danny Nikolic. It was leased from Danny by three men, one of whom was Bernie Evans, the former Sydney and Carlton footballer. Evans was on duty that Sunday night.

The Cricketer's Arms is an old wharfies' pub and a regular haunt for racing types. The pub is small and has a narrow front bar, but even so Evans could not recall seeing Samba in the bar; he was busy with the dining rooms and beer garden. The CCTV cameras were trained on the till. One patron did recall seeing the well-known horseman. He told reporters from the *Sunday Herald Sun* that he had seen Samba 'exchange angry words' with a couple of patrons in the pub.[3] He described the men as heavies. 'It was a bit hostile,' he said.[4] Samba had a couple of drinks and left.

After that, it seems Samba returned to the Crown Metropol – grainy CCTV footage captured him leaving his room again at

9.04 pm – and drove out to the affluent beachside suburb of Middle Park, near St Kilda. True to his word, he was going to meet a bloke.

Samba parked his car on the seafront at Beaconsfield Parade and walked 100 metres along the footpath, halting outside number 299, a white mock-Tudor home. The man he met just after 9.30 pm was in his twenties or thirties and had light curly hair protruding from a dark hat. He pulled out a handgun and shot Samba in the torso. Terrified, Samba turned and ran across the road towards the beach. Witnesses heard three or four shots. The father of two collapsed on the road. The remorseless killer went after him, stood over the horse trainer's prostrate body and, holding the gun in both hands to steady his aim, fired again.

Les Samba was dead. His body lay face-down in the street, bleeding from bullet wounds to the torso and the head.

'It sickens me that my dad died alone,' said his daughter Victoria. 'I wish I had the chance to embrace him again and say a few things before he died – remind him how much I loved and appreciated him.'[5] She had been called by her brother Jonathon, who was with their mother, Deidre, at her Sydney home the next morning. 'I was getting ready for work,' Victoria said. 'I was standing just there when I took the call. I started screaming hysterically and just shaking, shouting "No, no," over and over.'[6]

Just two days earlier, her father had told her how proud he was that she had landed a job at a major bank – a career outside of racing. She had been face of the Melbourne Cup in 2005 and head of marketing for Racing NSW, but her father had seen her academic potential early. He had been the one to encourage her pursue an arts/law degree at Bond University. 'I have nightmares,' Victoria continued. 'I can visualise it happening. I can see it all in my head ... What happened to him makes me sick in the stomach.'[7]

Detective Inspector John Potter was firm in his belief: 'It was a planned murder.' But he didn't think it was a professional hit – the street was too busy. 'We are not dismissing the possibility of more than one person being involved in the shooting and more than one involved in the planning. We think it is a possibility that he was lured there.'[8]

The trouble was finding a motive. There were plenty, including the fact that Samba was a notorious ladies' man, but were any of these potential motives right? If the meeting had been on the up and up, why didn't Samba arrange for it to be held in the comfort of the hotel bar? Clearly, who he met and why he met him was the key.

A year on, Homicide Squad detective Senior Sergeant Steve McIntyre was still calling for people to come forward – particularly anyone who had chatted to Samba at the yearling sales and might be able to offer a clue as to just who he was going to meet that night. 'He did have a number of criminal associates but they are not necessarily Melbourne identities, so working through which ones are viable suspects is taking time,' said the detective.[9]

Following the money was not easy either. 'He did not have a simple financial profile by any means,' McIntyre said. 'It has been one of those long, slow, slogs and it's going to be that way for a while yet.'[10]

He wasn't kidding. Les Samba lived a lot of his life in the shadows. One racing identity who had seen Samba at the sales on the day he died told reporters from the *Sydney Morning Herald*: 'There's a lot of people … who are shocked that this could happen to Les, but maybe they're being a bit naive. Those people that knew Les well must have known he was a heavy hitter in areas that might be best described as "shady". When something like this happens, you can't help but think of that saying, "If you live by the sword you die by the sword." '[11]

The police investigation began close to home. Danny Nikolic had no idea his former father-in-law had been in his pub on the night he died. Nikolic's brother Tommy lives in the same street, about 300 metres from where Samba was shot. Nikolic had been with his three-year-old daughter Hilary, Samba's granddaughter, all weekend and was dropping her off with his ex-wife, Victoria, when Samba was killed. He voluntarily went to see the police a couple of days after the shooting and spent two hours talking to detectives without a lawyer before being allowed to leave. The police said he was not a suspect. He said the killing was a shock in one way, but then again not in another. 'You never expect anyone to be killed like that, but he did mix in a lot of unusual circles outside racing,' said Nikolic.[12]

Police were told there was some tension between Samba and Nikolic over the split with Victoria. Samba was pushing for a pretty tough settlement in favour of his daughter. A month after the murder, police raided the Gold Coast home of Nikolic's brother John, a former horse trainer in Queensland, who had also been in Melbourne for the horse sales that weekend. He and his wife, Yvette, had already been interviewed by police for six hours and released under caution. This time, police took telephone and computer data.

This was the latest in a string of problems John Nikolic had suffered. He'd handed in his training licence to Racing Queensland and sold his stables in 2010 after an official inquiry was launched into horses he trained. Baby Boom was a $1.30 favourite when it came in fourth on the Sunshine Coast. Punter and commission agent Neville Clements bet the horse to lose and cleaned up more than $50,000 on Betfair. Other trainers came forward and said they were unhappy with some of Danny Nikolic's rides. It was a stressful time. Then, at the start of 2012, Danny faced a number of assault charges. He has strenuously denied the charges and intends to fight them in court.

Nikolic's problems did not end there. In August 2012 Victoria police offered a $1 million reward for information leading to the arrest of Samba's killers. The announcement came after the investigation was moved to the Purana organised-crime task-force, which had solved the infamous Melbourne gangland slayings and investigated drug kingpin and horse-lover Tony Mokbel. Fat Tony was rotten and, before his trip to the big house, had grown uncomfortably close to a number of jockeys – one of whom was Danny Nikolic. In August 2012 *The Age*'s investigative reporter Nick McKenzie put together a report for ABC's *Four Corners* that revealed information the police had asked him to keep under wraps for several months. Victoria police were looking at suspected race fixing at a meeting at Cranbourne on the outskirts of Melbourne two months after Samba's slaying. Nikolic had ridden a brilliant race to win on Smoking Aces. But police investigating Samba's murder turned up information that allegedly showed all was not as it should have been with the race. Punters associated with Nikolic reportedly pocketed a cool $200,000.

Detectives started investigations into possible race-fixing, focusing on Nikolic, a former trainer and several other racing identities. Jockey Mark Zahra was also investigated for conspiring to ride his horse, Baikal, in a way that favoured Nikolic. Adding to the general discomfort of those involved, the Australian Crime Commission stepped in to question people too.

Neither jockey would comment when approached by the media. As investigators probed deeper, the scandal widened to include several other jockeys, professional punters and racing identities across Australia. In one case, one of the nation's most famous jockeys was alleged to have bet thousands of dollars on a rival horse to beat him in a race. Betfair confirmed it was investigating at least two dozen races and another top jockey.

Senior Detective Superintendent Gerry Ryan was happy to talk about the investigation, reinforcing to *The Age* that police would leave no stone unturned to ensure racing became squeaky-clean. Tellingly, he added, 'Certainly, I believe that if we're able to solve the race fixing and solve the issues that are emerging, we will certainly solve the murder.'[13] Samba's murder was promising to unravel a major corruption scandal in Australian racing.

Earlier, police had also looked at the involvement of former top jockey Gavin Eades. He denied having anything to do with Samba's murder but said that being a police suspect was putting his life at risk. 'It's been full-on. I'm shattered. He [Samba] was like me dad. I don't know who knocked him,' he told the *Herald Sun*. 'I knew him since I was a 12-year-old kid.'[14]

The police had also spoken to Gavin's brother Travis 'the Albino' Eades, a convicted road-rage killer who had previously been named as a suspect in the attempted shooting of Des 'Tuppence' Moran. Travis was reportedly furious about the police leak that suggested his involvement and denied it strenuously to friends. The reality was that Les Samba had kept some very unusual company in his career on the turf. And, as Gavin Eades thoughtfully observed, 'No one gets knocked like that for no reason.'[15]

Les Samba was born in Salzburg, Austria, in 1950 and arrived in Australia as a toddler. His younger brother Imre Zambo, a South Australian businessman, confirmed to the *Herald* that his brother had changed his name at young age. As with many things about Samba, not everything was as it appeared.

He had no background in racing but loved every part of it. One of the early highlights of his career had been working as a strapper for Rain Lover when it won the Melbourne Cup in 1969. Samba then became a trainer in Adelaide and was quickly drawn into racing's seedy underbelly. He also worked on the door of a dodgy Adelaide nightclub owned by Australia's biggest purveyor of vice, Abe Saffron, the original 'Mr Sin'. Saffron's henchman and business partner was Peter Farrugia, known as 'the Black Prince', and his favourite horse trainer was Les Samba.

Farrugia would get Samba to take his horses all over the country to race. Minutes before the barriers opened, Farrugia and his bodyguards would stride into the interstate betting ring and organise a massive plunge on his horses, betting big at the last minute in order to catch the bookies unawares and secure the best possible odds. His punting syndicate, known as the King's Cross Connection, bet big money and had great information. They punted on Samba-trained horses, which always offered good odds, having performed badly the week before. They came home like rockets. Chemically enhanced rockets.

It is perhaps no coincidence that another associate of Farrugia and Samba was the Western Australian trainer George Way, known as 'Beyond 2000' because he'd been hit with a twenty-year ban. His horses had tested positive to the performance-booster etorphine, known at the track as elephant juice. Not that Samba restricted himself to making horses go faster. He and a small doping crew would also drive through the night from Adelaide to dope opposition favourites with a strong sedative cooked up by a corrupt pharmacist. The author of *Underbelly*, John Silvester, wrote in *The Age*: 'One night his doping plans were extinguished when a security guard relieved himself in grass next to a Flemington stable, unaware this was the spot where Samba was hiding. For Les, it was a long trip back to Adelaide with the window down.' After lawyers forced the deletion of the name of another colourful Sydney racing identity, Silvester lamented: 'Scum is scum, whether it rings a bath or rings a lawyer.'[16]

Samba's association with such unsavoury characters made it increasingly difficult for him to work. John Schreck, nicknamed 'the Sheriff', who was the chief steward at the Australian Jockey Club (AJC) during those turbulent times in the 1980s, said: 'He couldn't get a permanent licence for New South Wales in my time because the Australian Jockey Club wasn't satisfied with certain aspects … Everybody I've ever spoken to said he was very good with horses, but so was George Way, and the AJC wouldn't license him either.'[17]

The irony was that Samba was indeed good with horses; he was an excellent judge of horseflesh but, it seems, a poor judge of people. Take Farrugia, for instance. He too died from bullet wounds – in 1992 after a standover job in Queensland went badly wrong. Bundaberg real-estate agent Ronald Mathewson had seen Farrugia and a couple of Sydney heavies arrive at his sheep station 150 kilometres south-west of Goondiwindi. Rightly fearing that they were there to kill him, or at least beat him to a senseless pulp, he ran inside and grabbed the .38-calibre pistol a neighbour had given him for just such an emergency. The gun went off in the struggle that followed, the bullet passing through Farrugia's lung and aorta before coming out through his shoulder. The jury in Mathewson's trial in Toowoomba cleared him of murder and the lesser charge of manslaughter. Afterwards, he said: 'From the moment it happened I have never had a problem with what I did.'[18]

Two years later Samba found himself in court. He was charged with cultivating a cannabis plantation on his property at Nangkita in South Australia. The jury were not told that, a few years earlier, police had discovered another plantation at his property near the town of Peebinga, also in South Australia. The absentee landlord Samba expressed his astonishment and dismay at the discoveries. The jury agreed, failing to find a verdict, which led to Samba's discharge. The Adelaide District Court judge may well have intended a certain level of irony when he commented: 'It would seem Mr Samba is probably the unluckiest man in the state with his farming ventures.'[19] Charged with Samba over that Nangkita crop was a racing industry associate. Four days before Samba was killed, the associate was arrested by police over the discovery of 3000 cannabis plants on the same land near Peebinga where the original crop was cultivated. Police said this man was not a suspect in Samba's killing.

Samba was not mixing in nice circles. In the 1980s he had come under investigation by the FBI because of his links to the Mafia. Reporter Yoni Bashan in the *Sunday Telegraph* revealed that Western Australia's chief racing investigator, the late Ron Goddard, had been passed information by US agencies on Samba's links to American crime families. 'We understood he had links to the Mafia and flew frequently to America,' said Bashan's source. 'We're not certain what he did over there – but he wasn't buying milk and bread for them.'[20]

Western Australia's chairman of stewards at the time, Fin Powrie, confirmed having extensive talks with Goddard about Samba's criminal links, but he knew nothing about the Mafia. Others did, however. Samba's links to a well-known Italian Mafia figure attracted an enormous amount of attention from the authorities.

Samba's links to racing identities in Western Australia also piqued the interest of the police. Weeks before his death, he had paid a visit to Bruce Allan 'Squiggley' Morris, who was a member of the Mr Asia drug syndicate. Morris had done time in 1996 for freighting cannabis to Sydney.

And Samba seemed to be living well beyond his means. The National Crime Authority (NCA) and the Australian Tax Office wondered how he and his wife Deidre had $1.2 million in spending money between 1995 and 1998, given that Samba's declared income was just $20,000. Samba claimed it was from gambling. But when the NCA investigators looked closely at the winning tickets he produced, they found he was overseas at the time he was supposed to have bought them. Samba admitted to having stashed $850,000 in cash in secret spots; Deidre said that if anything ever happened to Les, she would never be able to find all the money. He didn't like banks, apparently.

There were also questions about the ownership of several top-flight racehorses. The NCA were particularly interested in the $2.5-million Shogun Lodge, for which Deidre was listed as a part owner. Samba explained that he had bought the horse for a friend, and his wife had never received any of its winnings. In the end, Samba rendered the fight with the tax man academic by declaring himself and his wife bankrupt in 2002. And then things carried on as normal. The *Herald* revealed that, just before his death, Samba lost $1 million in cash that had been tucked away on the premises of a suspected arms dealer. Police had unearthed and seized Samba's stash in a raid.

Of even greater interest were Samba's partners in horseflesh at the time of his death. He owned several thoroughbreds in partnership with Sydney businessman Ron Medich. It was a very successful partnership. However, in October 2010 Medich was charged with masterminding the murder of his former business partner Michael McGurk. In the week before McGurk was gunned down outside his home in Cremorne, on Sydney's lower north shore, in September 2009, Medich and Samba had been in New Zealand together to sell Guillotine, a half-brother to Melbourne Cup winner Efficient. They paid $400,000 for Sea Lord as a yearling. The month before Samba's death, Sea Lord was the subject of a betting plunge at Randwick that cost bookmakers millions. The horse was backed in at the track from $3.00 to $1.90 before its win on 5 January 2011. Medich and Samba also raced Defiant Dame together; Flying Pegasus was raced in the names of Medich and Victoria Samba.

After McGurk's murder in 2009, detectives from Strike Force Narrenga said Samba was spoken to as a business associate of Medich's and as a peripheral player. When Samba was murdered, Medich, who was out on bail and fighting charges in the McGurk case, passed on his sympathies to the Samba family. Detective Inspector Potter said police were looking at a number of motives for Samba's killing. 'If you ask me whether one of those is the McGurk case, I would say we can't discount that motive,' he said.[21]

After the murder, Samba's killer ran into Langridge Street in Middle Park, and that was the last anyone saw of him. He left a man dead and exposed the seedy underbelly of Australia's racing industry. 'It is about the only business that attracts high-class businessmen, politicians, prostitutes, pimps, and they all congregate together every Saturday,' said former chief steward Schreck.[22] To that list he could have added drug dealers, money launderers, standover men and killers.

From top to bottom, there has not been a single part of racing that has not been touched by evil. Of course, there are good people in the industry who simply love horses and racing. But they need to keep their wits about them because there are plenty of others who are on the lookout for the next quick fix – dragging the good name of the sport into the gutter. Men just like Les Samba.

RACE 2
LUCKY BREEDERS

Two-year-old colt Sidereus galloped into the 2008 Golden Slipper on a tide of victory and optimism. The week before the world's richest race for two-year-olds, Sidereus had silenced his critics. Doubters had wondered if the colt, sired by General Nediym, had the legs for the $3.5-million 1200-metre race.

Jumping out of barrier five in the Group 2 Pago Pago Stakes at Rosehill exactly seven days before the Slipper, Sidereus had shown his mettle. Jockey Larry Cassidy rode a masterful race, dropping the colt in third behind Brawled and Big Ethan, before timing his run beautifully. With 200 metres to go, Sidereus claimed the lead. Then came a storming challenge from Over The Wicket, which had run the race out wide and was belting home for a fast finish. Sidereus held him off, winning by a long head and securing a ballot-free berth in the Slipper.

Trainer Anthony Cummings was delighted with the result and had no fears that Sidereus would turn around easily for the race in a week's time. 'He is a very robust fellow, backing up next week will be a breeze for him,' he said.[1] Another who would have been delighted with the result was the horse's new owner, the Newcastle mining magnate Nathan Tinkler. He had just paid Cummings and a syndicate of owners $1.25 million for a fifty per cent share in the colt.

Unfortunately, things did not work out quite as planned.

Sidereus bombed in the Slipper, dawdling home second from last, while Sebring, trained by Gai Waterhouse, held off Von Costa De Hero in a nail-biting finish to take the money and the glory. Then it turned out that Sidereus was a 'rig' – a horse with only one testicle – which greatly reduced his value at stud. Cummings argued that he'd had no idea, but Tinkler was not happy. When he then found out that Cummings had a 'secret' ten per cent share of Sidereus, he went to war.

Cummings maintained that there was nothing secret about his ownership – it was there in black and white for all to see in the race book, where he was listed as an owner. But there were other problems – lots of them. And Nathan Tinkler, a man described as being evenly balanced – he has a chip on both shoulders – had the money and the anger to take the back-scratching old mates' club of Australian racing head-on.

Nathan Tinkler has loved racing since he was a kid, sometimes ducking classes to check out the track. Plenty of punters dream of owning a racehorse, but Tinkler found himself in a position to turn that dream into a very large reality. As a sparkie in Newcastle in 2003, he saw the opportunity to buy into what was considered a worthless coalmine in Queensland. When he sold Macarthur Coal to an Indian steel giant for $445 million in 2008, he was on his way.

Tinkler's first major foray into racing was a $7-million splurge at the New Zealand Premier Yearling sale. He topped that later the same year with a $19-million spending spree at the Magic Millions sale on the Gold Coast. 'The thing that stoked me up to do it was looking at those Woodlands guys as a kid and thinking they must be having the time of their life; having a runner in every race in Sydney and half a dozen in Melbourne,' he told the *Australian Financial Review*.[2] The 32-year-old quickly earned himself an unflattering sobriquet – 'the Whale', racing's description of a newcomer making a big splash with his cash. People in racing have seen a lot of big spenders come and go. In Nathan Tinkler, they saw an opportunity.

After starting out with a few horses owned in partnership with his father, Les, Tinkler moved quickly to become the biggest owner of bloodstock in the country. Many racing insiders, smoothing their ruffled feathers, argued that he had moved far too quickly. 'Nobody listens to me,' Tinkler raged after moving all of his horses to Melbourne and Queensland, following a very public dispute with the AJC over what he considered to be poor racing conditions at Warwick Farm in Sydney. 'I have got 25 years until I am fucking 60 and they tell me that's when I can have a say.'[3]

In just five years, Tinkler endeavoured to build a racing empire that would rival the legendary Woodlands Stud. It took the champion chicken farmers Jack and Bob Ingham a couple of decades to build up that stud before it was sold to Dubai's ruler Sheikh Mohammed bin Rashid Al Maktoum. But Tinkler did not want to hang around. In five years he spent $200 million buying horses and $70 million on farms and studs, including a 2025-hectare horse stud near Sandy Hollow in the Hunter Valley, which had once belonged to the late Robert Sangster.

The portly former electrician has an estimated worth of $1.1 billion – he sold just ten per cent of a coalmine he owned near Gunnedah in 2011 to pick up a lazy $370 million – but even so, the $20 million a year he spends on running costs must hurt. Tinkler insists that he is in racing for the long haul. It is a lifetime investment in an industry he feels has done him no favours. 'Sticking it up the pricks is half what it is all about,' he says. 'Standing there holding the trophy saying "fuck youse, don't youse hate this?".'[4] In 2008 alone, he spent $40 million on 155 horses – mostly young and unraced – in Australia and New Zealand. He expressed his feelings for the racing industry with names such as All Too Hard, Trusting, Frustrating, Count Your Fingers, Heard The Latest and Small Minds. Sticking it up the pricks.

His plan has been to emulate the big operations and turn success on the racecourse into money in the stud. For example, the Arrowfield Stud in the Hunter Valley – one of the biggest in New South Wales, and owned by the chairman of Racing NSW, John Messara – charges $137,500 for the services of stallion Redoute's Choice, which won the Caulfield Guineas. So far, Tinkler's stallions at his Patinack Farm are not in the same league. In 2010, according to the *Australian Stud Book*, sixty per cent of the mares covered by Patinack's six stallions were also owned by Patinack. That's a high-risk strategy; if the stallion does not produce winners, the mares are devalued too. One of Patinack's biggest stars, Wonderful World, in three seasons has only earned back just over a third of the $6 million Tinkler paid Bart Cummings for it.

All that cut and thrust can be put down to building the business. What has made Tinkler angry is the dirty dealing that goes on in the buying and selling of racehorses in Australia, and the tacit nod of approval those tricks receive from the authorities. 'If ASIC governed this industry, half of them would be in jail,' he told the *Australian Financial Review*. 'It's criminal some of the shit that goes on.'[5]

Well, it would be criminal in Kentucky, the American heart of the bloodstock industry, or in Britain, where legal eagles have condemned the kind of sharp practice Australians get up to. In 2007 Tinkler took a one-quarter stake in an auspicious $6 million colt called Shrewd Rhythm. The Melbourne Cup-winning trainer David Hayes and his nephew Sam were looking after the sprinter and putting together the deal that brought Tinkler in. The only problem was that Shrewd Rhythm lost its rhythm pretty quickly; Tinkler was not feeling very shrewd when he learnt that David Hayes' stud had bought the horse for $2.3 million just months earlier.

Tinkler angrily said that the giant markup had not been disclosed, a fact hotly denied by Sam Hayes and other members of the syndicate. The group had done nothing illegal. The problem was that they had more than one role in the deal; unlike in America, there was no formal pressure for them to disclose in writing that they were simultaneously the owner, trainer and principal in the deal. It is a murky world. Tinkler took no legal action against the Hayes group but he was perfectly primed; when he felt wronged by Anthony Cummings, he went off.

It had all started very promisingly – two rich men having a bit of fun together. Tinkler was happy to have a Cummings, the son of legendary trainer Bart, taking care of his interests, and Cummings was happy to have a big spender on board. And did they spend big! Cummings helped Tinkler part with $55 million on yearlings to stock his lush new paddocks in the Hunter Valley.

Then Tinkler heard whispers that his man Cummings was really Cummings' man Cummings. The trainer was allegedly taking secret commissions on the sale of horses he was advising Tinkler to buy. This is one of those commonly accepted practices in Australian horseracing that Tinkler is so rightly riled about. Buyer's agents, usually trainers, are paid a commission of between five and ten per cent of the value of the horse they recommend to someone as a good buy. It is handed over by the breeder once the sale is complete. Usually they don't bother the actual buyer with any of this tiresome detail. Tinkler was furious – this was on top of his discovery that Cummings also owned ten per cent of Sidereus.

Despite his enormous wealth, Tinkler has also developed a reputation for being a bit slow at paying the bills. Eventually, Cummings sued him for $351,000 in unpaid fees – plus a ten per cent commission on two stallions he bought for him, Wonderful World and Teranaba, for $6 million. Tinkler launched his lawyers into the fray, refusing to pay the $1.25 million for Sidereus and seeking to recoup $700,000 in kickbacks he claimed were trousered by Cummings.

Tinkler initially alleged that Cummings had received $2.3 million in secret commissions but then revised the figure down. He forced fifty-two prestigious auction houses and studs to hand over their financial records, hoping they would prove his case. Just six weeks before the case was slated for a fifteen-day hearing in the New South Wales Supreme Court, Tinkler's barrister, Robert Dubler SC, was asking that Cummings' own records be released in an attempt to find proof of $483,000 in secret commissions.

For his part, Cummings played a very cautious hand, all the time affirming that nothing outside the rules had happened. He said he had received at least $300,000 in commissions perfectly legally. What's more, he claimed, he had told Tinkler about the commissions and the billionaire had said he was happy for him to take any that were under five per cent. If they were over five per cent, Tinkler wanted half.

Despite his apparent calm, Cummings lacked Tinkler's financial firepower and was staring at ruination – legal fees of at least $700,000 and an investigation by Racing NSW stewards into his licence – if he lost. 'If I thought blowing up would help, I'd blow up but I'm yet to see how that improves things,' he said coolly as the deadline for the case in the middle of the Melbourne Spring Carnival loomed.[6] Clearly, something had to be done. The airing of all that dirty laundry in the courts and on the front pages of every newspaper in the land would do nothing for the already tarnished reputation of the racing industry.

At the eleventh hour, a saviour stepped forward in the form of Gerry Harvey, the hands-on retail king and owner of Harvey Norman. Harvey has had a lifelong passion for horses. 'In 1972, I bought my first five mares at horse sales in Sydney; of the three horses I sold at the sales, one won 18 races, one won second breeders' place and the third won races too,' he said. 'I thought "this is a piece of cake" so I bought more and more and I raced them and after a while, I joined the Sydney Turf Club (and) was a director there for five years.'[7] He went on to own 1000 horses at five studs in Australia and New Zealand. Crucially, when the Magic Millions went into receivership in the 1990s, Harvey bought it and turned the Gold Coast horse sale into a hugely successful event.

Obviously, a public stoush between a wealthy owner and a famous trainer over dodgy commissions would not be good PR for any of those auction houses. At Tinkler's behest, Harvey arranged a lunchtime meeting in a private first-floor room of Darcy's restaurant in Paddington in Sydney. The three men, Harvey, Tinkler and Cummings, sat down to a meal of pasta and fish, washed down by a $58 bottle of Cloudy Bay sauvignon blanc. The four hours of discussion remained private, but the *Sydney Morning Herald*'s Tom Reilly, who has followed Tinkler's every move since he soared to prominence, had a source on hand to spill the beans.

It appeared that Tinkler was upset that Cummings had refused to work for him exclusively. Cummings had wavered because he was naturally reluctant to tie himself to just one source of income. Tish tosh – Tinkler would have given him a watertight contract to guarantee his finances. 'Tinkler then admitted that he hadn't properly explained this to Anthony at the time,' said Reilly's source, who knew both men.[8]

In the end, it was all smiles and handshakes. Tinkler agreed to pay Cummings more than $1 million – although his legal team later said it was much less – and $800,000 for the rig Sidereus. 'When they were leaving the restaurant, Tinkler told Anthony that if he finds a "good stallion" to give him a call,' said the source.[9] Phew – all that nasty news swept back under the carpet.

But not for long. In August 2012, Tinkler's bête noire, reporter Reilly, put him on the front page of the *Sydney Morning Herald* once again. Despite BRW estimating Tinkler's wealth at $915 million, he had apparently not been paying all his bills. In the previous ten months, seven businesses had successfully taken legal action to get their money out of Patinack Farm and Tinkler's building company, Bolkm. Others sent in debt collectors or took assets in lieu of payment. Worse still, staff at his racing concern were reportedly on the point of mutiny over his failure to pay their superannuation since the previous

November. One worried worker said, 'This guy's supposed to be a billionaire, so why can't he pay people what they're due? There's a lot of anger and frustration among the staff. There's a sense that the whole Tinkler house of cards could collapse. People are definitely worried we won't ever see this money.'[10]

Tinkler's PR department lumbered into action, and creditors named in the stories were paid. There was no explanation as to why it had taken so long. But it was known that Tinkler had tried to sell his entire $300 million racing empire to Qatari royal Sheikh Fahad Al Thani, owner of Melbourne Cup winner Dunaden, at the knockdown price of $200 million. 'People often come to us with offers and we reject nearly all of them,' explained the Sheikh's bloodstock advisor David Redvers.[11]

Fortunately Tinkler's old mate Gerry Harvey was able to lend a hand again – reportedly advancing $20 million against the sale of 350 Patinack Farm horses at a special Magic Millions reduction sale on the Gold Coast later in the year. Elsewhere, Tinkler's business empire was collapsing. It clearly wasn't helping that bills for his horse-racing empire were coming in at an estimated $500,000 a week. The former electrician was learning the hard way why racing is known as the sport of kings and the business of knaves.

Undeclared commissions are not the only dodgy deals that go on at Australian horse auctions. The other wicked wheeze is a neat trick called a buyback. This is all about manufacturing a market and creating a false value for a horse's bloodline.

It's simple. A stud puts in bids for its own horses, pumping up the price. They pay the auction house the commission on the sale, then syndicate or race the horse themselves. The first ever million-dollar yearling sold in Australia was a buyback.

Fortunino was sold and bought by the late concrete magnate Tristan Antico for $1.1 million at the 1988 Inglis Easter Yearling Sale. It was unraced and later sold for just $6000.

Not a great start, but the technique has been perfected since then. At the 2009 Inglis Easter Yearling Sale, the top-priced colt was a buyback. The colt, by Encosta de Lago and out of Show Dancing, was sold by Emirates Park Stud for $1.8 million to Dynamic Syndication. The colt was renamed Mutamayez and began racing, not particularly well, with the owner clearly listed as 'Emirates Park No. 2 Syndicate'. That would be the syndicate of Hussain Lootah, who happens to be the son of Nasser Lootah, the owner of Emirates Park Stud.

The stud's chief executive, Trevor Lobb, got very shirty when *Australian Financial Review* reporter Angus Grigg asked him about the buyback deal. He later claimed to have been misquoted when explaining that deals such as this were 'commonplace', and that it was really jolly unfair to pick on his stud. 'You would probably find 50 or 60 horses in any sale just like this one,' he said – the logic being, presumably, that fifty or sixty wrongs make a right.[12]

Lobb refused to speak to Grigg when he reported that Emirates Park Stud had orchestrated another buyback with its $1-million payment for the top-priced horse at the 2011 Inglis Easter Yearling Sale. After the auction, William Inglis & Son said the buyer was Sydney trainer Gerald Ryan. An Inglis press release at the time said Mr Ryan had 'set the early benchmark'.[13] That early benchmark, of course, serves to put the buyers in the right frame of mind to part with their cash. Mr Ryan insisted it was a genuine sale, saying the Emirates Park proprietor, Nasser Lootah, had actually bought the horse from his son Hussain. Er, right, so that's okay, then?

Apparently it is. Following a complaint by participants in the industry, the Australian Competition & Consumer Commission (ACCC) sent its officers to the 2011 Inglis Easter Yearling Sale but then walked away from the investigation. It said it needed state legislation to stop the practices that were commonplace at the Inglis and Magic Millions auctions. Policing the auctions remained in the hands of the racing chiefs; that is, the poachers were in charge of the gamekeeping. Happy days!

A completely toothless 'Thoroughbred Code of Conduct' was drafted up in place of legislation. The chief executive of Thoroughbred Breeders Australia, Peter McGauran, said in a statement introducing the code: 'Complaints against agents – defined as any person representing or advising a buyer or seller at a sale – are infrequent to the point of being rare but all of us have a vital interest in maintaining confidence in the sales system and answering any criticisms however ill-informed or unjustified.'[14]

The key to the success of the code is a complaints resolution panel, which unfortunately has no power to enforce anyone to actually turn up. Nathan Tinkler had predictably strong views on just how the code could work: 'We need to see some early scalps to send a message to people that change is here and those who continue to do the wrong thing will be punished.'[15] Of course, that's not going to happen.

At the 2011 Magic Millions sale on the Gold Coast, Melbourne Cup-winner Makybe Diva's owner Tony Santic bought and sold a couple of his own horses. Afterwards, Makybe Racing & Breeding produced an ad that bragged about the fantastic value of its stallion Purrealist: 'His first crop sold at the major yearling sales throughout Australia and averaged a staggering 10 times his service fee.'[16] The ad said that Domovino sold for $240,000 and Anjea for $110,000. Close inspection of the registration documents, however, shows that Makybe Racing & Breeding was both the buyer and seller for both horses, which puts a very big question mark over the true value of Purrealist as a hiring stallion. Stud manager Stephan Putter later explained that the horses had failed their veterinary tests and were therefore retained by the stud. Funny how that did not make it into the ad ... so much for the Thoroughbred Code of Conduct! It's business as usual.

And what a business! The 2011 *Australian Racing Fact Book* said that in 2010–11, 4646 yearlings were sold for a total of $246,880,314. That's an average of $53,138 a horse. The top price was for a yearling by Casino Prince and out of Helsinge, which fetched $1.025 million at the Inglis Easter Yearling Sale. By type, broodmares fetched $45 million, weanlings $14.5 million and two-year-olds $10.5 million. No wonder the breeders reacted so ferociously when the issue of artificial insemination came up.

Former bookie and head of the Sydney Turf Club Bruce McHugh launched a legal challenge in the Federal Court to lift the ban on artificial insemination in the thoroughbred racing industry. The breeders went ballistic. Thoroughbred Breeders Australia chief executive McGauran, a former minister in John Howard's federal government, explained that it would destroy Australia's international market: 'If Australia goes unilaterally and is the only country in the world to introduce artificial insemination, then we would be excluded from the major jurisdictions such as the United Kingdom, France, the United States and much of Asia. Australia depends very heavily on more than two-and-a-half thousand exports of horses in the region of around $200 million each year. It would be insane for Australia to do it.'[17]

At present, to be eligible to race, a thoroughbred must be registered in a stud book. Australia's stud book was begun in 1878 by the sports editor of the *Melbourne and Weekly Times*, William C. Yuille. It cooperates with over seventy stud book authorities around the world, all members of the International Stud Book Committee. This ensures the integrity of the thoroughbred breeding industry, which only allows for thoroughbreds to be bred naturally. The breeders argue that allowing artificial insemination (AI) would drastically reduce the number of sire lines and diversity in the industry: the owners of broodmares would flock to have the services of just a few champion stallions. 'AI would decimate the thoroughbred population,' wrote Carrie Brogden, who with her Australian husband, Craig, runs a thoroughbred farm in Lexington, Kentucky, in an email to *Bloomberg Businessweek*. 'The ramifications of this are staggering.'[18]

Of course, the current system works very well for a few very wealthy breeders, such as Dubai's ruler, Sheikh Mohammed bin Rashid Al Maktoum. It's no problem for him to send his shuttle stallions to cover mares around the world at up to $330,000 a pop. McHugh was speaking up for the little people, those owning two or three mares, who would love to have a cheap way of mating them with, say, an American champion. What he proposed threatened a multi-million-dollar global industry that is the playground of the rich and royal. If the decision went his way, it would either see Australia isolated or other countries follow suit; either way, the breeders' cosy market would disappear down the economic toilet. The decision is not expected until mid-2012; regardless of the result, it is likely to go to appeal.

But can the market have too much of a good thing? Take Fastnet Rock, for example. Plenty of breeders had seen the potential in Coolmore Stud's young stallion, which had been sired by Danehill. He was a busy horse, with over 100 foals sired by him up for sale in the Magic Millions Gold Coast, the New Zealand National, the Melbourne Premier and the Inglis Easter Yearling Sales in the first half of 2012. That's an awful lot of sons and daughters of Fastnet Rock hitting the racetracks all at the same time, which seems to shoot a hole in the arguments against artificial insemination.

That is, of course, until you consider that he is hired out at $132,000 a time, thus earning Coolmore Stud almost $1.5 million for just the current crop trotting around the sale rings. If the owners were worried, they could take heart from the performance of Fastnet Rock's offspring on the track. The pick of the litter was Mosheen, winner of the Group 1 VRC Oaks in November 2011 and producer of what was described by the *Daily Telegraph* as 'Randwick's ride of the decade'.[19]

In the $500,000 Randwick Guineas, Mosheen was held up between horses at the top of the finishing straight. Trainer Robert Smerdon knew she had the legs for a fast finish but did not think she had enough time to pull it off. Jockey Danny Nikolic thought otherwise, however, and so did Mosheen. Boxed in, it looked as though she had nowhere to go. Nikolic pulled her wide and blazed down the outside for a barnstorming finish that had the caller stunned – she had come from nowhere. Smerdon said: 'On Thursday morning Danny rode her in a gallop and she was supposed to come home her last 400m in about 26 seconds but she did it in 22.8 on her ear – that's what separates these really good horses from the rest.'[20]

The other thing that separates them is the price. On the same day Mosheen set the track alight, his brothers were firing up the International Sale in Hong Kong. The first Fastnet Rock gelding into the ring, from the mare Verdict Declared, fetched a new Hong Kong record of HK$8 million ($973,000). The next Fastnet Rock gelding into the ring, out of the mare Undercover, broke that record with a sale of HK$9 million ($1.095 million). Not a bad improvement on the $230,000 that the Hong Kong jockey club paid his New Zealand owners. Western Australian breeder Dawn Quackenbush, who bred the colt and sold it as a nine-month-old weanling for $160,000, said with smiling understatement, 'We were very pleased when that result came up.'[21] Meanwhile, Fastnet Rock yearlings were bestsellers at the Magic Millions Gold Coast ($960,000 for a colt out of Rose of Cinnamon), the New Zealand National ($1.355 million for a colt out of Nureyev's Girl) and the Melbourne Premier ($500,000 for a colt out of Bellevue Lady).

Clearly, breeders have bagged the jackpot. They have long been accused of running a very lucrative and cosy exclusive club that is subsidised by the little people – small breeders, hobby owners, punters and poorly paid workers. It's a mug's game. The Sydney *Daily Telegraph* racing writer Brent Zerafa crunched the numbers. Of the 17,723 foals born in 2009, just 1524 made it to the track as two-year-olds. Sixteen of those got into the $3.5 million AAMI Golden Slipper in 2012 – that's just 0.09 per cent of the generation.[22]

It is a massive business, with very few winners. To put Australia's thoroughbred industry into perspective, it is the second-largest in the world, behind only that of the United States. However, there are well over 300 million people in the USA, compared with just 22 million in Australia. The Productivity Commission's 2010 report into gambling took a long, hard look at the way the racing industry was funded. It found: 'Australia's thoroughbred racing industry, in particular, is unusually large by international standards. For example, Australia has the greatest number of thoroughbred racing clubs in the world (379) and is amongst the top three countries in terms of the number of races held, prize money and foals born.'[23] The report looked at the threat posed to racing by the emergence of corporate bookmakers, and the subsequent loss to the racing industry of gambling proceeds from the TAB.

The problem was that the big corporate bookmakers came in and offered punters new ways to gamble on horseracing across Australia. And the punters loved it. The difference was that the TABs were pumping a hefty wedge of the money they took back into the industry, while the corporate bookmakers were 'freeriding' and not contributing to the industry from which they derived their massive income. The states countered this by introducing 'race fields legislation', which made it an offence to print the copyrighted race fields without paying a fee – and it is hard to have a punt if you don't know who is running. That put money back into racing, and the corporate bookmakers now contribute between ten and twenty per cent of gross revenue in each state – except in New South Wales.

Racing NSW's chief executive, Peter V'Landys, wanted the much larger sum of 1.5 per cent of the corporate bookmakers' turnover – that is, $1.50 for every $100 wagered, win, lose or draw. 'No one likes conflict but at the same time I am not going to let people down,' said V'Landys, who polarised opinion in the racing industry. 'People have trusted me in this position to look after their interests and, no matter how much stress and heat there is, I have got to take up the fight.'[24]

V'Landys, an affable and enjoyable raconteur, has made his fair share of enemies. That does not worry him, though – he is tough. He likes to recount the story of a young accountant who walked into the office of the supervisor at Harold Park Raceway twenty years ago; the supervisor was lounging with his feet on the table, and the accountant asked what he did for a job. In no uncertain terms, the supervisor told the young man where to go. A week later, the supervisor discovered that the accountant was Peter V'Landys, the new CEO of Harold Park Raceway – and also that, by the way, he was fired. 'I could take him being rude to me as the CEO but he thought I was a customer and I could not tolerate that,' said V'Landys.[25]

The issue the corporate bookmakers have with Racing NSW is the accounting method it uses, which effectively means they will be paying sixty per cent of their income to the racing authority. 'And that's just not fair,' said the Tasmanian-based chief executive of Betfair, Andrew Twaits. 'If we are required to pay this fee on a long-term basis our racing business will be decimated. We believe we should pay a fee to the racing industry but not one that is six times more than our competitors, the TABs.'[26]

While the case was being decided, the bookmakers were making the larger payments; the cash was being held in a rapidly expanding account, just in case it had to be paid back. Matthew Tripp, chairman of Sportsbet, based in the Northern Territory, pledged that, if the case went his way, 'I am not going to demand they give back every dollar, just the difference between the 10 per cent of gross profit they should be charging and the 1.5 per cent of turnover they are charging. The point is that we do want to contribute to the industry but only what is fair and equitable.'[27]

The vexed issue prompted the Victorian deputy premier and minister for racing, Rob Hulls, to call for national legislation to prevent freeriding by corporate bookmakers. 'I've got news for them – the thousands of Australians who rely on a vibrant and growing racing industry and invest their blood, sweat, tears and dollars in putting on the show rightly expect corporate bookmakers and betting exchanges to pay a fair share of that cost,' he fumed. 'Over the past decade we have seen corporate bookmakers on the one hand saying "we are happy to pay our way" and on the other pursuing litigation in any court available to them to avoid it. This could go on for years while our racing community faces heavy revenue losses.'[28]

At the end of March 2012, the seven judges of the High Court delivered Racing NSW the mother lode. While other racing authorities had crumbled and taken the smaller gross-profit model, V'Landys' massive punt had paid off. 'This is not a victory for Racing NSW, it is a victory for the industry's 50,000 participants,' he rejoiced.[29] It was the end of a four-year ordeal, and it meant the $100 million paid into a trust fund by the corporate bookmakers could immediately flow through to all those involved in racing in the state. 'Safeguards will be put in place to make sure strappers, for the first time, get a share of the winnings,' said V'Landys. 'I'd love to be the strapper of next year's Golden Slipper winner.'[30] It would see around $40 million more flowing into racing every year; effectively, it was a $1-billion decision for racing over the next two decades.

Other states, notably Victoria, were quick to jump on the bandwagon. Victoria's new racing minister, Denis Napthine, said legislation would be brought forward to ensure that the state could cash in on the decision. Racing Victoria's chief executive, Rob Hines, reckoned Victoria had been right all along, but explained: 'If we got out of sync with NSW and continued with the revenue fee, the corporates and Betfair would probably target Victorian punters and we would be more likely to lose [turnover on] the tote.'[31]

Others wondered aloud why Victoria hadn't just backed up New South Wales in the first place. Betfair whined that it would now be six times more expensive for it to operate in New South Wales, and that it might have to withdraw from the state. Yeah, right. But Sportsbet's chief executive, Cormac Barry, was moving on. 'We will sit down with Racing NSW … we'd love to be sponsoring the Golden Slipper in a couple of weeks, we'd love to be sponsoring Randwick,' he said.[32] Exclusive advertiser Tabcorp might have a word to say about that. Meanwhile, pundits were talking excitedly about resurfaced tracks, increased prize money and racing centres of excellence. If it comes off, it would be fantastic because, traditionally in racing, the money and the power has always been held by a lucky few.

The Productivity Commission's report highlighted an alarming disconnect between those running racing and those using it, asking: 'Who is the racing industry for?' The report said: 'Some participants have argued that the racing industry does not merely exist to meet the demands of consumers [punters] and provide them with the services they want at the lowest feasible prices – as generally accepted in other industries – but rather to: provide employment [and] serve the needs of a broader group, which includes industry stakeholders themselves.'[33]

Translation: the racehorse industry exists to provide jobs for the people who breed horses and work in it, and sod everybody else. Oh, as long as they keep paying, of course. This was referring to a submission from the National Horse Racing Alliance. A co-convenor of the group, Michael Sissian, told the commission: 'We are a national lobby group. Our current mission is to protect the funding base of the Australian racing industry.'[34]

That sounds good – until you take a look at just who makes up the group's membership: Thoroughbred Breeders Australia, the Thoroughbred Racehorse Owners Association, the NSW Trainers Association, William Inglis & Son Ltd, Magic Millions Pty Ltd, the Randwick Equine Centre and the Federation of Bloodstock Agents Australia. Can we pick a theme here?

Patrick Smith in *The Australian* certainly did: he renamed the breeding interests' lobby group 'the Rich Racing Toffs Alliance' and tore into them. Sissian had written to the Productivity Commission: 'In the time available to the NHRA, we have not been able to accurately estimate the net subsidy of the racing product by breeders, who bear the cost of rearing 18,000 foals for two years, on average, before they go to sale or into training. On balance it is most likely that both owners and breeders subsidise the racing product heavily and that their contribution is, at least, the equal to the contribution made by the punters.'[35] Smith was outraged: 'Really? Breeders subsidise racing? How? Who does a cattle breeder subsidise while he waits for his animals to go to sale? Or a pig farmer, or a sheep farmer?'[36] He dismissed Sissian's arguments as being without merit or substance.

Much the same conclusion was drawn by the Productivity Commission itself, which explained that most other industries do not offer any guarantee of return to those who choose to invest in it. What's more, buying a horse is a recreational activity, but one with the added bonus of a substantial potential for a subsidy through prize money.

Imagine any other business justifying its existence so loftily ahead of the people who consume its product. You would have to imagine it, in fact, because it would not survive for very long. To highlight the point, Smith returned to the Productivity Commission submission by the Rich Racing Toffs Alliance's QC, Martin Einfeld: 'But the majority of punters are not sensitive to whether they are able to receive 10-9 or 9-1 from this bookmaker or the next. What drives them? Who knows?'[37] What's the weather like on your planet, Mr Einfeld? It's a lovely place, clearly, where the idea that punters look for better odds is a total fallacy. 'It just doesn't exist. It is not the reality,' Einfeld said.[38]

No wonder the corporate bookmakers are cleaning up. Fortunately, the Productivity Commission saw through such errant nonsense. 'Attempting to advance the consumer interests of owners, at the expense of punters, is counterproductive. It essentially penalises the subsidy provider (punters), who in the long run will reduce betting, with negative implications for prize money and the costs of "consumption" for race horse owners.'[39] Therefore, favouring TABs over other wagering operators is not sensible or acceptable. Competition exists in a free market, whether the breeders like it or not.

Of course, in New South Wales the king of the Rich Racing Toffs is in charge of the whole kit and caboodle. The appointment of John Messara as chairman of Racing NSW in December 2011 was met with howls of protest as an example of the old mates' club in action. Ken Callander in the *Daily Telegraph* commented: 'John Messara claims he has experience in all aspects of racing. I don't believe that to be quite correct. John is a member of what they call in the US the "one per cent club".'[40] The one per cent club, he went on to explain, is the group of wealthy breeders who breed racehorses and the fantastically rich owners who race those horses. The ninety-nine per cent club are the lowly paid workers and the punters who cough up the cash to keep the sport in business.

'I find it embarrassing there are people who think punters should be the ones happy to subsidise a rich man's pastime,' wrote Callander, who went on to attack the appointment by New South Wales racing minister George Souris as an old mate giving jobs to the boys.[41] He referred readers to the minister's press release, which stated that board membership was expressly prohibited if the person has a pecuniary interest in conflict with the role of board member. Naturally, this does not apply to Messara, whose stallions at his Arrowfield Stud receive some of the highest service fees ever known in Australia.

Callander later wrote of the enormous support his articles opposing the unpopular appointment received: 'I am haunted by remarks Messara made to Caroline Searcy in March 2010 when he described punters as recreational. To me it sounded elitist, particularly when you realise the majority of owners are recreational.'[42] Indeed, the people making the real cash in racing are the major breeders, who make the big money in yearling sales and stallion fees. In New South Wales, at least, those people now have a sympathetic ear at the top.

And they might need it sooner rather than later. Trainer John O'Shea was left considering his future in racing after advice he gave to an owner went pear-shaped. O'Shea advised owner Humberto Vieira, a debt collector, to buy a seventy per cent share of the $330,000 horse Dashere at the Magic Millions sale in January 2007. Sensibly, O'Shea asked vet Richard Humberstone to give the nag the once-over. Dr Humberstone reported back to O'Shea that the horse was a low risk, providing it was given six months to rest. He was slightly concerned about Dashere having a dicky knee, the legacy of a cyst that had been treated with an injection. In January 2007 Vieira asked O'Shea if 'the vet says [the horse] is OK?'; O'Shea replied: 'Nothing wrong with him. The horse is good.'[43]

Wrong! At least, according to the Court of Appeal, which said O'Shea was in breach of contract and had to pay Vieira more than $500,000 in legal costs and damages. The horse took a long time to recover and only managed a win four years later in a Quambone maiden. O'Shea was gutted by the decision, the costs of which he would largely have to meet out of his own pocket since the Australian Trainers Association's public indemnity insurance topped out at $75,000. 'I'm assessing my future and whether I continue in the industry,' O'Shea said afterwards. 'I have been struggling with this [case] for the past four years, and all my fight is just about gone. It has major ramifications for the industry and trainers or agents that buy yearlings and then sell them to clients.'[44] He then carried on anyway.

Former AJC and Hong Kong Jockey Club chief steward John Schreck felt compelled to warn that the case could provoke major changes in the future. In an email to *Sydney Morning Herald* racing writer Craig 'Stinger' Young, he said the trouble lay in finding the ethical line in the large grey area of selling horses. 'The racing game is played by all sorts and can be a tough, selfish business,' he wrote. 'Let's be fair dinkum, greed is everywhere in our sport. And if the need is great enough, some selfish sellers tend to forget ethics.'[45] After a lifetime policing the industry, he should know.

Now a dabbler in horseflesh himself, Schreck said: 'Horse dealers have been taking advantage of horse buyers since commerce began. Let's not kid ourselves – the fact is that abuse in horse sales is not uncommon. Sellers profit from their misdeeds and, regrettably, innocent buyers are the ones hurt.' He went on to point out, however, that buying and selling horses is far from an exact science. One man's champion is another man's dog. If a racehorse breaks down, could its owners demand their money back? 'Where does it end?' Schreck asked. 'In court, and O'Shea is the fall guy. The racing industry should be concerned.'[46]

There are some who might say: 'At last.'

RACE 3

HOOP OR DUPE?

The New Zealand mare Jezabeel came out of the gates fast for the 1998 Melbourne Cup, with jockey Chris Munce feeling like a million dollars in the saddle. 'She was enjoying herself as well, I could tell that just going into the barriers,' he said. 'She was in for a one hell of a race.'[1] They were drawn wide but, unusually for a stayer in a two-mile race, Jezabeel had superb gate speed. And it counted. By the time they thundered past the winning post in front of the stands for the first time, she had crossed the majority of the field and was actually leading.

Munce concentrated on safely negotiating the first sharp turn, then allowed six or seven horses to move in front of him. 'I was three or four pairs back and one off the fence which was exactly where I wanted to be,' he said in a commentary of the race afterwards.[2] Munce focused on letting the mare, which was trained by

Brian Jenkins, get into her rhythm and allowing her to breath – coasting until the genuine work began in the legendary race. The pressure kicked in early, at the 1200-metre mark, as two European horses piled on the power. They had been four or five horses out, and Munce expertly guided Jezabeel into their slipstream. 'By the time I had turned home I hadn't even clicked her into fourth gear. I was just really coming up into the race beautifully,' he said. He told himself repeatedly: 'I can't go yet, I can't go yet.'[3]

When he finally gave Jezabeel her reins, she lengthened her stride comfortably and the crowd was on its feet, howling for victory. But the race was far from won – fellow New Zealand mare Champagne came hurtling up on the outside. 'From the 300 to the 100 was probably the most stressful time of my life because Champagne had got to my outside and had actually headed me,' said Munce.[4] Despairingly, he resolved himself to running second or third.

But Jezabeel was a genuine stayer: she dug deep and held her pace, outstaying Champagne to dramatically pass the winning post in front by a neck. 'I was just over the moon to be able to say that I had won a Melbourne Cup,' said Munce.[5]

Queensland-born jockey Chris Munce had it all. He built on his Melbourne Cup victory with wins in the Golden Slipper Stakes in the same year, with a brilliant strategic ride on Prowl, and again in 2004. Then he turned that success into a hugely lucrative gig riding in racing-mad Hong Kong. In his first season in the former British colony, Munce blitzed it. He rode fifty-one winners and finished third on the 2006 premiership table. His mounts secured HK$34 million ($5.53 million) in stakes, and Munce himself pocketed nine per cent of the prize money – almost double the amount jockeys take in Australia – at a very favourable tax rate. But it wasn't enough.

Munce got greedy.

At the end of that first season he stopped at the luxurious Royal Garden Hotel on his way to the airport to fly home to his wife, Cathy, and their three young children. He did not make the flight. Hong Kong's powerful Independent Commission Against Corruption (ICAC) had been keeping the 37-year-old Australian under surveillance. When they burst in on Munce, the ICAC investigators found he had HK$250,000 ($40,000) stuffed into his jeans pockets, along with slips of paper that ICAC's code-breakers claimed were betting tips. Munce said the money was a going-away present. Later he explained: 'I said all along I didn't think I had done anything wrong so I was up front and honest with them from the start. Looking back, that was probably my mistake. I never hid anything, I was always transparent. If I was guilty of anything, it was probably that I was a bit naive in regards to the people I associated with.'[6]

Hong Kong takes a very tough line on corruption. ICAC has more powers than the police and states that its mission is to 'pursue the corrupt through effective detection, investigation and prosecution; eliminate opportunities for corruption by introducing corruption-resistant practices; and educate the public on the evils of corruption and foster their support in fighting corruption'.[7]

Even after the anti-graft squad pounced, Munce was not worried – but he should have been. On the same day that he was arrested, a 51-year-old woman was jailed for four months for attempting to bribe her driving instructor with $86 to make sure she passed. Munce's crime was far more serious.

Jockeys are treated like gods in Hong Kong, where any information they pass on is pounced on by a gambling-addicted public desperate for the inside line. Jockeys themselves are banned from placing bets. ICAC alleged that Munce got around this irksome rule by approaching a 31-year-old Indian businessman and racing enthusiast, Dinesh Daswani. He in turn passed Munce's tips on to an elderly local businessman, Andy Lau, who placed the bets. Lau absorbed the losses and passed on the winnings; Daswani took thirty per cent for his trouble. ICAC alleged that, during the Hong Kong season, Munce had offered tips on thirty-six horses, eighteen of which had won, and that his share of the HK$600,000 ($103,000) bets that Lau placed on his behalf would be HK$1.6 million ($276,000).

The Australian racing authorities took a much more lenient view of Munce's alleged transgressions. Racing NSW granted him a licence while he was on bail, and he rode two Group 1 winners at the Spring Carnival before returning to Hong Kong to face trial. Munce's lawyer, John McNamara, argued that the matter should be dealt with by racing authorities rather than in a criminal court, and claimed it was a victimless crime in which no one had suffered financially. 'What is alleged, what's been proven doesn't deserve the penalty that would ruin the life of this man and the life of his family,' fired McNamara.[8] The District Court judge, Kevin Browne, disagreed: 'What about the reputation of racing? It attracts huge public interest,' he said.[9]

As Munce stood in the dock in a black suit, blue shirt and pink tie, Judge Browne told him that he had 'undermined the integrity of racing', and that he was satisfied beyond reasonable doubt that Munce had agreed to swap tips for bets that would be placed on his behalf.[10] This was in breach of his contract with the racing authorities, and was therefore a crime. 'For an offence of this kind, an immediate custodial sentence is inevitable,' the judge said, before sentencing Munce to thirty months' jail.[11] Cathy Munce broke down in tears, and as she left the courtroom screamed out: 'You'll never get anyone here again' – meaning that the tough sentence would scare away foreign jockeys.[12] (She was wrong.)

Munce was marched away, his emotions reeling from anger to disappointment to sheer disbelief. 'I couldn't understand what I was doing in prison,' he told the *Daily Telegraph*. 'Those first nights there was a lot of anger and disappointment. I was in shock. I didn't have a chance to think of my family. That came after a few days.'[13] He was placed in a stifling cell with thirty other inmates, sleeping two to a hard wooden board bed with no mattress. And he stood out. Not only was he one of the few white faces in the jail, but every inmate knew he was a famous jockey. It meant they were watching him, as were the guards.

Munce coped by withdrawing into himself, reading books to escape and desperately trying not to think of his family. When Cathy did come to visit, he suffered. 'They were my worst days, as much as they should have been my best days. Even talking about it now makes me emotional and a bit upset,' he said. 'Because of the travelling, Cathy couldn't see me often and the occasions she did come to visit, I could only see her for half an hour and there was no contact. It was a very tough time for both of us.'[14]

Munce was transferred back to Australia and served out the remainder of his sentence – which was shortened to twenty months for good behaviour – in the minimum-security wing of Silverwater Prison in New South Wales. He emerged from jail raring to get back into the saddle, his appetite for horse-racing undiminished. The Hong Kong Jockey Club had other ideas. It had not yet punished Munce for his part in the 'tips for bets' scandal. It banned him from racing for thirty months; the sentence was backdated, but it still meant Munce had nine more months to wait before he could race again.

Racing NSW's chief executive officer, Peter V'Landys, was having none of it. 'We could not under natural justice processes continue with the penalty of 30 months because it doesn't apply in Australia. It is a breach of the [racing] rules in NSW to tip for cash but he would not have ended up in jail. It is not a criminal offence in Australia, it is in Hong Kong. We believe he has served his time in jail, he was taken away from his family for two years. He couldn't provide for his family for two years, that is a pretty stiff penalty.'[15]

Munce was delighted by V'Landys' support. 'I've got no reason to hang around now. I'm fit and well, why wait? If I can get rides I'll kick off at Randwick and then ride at Rosehill on the Saturday and Hawkesbury on Sunday,' he burbled excitedly. 'I've always had confidence Australian racing authorities would recognise the Hong Kong penalty was manifestly excessive and that I'd more than paid the price.'[16]

However, the Australian and Hong Kong racing authorities have a reciprocal agreement. They each must uphold the other's decisions and penalties under Article 10 of the Agreement on Breeding, Racing and Wagering, which is published by the International Federation of Horseracing Authorities. Winfried Engelbrecht-Bresges, the chief executive of the Hong Kong Jockey Club and the chairman of the Asian Racing Federation, was not happy. 'The Hong Kong club is surprised to learn that while the Australian Racing Board is a signatory to the agreement, Racing NSW, as a principal racing authority, is not,' he said.[17] Furthermore, he warned that Racing NSW's decision to allow Munce to ride threatened the relationship between Hong Kong and Australia, and the integrity of international racing.

Racing NSW stuck two Australian fingers up to that one, and Munce, the golden boy, was back in the saddle. Like so many other jockeys, he had taken a gamble and lost. Yet, compared with some of his fellow professional jockeys, Chris Munce was lucky.

The common perception among racegoers is that jockeys earn good money. They point to champions like Craig Williams. Halfway through the 2011–12 season, he had already trousered more than half a million dollars. Admittedly, it was a great run, complemented by a six-week stint in Japan that saw him finish a close second in the Japan Cup, earning him almost $60,000, and first in Hong Kong on Dunaden in the Hong Kong Vase, which won him almost $50,000. His wins on Southern Speed in the Caulfield Cup netted him $82,500, on Pinker Pinker in the Cox Plate $92,500, and on Ortensia in the Winterbottom Stakes $15,000. And he would likely have won even more if he had not been suspended and missed riding Dunaden in the Melbourne Cup.

Good jockeys get good rides, and Williams cleared the cash from just thirty winners. Australian jockeys get just five per cent of the prize money awarded for a race win, but that's not bad if you are Kerrin McEvoy, whose forty-eight wins in the 2011–12 season generated $4,944,973, or Craig Newitt, whose wins for the same period produced $3,913,873.

For the majority of jockeys, however, it is a very different story. The prize money for the Melbourne Cup glitters in the publicity spotlight at $3 million, but for a country race it might be just $4000, which would give the winning jockey the princely sum of $200. But that's only if he or she wins, and only one jockey can ride the winner in any race. Their income comes from a riding fee, which varies, depending on the state, from $130 to $160. That's not a lot of money when you consider that most jockeys put in around fifteen hours a week of unpaid track-work to ensure they get rides in the first place.

The Australian Jockeys' Association (AJA) did a survey of a typical race day at Randwick in Sydney. Of the twenty-nine jockeys at the race, only nine rode winners and got a share of the prize money. The other seventeen derived their income from the riding fee. Nine of the jockeys only rode in one race, meaning they earned just $130 for the day. After they took out tax, insurance and expenses, they would barely have enough for a round of beers and a bus fare home.

The AJA surveyed its members and found that half earned less that $1000 a week (gross); in 2006–07 eight out of ten jockeys reported their income as being $40,000 or less. That figure is still no more than $60,000 today. Six out of ten jockeys said that at some stage in their careers they had been unable to pay for food and bills. A survey in 2008 found more than half had no private health insurance, and more than a third had no superannuation scheme. It should come as no surprise, then, that jockeys are bailing out in increasingly large numbers – their numbers have almost halved over the past decade.

But without them there would be no racing industry. With money pouring into the bookmakers' pockets, the AJA's chief executive officer, Paul Innes, is perplexed as to why the industry has been so reluctant to hand over even a tiny proportion to reward the very people upon which it relies. In Great Britain, Singapore, Korea and South Africa, jockeys get at least seven per cent of the prize money, while in the United Arab Emirates, Macau, Hong Kong and Ireland they receive ten per cent. Australian jockeys used to get an unofficial five per cent 'sling' on top of their standard five per cent for winning, but the practice has virtually stopped because of resistance from owners and trainers. That was worth $19 million a year – an average of $22,000 per jockey. Meanwhile, the national prize pool has virtually doubled; the horseracing industry clocks up an annual total economic benefit of $14 billion.

Paying jockeys so badly makes them vulnerable to corruption. It must seem to the average impoverished jockey that everyone is making a buck out of the racing game except him or her. With so little cash around, the temptation to place an illicit bet or take a bung to fix a race is never far away. Unfortunately, there is always some poor hoop (racing slang for jockey) who is ready or desperate enough to do the wrong thing.

It is illegal for licensed jockeys to bet on a race, even if they are not competing in it. That did not stop top jockeys Blake Shinn and Peter Robl from turning over a massive $300,000 in a Tabcorp account in just six weeks. The account was held in the name of Elaine Robl, the older jockey's wife and a trackwork rider, and the money was poured into it by Shinn's mother, Carol, the wife of Victorian trainer Lee Hope and herself a licensed stablehand. When the two jockeys were first confronted by racing stewards, Robl lied, trying to cover for his 23-year-old Melbourne Cup-winning accomplice.

Shinn may have been gambling but he adamantly told the stewards he had only ever had one bet on a horse he was racing against, and that had resulted in a $2500 loss. Nevertheless, Racing NSW's chief steward Ray Murrihy was not impressed. 'Here we have one of the best jockeys in Sydney, a Melbourne Cup winner, putting $2500 on the head of another horse,' he said.[18] Shinn had backed Giresun at Randwick on 18 August 2010 while he was riding Diamond Jim in the same race. Giresun came home second and Shinn trailed in fourth.

But Shinn insisted it was not about race-fixing. Rather, the betting was informed. For example, he instructed his mother to put $1300 on Venus Dream at Wyong on 26 August 2010. The horse was odds-on early, but by betting late, Shinn secured odds of $11.20, which paid very nicely, thank you very much, when the horse romped home first. Robl was also riding in that race but denied any knowledge about the Venus Dream bet. Shinn did like to back himself, however, once putting $1500 on the Clarry Conners-trained Best Choice, which won its debut at Canterbury. He also put $50 each way on Olivia Blue, which his girlfriend, Kathy O'Hara, was riding in Canberra. His biggest single bet was a $10,000 plunge on Aussie Crawl in Muswellbrook.

Murrihy conceded that both jockeys were remorseful, before handing out lengthy bans – Shinn for fifteen months and Robl for a year. On appeal, it emerged that Shinn had been suffering from an $1800-a-day gambling problem that had seen him blow $1 million over two years on the gallops, dogs and trots; he believed that the Robls, who were family friends, had no idea of the extent of his punting. He was caught on CCTV footage at TABs in Randwick, at the South Sydney Juniors Leagues Club, and in Moorebank and Kensington. And it did not stop there – Kathy O'Hara was caught on film with Elaine Robl withdrawing $9000 from a Moorebank TAB, and a further $2000 the following day.

Shinn's ban was reduced on appeal to allow a three-month ban for using a mobile phone in the changing rooms to run concurrently. O'Hara copped a $2500 fine for being on the phone to him in the changing rooms, although the stewards conceded that they were simply murmuring sweet nothings rather than fixing races. Elaine Robl and Carol Shinn were each fined $7500.

At the appeal, Murrihy quoted Shinn's own defence counsel, Dr Cliff Pannam QC, from years before: 'Whenever you put together a man, a horse and a bookmaker of course you have circumstances alive with the prospects of dishonesty.'[19]

The extent of Shinn's remorse was not that evident when he finally returned to the track, however. Pulled up for a lousy ride on Hussousa in the Reisling Stakes in March 2012, Shinn displayed a stunning disregard for the stewards. Trainer John Thompson said: 'He got outridden.'[20] Shinn clearly disagreed, and he sat in front of the stewards calmly leafing through the newspaper's form guide as they dealt with him. 'You are showing a great respect for the stewards,' Murrihy fired sarcastically, before ordering Shinn to return after the last race.[21] He was left waiting for quite a while, too.

Murrihy had said earlier that the volume of the betting by the two jockeys was something he had not seen before: 'Some people have thumbed through trying to find examples and they have gone back to George Moore. Well, George Moore finished as I started in racing [more than 40 years before]. It is too late to get George, but for any other riders who are like-minded or family members who want to help [them bet], then the stewards will eventually find them.'[22]

He was referring to racing giant George 'Cotton Fingers' Moore, an Australian champion who rode the legendary racehorse Tulloch to victory in nineteen of its thirty-six wins. Moore won the AJC Derby six times in a career that clocked up 2278 victories from his apprenticeship in 1938 to his retirement in 1971. His record of 119 Group 1 wins remains unsurpassed, and he is hailed as one of the greatest jockeys Australia has ever produced. Overseas, Moore rode for the Aga Khan and replaced Lester Piggott as stable jockey for the highly regarded

Warren Place Stakes in Newmarket in the United Kingdom in 1967. That year he took out the English classics, winning the 2000 Guineas and Derby with Jim Joel's Royal Palace, and the 1000 Guineas with Fleet, before going on to win the Eclipse Stakes at Sandown and the King George VI and Queen Elizabeth Stakes at Ascot.

But Moore left the United Kingdom after just one year, following phone calls threatening that his wife, Iris, and daughter, Michelle, would be killed unless he won or lost to order. The final straw came when his London flat was broken into and his clothes slashed to ribbons.

Moore may have had a gossamer touch on the reins – hence the sobriquet 'Cotton Fingers', given to him by Tulloch's trainer, Tommy Smith – but he was less than puritanical in his approach to the rules. On one occasion he thumped another hoop as they sat in the barriers. In 1954 he was banned for two and a half years for betting on a horse called Flying East, which went on to win its race at Hawkesbury. There were two big problems with this, apart from the betting. Firstly, Moore was the registered owner of Flying East, and secondly, Moore was riding another horse in the same race.

Shinn and Robl were treading a well-worn path. Over a two-month period from 28 November 2009 to 28 January 2010, country jockey Danny Peisley received a five-month ban for placing forty-eight bets on his mother's account, and for attempting to place two more on the Taree Jockeys Challenge. That followed his twelve-month ban in 2008, when drugs were discovered in the Gold Coast jockeys' room; Peisley was banned after refusing to provide a urine sample. His pal, Sydney jockey Willie Pearson, received a three-year ban when he was caught with cocaine and speed in the same incident.

Even that was not the first time he had been in trouble. Pearson was riding the Gai Waterhouse favourite No Penalty at Rosehill on 30 October 2004, when it lost to the heavily backed Lord of the Land by half a neck. The stewards found no fewer than nine points of concern with his riding. The nineteen-year-old was at the top of his game and had won the previous race on the favourite, Crown Princess. But somebody seemed to know something about Race Nine at Rosehill in the minutes before the jockeys and their mounts entered the barriers. Suddenly, No Penalty was not the short-priced favourite anymore. Lord of the Land's odds shortened from 7/1 twenty minutes before the start to just 3/1 when the race began. The betting was huge – $2.5 million on the TAB win tote alone, $300,000 of which appeared in those final twenty minutes. Someone made a lot of money that day.

Before the race began, Waterhouse's racing manager, Steve Brem, congratulated Pearson on his winning ride on Crown Princess and said that it would be great 'if he could ride the mare like that in the box seat. If something was fortunate enough to come up the inside of him so that she was one off [the fence], so much the better.'[23]

At his appeal the panel noted: 'Unfortunately, as the film shows, those instructions were not followed. Indeed, the opposite to those instructions was the manner in which the appellant rode No Penalty.'[24] Pearson came out of the gates slowly, holding the horse's head tightly, and took up a position at the rear of the field. He stuck to the rails at the back and, rounding the home turn, he deliberately steered No Penalty from a clear and uninterrupted run up to the back of the leader, Lord of the Land. Instead of taking the clear runs afforded him between 480 metres and 200 metres to go, Pearson tucked in behind He's Latin and Time Off, giving No Penalty no chance at a clear run.

Gai Waterhouse told the stewards' inquiry on 12 November that the handling of No Penalty was: 'Just a very poor ride. I could expect much greater ability by that young man. He just seemed to have completely misjudged the pace. I don't know quite what he was thinking about when he was riding the mare.' She added: 'I just think throughout the whole race he misjudged it. I think every section of it. There were plenty of times he could have given her a kick in the ribs and moved her up and put her into a competitive position.'[25]

She was dismissive of Pearson's claim that his lack of vigour could be explained by exhaustion. He argued that he had weighed in at fifty-three kilograms at the start of the day and was still riding at the same weight by the end. He really just wanted a drink. Despite the poor riding, with fifty metres to go No Penalty was still in contention. Given that the horse only finished half a neck behind the winner, it is astonishing to think that Pearson eased off on the whip and reduced his effort in the saddle.

At the stewards' inquiry, Waterhouse asked Pearson why he had used the whip in his left hand. 'Why did you choose on my horse to ride the horse with the left hand, your weakest arm, and yet in the race before when you won the race you used your right hand? You changed the whip over coming into the straight. In the race before that you won the race. Yet on my horse you chose to keep it in your left hand or change it into your left hand that you knew was your weakest arm?'[26]

Pearson told her: 'Well, as I said, things hadn't gone right in the run and all the way, in losing my running and having to switch back to the inside it was in my mindset to just hit the horse and get going. I really – I didn't even think about pulling the whip through. Sometimes when I pull the whip through, you've always got time to think about it, you know, and rein up and pull it through.' Clearly, the stewards thought that was a load of cobblers. Pearson's appeal was overturned and his ban of ten months for not allowing No Penalty to run on its merits stood. Many gambling racegoers who lost out on that day felt that he'd got off lightly.

There are many punters who feel that jockeys should be allowed to bet, and that it would be easier to regulate if jockeys' gambling was out in the open. The concern is that letting jockeys punt can lead them to manipulate the results – race-fixing. When jockeys and punters get together, the outcome is seldom good for either party, or for racing in general. Just ask Queensland jockey Bobby El-Issa and his professional Sydney punter mate Stephen Fletcher.

El-Issa was picked to ride Bold Glance in the $100,000 Falvelon Stakes at Eagle Farm on 26 February 2011. He already had fantastic form on Bold Glance, having roared down the straight with his whip flying to win the horse's previous start on the Gold Coast. This time, he appeared to ease off on the final straight as the odds-on favourite, Essington, challenged hard. The stewards noted the lack of movement through El-Issa's torso and legs, and his decision to use the whip backhanded just three times to the finish. 'Each member of the panel has observed Jockey B. El-Issa's riding over several years and is very familiar with his ability to get the best out of his mounts whether it be through riding with the whip or by hand and heels riding,' reported Racing Queensland's stewards.[27] They found that El-Issa had not allowed the horse to race on its merits and banned him for two years.

What is interesting about this case is why El-Issa did it. The stewards found that he and his punter mate Stephen Fletcher were in regular close contact before the race. They said El-Issa was well aware that Fletcher had wagered on Essington to win, and that he'd opposed Bold Glance on Betfair. If El-Issa ensured that Essington won and Bold Glance came in second, Fletcher would pocket more than $30,000 and keep his $55,000 stake. Nice work if you can guarantee it.

Fletcher argued that he bet on certain jockeys all the time. 'It doesn't matter what odds they are, as long as they are less than what the correct true market is, I'm happy to lay it,' he said. 'And I've found that with Bobby, with Stathi, with Ben Melham in Melbourne, with Josh Parr in Sydney, with Tim Clark in Sydney and a couple of others, and William Pike in Perth, I can show you evidence where I have laid them significantly and consistently for similar amounts at great odds, in my eyes.'[28]

The stewards looked in to that. Unlike in Queensland, Fletcher's top ten risks in Victoria included six different jockeys. Ben Melham rode five of the horses he laid, with three coming home successfully. That appeared to be completely different to his relationship with El-Issa in Queensland. There, El-Issa rode all ten of Fletcher's heaviest betting risks, and every one of them was successful. 'This, in the opinion of the Stewards, serves to seriously discredit Mr Fletcher's explanation for the correlation between his lay bets and Jockey El-Issa's rides. Stewards rejected Mr Fletcher's suggestion that Jockey El-Issa is the only jockey in Australia that has a following of punters willing to take "under the odds".'[29]

Fletcher, who had previously hit the headlines with a greyhound sting on the Gold Coast in 2005, was banned for twelve months because he was a significant financial beneficiary of

El-Issa's actions. Under Australian racing rules, bookmakers are not allowed to take bets from a disqualified person; the ban also extends to all TABs. The professional punter was also barred from attending racetracks. In September 2011 Fletcher's disqualification was lifted on appeal and he was cleared of the charges.

It is easy for jockeys, even those at the top of the game, to fall into bad company. They have to be careful, because you never know who is listening.

In 1994, members of the Australian Federal Police were eavesdropping on the conversations of a man they suspected to be planning a major drug deal. Then aged fifty, Victor Thomas Spink was a former shoplifter who had done time for a post office job in Port Macquarie on the north coast of New South Wales. Unfortunately for some of Australia's top jockeys, Spink was also an avid race fan and spent a great deal of his time talking about racing – specifically, about exactly which races were fixed or could be fixed.

The information that came out of the 40,000 hours of police monitoring tapes helped put Spink behind bars for leading a $225-million cannabis importation. Some of his conversations also threw light on another unsavoury matter. They became known as 'the Jockey Tapes' and plunged Australian racing – and star riders Jim Cassidy, Kevin Moses and Gavin Eades, in particular – into a world of hurt.

Spink and the jockeys spoke by mobile phone, erroneously believing they could not be bugged. It was their downfall. The publication of one tape in particular, recorded at 5.35 pm on 22 March 1994, sparked Australian racing's biggest ever shakeup. The tape begins with Spink getting on the phone to Cassidy. Spink immediately asks him if he had received the signal and put money on the last race. Cassidy says he looked everywhere for him and couldn't see him.

Spink asks: 'You had Kevin Moses, did you?'[30]

Not just fellow jockey Kevin Moses, boasts Cassidy, but 'strike me dead, I had four fucking helping me'. The horse had romped in at 'eleven to two'.[31]

This was heartbreaking news to Spink: 'Yeah, I wasn't there, mate. I left dead-set because, you know, if I hadda thought, I woulda … stayed.'[32]

And, he adds, put $50,000 on the winner. Despite losing his $300,000 payday, he agrees to pay each of the jockeys $1000 for fixing the race. Spink then complains to Cassidy that he lost $30,000 on one of his rides on Saturday and wonders what went wrong. Before the line drops out, Cassidy tells him that he isn't sure what had happened but next Wednesday was looking good. Spink vows to splurge $50,000.

Spink calls Cassidy back ten minutes later, still bemoaning the fact that he had not received any 'mail' in time to get his money on the last race. He asks whether they have a horse for tomorrow.

Cassidy thinks so. 'Three of us gunna get our heads together, me, Kev and [third jockey],' he says.[33]

Spink tells him: 'Right, but you'll know who'll help [names well-known jockey], he'll help too, if you wanna hand.'[34]

Cassidy replies: 'Yeah, but he's got a big fucking mouth.'[35]

Then the drug dealer and the jockey set up a meeting in a backstreet close to Sydney's Canterbury racecourse. They want to decide which race to fix so that Spink can put on $40,000 to $50,000. He promises to give Cassidy $20,000 to split between the four crooked jockeys. 'You know, that's not a bad little fuckin' day's effort,' says Spink.[36]

'Fuck, yeah,' says Cassidy.[37]

Spink adds: 'It may as well be in your pocket than all those other pockets, or even the bookies' pockets.'[38]

'Exactly,' says Cassidy.[39]

Spink then gets on the phone to Kevin Moses, who at forty-two was at the peak of his career, having been Sydney's premier jockey for the past three seasons. Spink is still moaning about not having a cent on that afternoon's winner. They agree to try again tomorrow. 'Just a nice few bob here and there, it's fucking lovely, isn't it?'[40]

'Yeah,' says Moses.

The horse they all decide on in the end is Nurmi. The race results for 23 March show that Cassidy rode it to victory in the eighth race – and there had been a big betting splurge on the horse moments before the race began. Ker-ching!

Except for the fact that the *Sydney Morning Herald*'s top investigative reporter, Kate McClymont, got hold of the tapes and printed the transcripts – at first with names removed – in the newspaper in April 1995. They caused a sensation.

A whirlwind AJC stewards' inquiry headed by John Schreck took just four days to disqualify Cassidy for three years and Moses for one. But the bans were not for race-fixing. Instead, the stewards found that the jockeys were *pretending* to fix the races. It was apparently an audacious sting on the drug baron by Cassidy, who was financially stretched with car and mortgage payments despite pocketing $250,000 in prize money that year. Moses was guilty of participating in the sting by backing up Cassidy's stories. Spink certainly believed them – during the court case for the drug offences, it emerged that he had spent $700,000 with a licensed bookmaker in the five months before his arrest and had managed to buy fifteen properties worth $4 million. On one day at the races he had lost $400,000.

When the Jockey Tapes story first broke, Cassidy was furious. He contacted a corrupt copper, Detective Sergeant Alan Robert Thomas, for information. They agreed to meet in a lane in Burwood. 'I got the impression that Jim Cassidy was worried about these jockey tapes and whether they'd be any criminal charges and I said to him: "I can make inquiries and find out",' Thomas later told police.[41]

Cassidy was also worried about jockey Shane Dye. 'I need to know whether young Dye has been giving me up,' Cassidy allegedly told Thomas.[42] The corrupt cop wanted $50,000 for his efforts, but Cassidy eventually opted to take care of matters in his own way.

This only came out later, in 1997, when Thomas was tried and jailed for a host of corrupt practices. Once again, Cassidy got caught in the crossfire. His feelings about all this were summed up by his actions when his appeal against his ban was turned down by the AJC. Muttering under his breath as he left the club's committee room, he saw McClymont with her back to him – so he spat on her.

Cassidy, Moses and Eades were all suspended, but New South Wales' director of public prosecutions found that there was insufficient evidence for a criminal case.

The response of AJC chief steward John Schreck when he first heard about the Jockey Tapes was remarkably sanguine. 'Since I have been in Sydney for 13 years, I have been hearing this sort of thing day after day, and I am sick of it,' he said. 'It is nothing new. A lot of people mightn't condone it but some of the most influential people in Sydney talk to jockeys every Saturday morning.'[43] Besides, he added, it is not a crime for jockeys to speak to underworld figures. No, but it's clearly not very desirable either, John.

The reaction to the racing sting was probably best summed up by one of the AFP officers involved in recording the tapes. He said the extent of the rigging had shocked even the police. 'I used to have a bet, but now I would never bet on the races again,' he said.[44]

Many of the jockeys involved are still racing today. Has much changed?

RACE 4

WASTED

Everyone loved Stathi Katsidis. In 2010 he was at the top of his game. He had put troubles and injury behind him to turn in an amazing season. More wins – 171.5 (the half was for a dead heat) – than any other jockey in Australia. And he was all set to pilot the four-year-old gelding Shoot Out to victory in the Cox Plate at Moonee Valley in just a few days' time. The 31-year-old was brimming with confidence and enthusiasm. The $3-million Cox Plate would be the launching pad for Katsidis and Shoot Out to take out that year's Melbourne Cup.

Katsidis told Brad Thompson of the *North West Star* exactly how he would handle Shoot Out on the tight turns of the 2040-metre Moonee Valley course. The race favourite, So You Think, trained by Bart Cummings, was firmly in his sights. 'It should be genuinely run, it will give him [Shoot Out] his chance to fly home late,' Katsidis predicted. 'I'll give him one last shot at them, hoping they start reeling off some quick sectionals from the 1000m. I'm hoping to tag onto the back of a couple of horses going forward from about the 700m, and I'll stay on their backs until probably inside the 400m. Then I'll look to peel to the outside and have one last run at them when we come down the straight. I'm of the belief that when he sees So You Think or More Joyous [second favourite] in front of him that he will try and attack them. It could be a great showdown and I think we're a great knockout chance.'[1]

It would have been a great race, but Stathi Katsidis was found dead on his living room floor just a few days before it was run.

'It's just very, very sad,' said his friend and fellow jockey Danny Nikolic. 'I wouldn't think he would have had many or any enemies in the jockeys' room. He was a pretty quiet sort of guy, but he was the sort of guy that you could not help but like. It was rare to see him get upset or flustered. He was a terrific bloke, an A1 bloke, an A1 jockey and an A1 family man. I know he copped some criticism for some of his Shoot Out rides, but he didn't make too many mistakes.'[2]

That year Katsidis had piloted Shoot Out to victory in the Group 1 Randwick Guineas and the AJC Derby, which Katsidis and many racing observers believed was the race of his career – better even than his first ever Group 1 win, as a 21-year-old on Show A Heart in the T. J. Smith Classic in 2000. The tragedy of his sudden and unexpected death was that he seemed to have put his 'wild child' days behind him.

Katsidis had developed a love for racing from a very young age. By the time he was thirteen years old he was getting up at two am to clean out the stables of trainer Graham Banks in Toowoomba in Queensland. At fifteen he had quit St Mary's

College and ridden his first winner, Boneset, which was trained by his grandfather Alan. He was a quiet and respectful apprentice who listened hard to the other jockeys.

But he had a wild streak. In February 2008 Katsidis was stopped by police and breath-tested – his blood alcohol level was three times the legal limit. He was fined $1000 and disqualified from driving. Two months later, he tested positive for ecstasy during a random drug test at the Ipswich races.

In November 2008 Katsidis' left leg was shattered when a three-year-old he was breaking in at Pinnacle Park in Beaudesert fell backwards and landed on him. There were serious doubts that the jockey would ever be able to use the leg again, let alone ride. But strangely, the accident turned out to be a blessing. It gave him focus.

Each week, Stathi's brother Michael, a world-champion boxer, sent him $500 from his base in America and encouraged him to fight back. Eventually, with a steel rod in his leg, Stathi returned to the track and outrode every jockey in the country. His wins included a memorable victory in the Magic Millions on Military Rose.

'After spending 18 months on the sidelines through suspension and injury you have a lot of time to think and I realised that "I am really good at being a jockey",' Katsidis said in that tragic final interview. 'I realised I want to be as good I can and not squander it. That's what I've done and over the last 12 months I've had quite a vigorous schedule and think I've found a nice balance between work and enjoyment in life. I want to try and keep that going and just really try to simplify life. I really love riding and that's why I ride so much. I just try and ride as much I can.'[3]

At lunchtime on Monday, 19 October 2010, just five days before his rendezvous with Shoot Out in the Cox Plate, Katsidis went drinking with some friends at the Hamilton Hotel in Brisbane's north side. After three hours of solid boozing, he left with two friends and fiancée Melissa Jackson to return to their Hendra home. There he started taking drugs.

In a twelve-hour binge, he took fantasy, ecstasy, cocaine and crystal meth. The designer drug fantasy, which Katsidis was swigging from a bottle mixed with orange juice, is considered to be a powerful aphrodisiac. Also known as GHB (gamma-hydroxybutyrate) – or colloquially as 'grievous bodily harm' or GBH – it is dangerous because of the fine line between a high and an overdose.

As Katsidis' binge continued, Jackson became worried and they fought. She wanted his friends gone. 'I just didn't think they should have been there. I didn't think it was right coming up to the Melbourne Cup,' she said. 'I was just looking out for Stathi's career, his health, my son. I really wish I didn't have a fight with him that night ... but I think I had some sort of right to be a little upset.'[4]

She took her five-year-old son, Brooklyn, and went out to look for a motel for the night. Later, she came back and found Katsidis swaying and swearing on the couch in the lounge room with one of his friends. He was drinking vodka-based drinks from a cider or vinegar bottle, which, he told her, also contained fantasy. He refused to go to bed. Jackson did go to bed but got up an hour later and asked the friends to take Katsidis to hospital. One promised they would, but instead they left the house at around two am.

Worried, Jackson went out to the lounge room again and found Katsidis snoring loudly on the couch with the TV blaring. The next morning she emerged to find him face-down on the living room floor; he had turned purple. She screamed to their neighbours to get help. When ambulance officers arrived at 7.59 am – nineteen hours after the bender began – Katsidis could not be revived and was pronounced dead. Coroner John Lock found that his death was caused by 'mixed drug and alcohol toxicity'.[5] Katsidis had a high blood alcohol reading of 0.146, as well as fantasy in his blood at a concentration of 258 milligrams per kilogram. It has been proven fatal at just twenty-seven milligrams per kilogram.

Katsidis was not the only hoop to be seduced by drugs. Jockeys, schooled from a young age to live with the highs and lows of racing, are in fact prone to drug-taking. Michael Jackson, the brother of Katsidis's fiancée, told how he regularly partied with Katsidis and other jockeys. 'I've been 14 years in the racing game and there's not a jockey I know that hasn't done it,' said the former strapper. 'If they went through 100 per cent of the jockeys every Monday morning, they'd get close to 30 per cent.'[6]

For one thing, drugs have fewer calories than beer, and jockeys have to keep their weight down. But there is a lot more to it than that. In 2011, on the eve of an unprecedented compulsory seminar organised by Racing NSW for apprentice riders, jockey Christian Reith revealed the dangers of addiction. 'I don't mind admitting I'm an alcoholic and drug addict but I know how to manage it now,' Reith told *Sydney Morning Herald* racing writer Craig Young. 'I'm not ashamed to say I'd finish riding on a Saturday and get home on Tuesday. It was easy to go through $5000 on a weekend, you drink like a fish, you snort like you're a drug kingpin.'[7]

The Queenslander once received an eight-month ban for snorting cocaine while riding in Macau. But he stayed hooked on the lifestyle, with plenty of 'associates' happy to tag along for the ride until his performance in the saddle was affected and he could no longer afford to pick up the tab. Before Reith knew it, he was taking drugs every day. 'You become paranoid you're going to be drug-tested, paranoid someone will see you out at night,' he said. 'The anxiety builds up, it snowballs and it becomes a problem. It is the chemical age, people pop pills but it is the after-effects that hurt you. I don't think people realised how bad I was. I had a choice: clean myself up, get better or end up in the gutter, worse still I could've ended up dead.'[8] The support of his wife, Betina, and the arrival of his daughter, Scarlett, helped him learn to control the cravings.

Drugs are a massive problem for young jockeys cast adrift in a world where predators are always looking for an opportunity to exploit them. A typical scene in Sydney after the Canterbury races will see jockeys being feted by so-called punters at the plush Golden Century restaurant in Chinatown. A mentor and counsellor to apprentice jockeys in New South Wales, Pat Webster, says the 'punters' are really 'scumbags' who manipulate the jockeys for money.[9] They pick up the tab, provide the recreational drugs and in return ask for inside information – and even, when they can, for a race to be fixed.

The more successful the young jockeys are, the harder it is for them to handle the out-of-control life that is sweeping them along. Although many struggle by on a meagre slice of the winnings, a very few superstar apprentice jockeys still in their teens can earn $500,000 a year. While most of their mates are taking the bus or saving up to buy a 1987 Toyota Corolla, they are paying cash for brand-new Lexus sports cars.

In 2011, eighteen-year-old Josh Adams was the number-one apprentice, having ridden 150 winners. 'You get your pay every two weeks – there's always 10, 11, 12 grand there on a slow week,' he said. 'I was 18 and I was making 14 grand a fortnight, at least. I remember one fortnight I was having a good run and I made 24 grand. It's a bit full-on really – that's a lot of money.'[10]

Adams had good advice from his parents, he was well-mannered and thoughtful, and he drove a sensible car. He realised that punching $200 through the pokies as your mates watched on was insensitive. Even so, one night he went out for a drink with his mates and, in the blur of the evening, took something that turned up positive in a random drug test at the Gosford races on 5 April 2011, the morning after the Golden Slipper. 'The lowest point for me was when I had to sit in that room with three stewards,' he said. 'That's when I had to hear they had given me seven months. That was pretty tough to take.'[11]

The pressure can simply become too much. Daniel Ganderton was the 2008–09 champion apprentice, with winners worth $6 million in prize money under his belt, when he walked away from racing. 'I felt smothered,' he said after returning home to Tasmania to take stock of his life. 'The pressures of riding race day never got to me. I always felt I should be allowed my release when I go out but you are probably never afforded that. Some days I would go to the races and the stewards could tell me where I was, there were rumours people were sent to follow you. They would say, "I saw you here doing this and that."'[12]

In his short time in the saddle, Ganderton had plenty of brushes with authority. Comments on his Facebook page earned him a $1000 fine, then he lied and said he was waiting for the NRMA to fix his car when he should have been at a race meeting in Wyong, before getting caught by police close to the Hawkesbury racetrack for driving while suspended. They're mistakes any teenager could make, but they are magnified in the goldfish bowl of publicity that surrounds a young jockey.

Melbourne Cup-winning jockey Darren Beadman was actually relieved when his nineteen-year-old son, Mitchell, called him from Hong Kong and asked for help. The weight of the family name and the pressure of a life as a successful young jockey had taken their toll. 'I think he's trying to be a normal teenager,' Darren said ten days after taking the anguished call. 'This game doesn't allow you to be a normal teenager. It's a very hard game ... as I explained to Mitchell the other day: "Mate, you're like an Olympic athlete, you've got to train seven days a week and 365 days a year."'[13]

Mitchell Beadman walked away from racing, taking time out at a health retreat to regroup and rethink before heading back to the track in Hong Kong.

At Racing NSW, Peter V'Landys has programs in place to help young jockeys deal with the pressures of drugs, alcohol and money. Their wages are now paid into a trust account in order to temper those wild spending sprees. 'All the money goes into a trust and they won't get it until they finish their apprenticeship or turn 21, whatever comes first. Say he wants to buy a car or buy a property, we'll give it to him ... it has to be a necessity of life,' said V'Landys.[14]

But for some young stars who think they are bulletproof, it is not enough. 'Unfortunately no matter how many sessions of counselling or lectures you have, some of them are unfortunately going to be led down the wrong path,' said V'Landys.[15]

Riding racehorses is a dangerous business. In just over 150 years of organised racing in Australia, at least 314 jockeys have died while riding. Their names are engraved on the monument to the fallen at Caulfield racecourse. But racing historian John Adams says the reality is actually far worse. He has dug through the files and identified a further 195 jockeys who have died while racing, which makes the total number of deaths 509. 'It's a staggering figure when you think about it,' Adams said on National Jockeys' Celebration Day in September 2012. 'These jockeys face all sorts of risks and a lot of them go unnoticed.'[16]

In 2008, Paul Innes, CEO of the AJA, said: 'Over the next decade we can expect another 12 to 15 to die on the job. Many more will suffer horrific accidents resulting in permanent disability.'[17] Innes claimed that the true number of jockeys who had died in Australia would never be known. Records are poor, but research the AJA commissioned into early races in Victoria suggested that there could be another sixty names to add to the 'Fallen Jockey' monument at Caulfield Racecourse. 'When we started doing the research six to eight years ago not one race club in Australia could tell us the names of the jockeys who had died on their racecourse,' he said. 'I think that's a pretty sad indictment of the regard they have for the riders in this industry.'[18]

Research by Associate Professor Leigh Blizzard of the Menzies Research Institute in Hobart, Tasmania, found that riding racehorses was one of the most dangerous jobs in Australia. His report followed on from American studies that said: 'Jockeys have a higher risk of fatality than pilots and flight engineers, logging workers, structural metal workers, roofers and truck drivers, or participants in sports such as skydiving, motorcycling and boxing.' The Australian researchers concluded: 'Being a jockey carries a substantial risk of injury and death.'[19]

Talented Mount Isa jockey Corey Gilby escaped a brush with death in 2005, when he was struck by lightning as an eighteen-year-old apprentice. He was riding out for trackwork in Tocumwal, on the border between New South Wales and Victoria, when he took the full force of a chain-lightning strike that threw him from his horse but left him otherwise unscarred.

His luck didn't hold. In November 2011 Gilby had just crossed the finish line during a trial gallop at Julia Creek, in north-west Queensland, when the bandages on his horse's legs appeared to come loose and trip the horse. Gilby went down, and the struggling horse rolled over him several times. He was rushed to hospital in Townsville, where his family made the heartbreaking decision to turn off his life-support machine. He was the eleventh jockey to die in a race-related fall since 2000.

Gilby had only just moved to Julia Creek, having linked up with local trainer Kerry Krogh. 'He didn't drink, didn't smoke and was a very quiet sort of bloke ... a very nice young bloke,' Krogh said. 'He loved anything to do with horses. He would go to work of a morning and afternoon. He was a very, very capable rider and would ride any horses. No horse would phase him. He was just a good bloke. Only young, it's very sad.'[20]

Jason Oliver was riding an unraced two-year-old, Savage Cabbage, during a trial at Belmont in 2002 when the horse broke a bone in its foreleg. Oliver was thrown over the front of the horse, which then skidded along the track with the 33-year-old jockey trapped underneath. He died in a Perth hospital from his head injuries without ever regaining consciousness.

His death would have generated very few headlines, but for the fact that, just days later, his brother Damien went on to ride Media Puzzle to victory in the Melbourne Cup. In an interview with *60 Minutes* reporter Peter Overton, Damien later said: 'I was thinking to myself, "What would my brother have wanted me to do?" And I thought if I was sitting at home watching that race on the couch, he'd have been thinking to me, "You idiot, why did you do that?" So it was because of him that made me want to become a jockey. As soon as I crossed that line, I looked up to the sky and it was almost as if he was there with me and it was a great tribute to my brother.'[21]

The anguish of that time and Damien Oliver's decision to ride has now been made into a movie called *The Cup*. The Oliver family knew the dangers of racing. They had been there before: the brothers' father, Ray, died in a racing accident in Kalgoorlie in 1975.

In March 2012 Damien Oliver was sickeningly speared into the turf when Like An Eagle broke a leg 200 metres from the start at Moonee Valley. He survived that fall, which came seven years to the day after a fall at the same track had resulted in titanium rods and screws being inserted into his back.

Research compiled by the AJA reported that of the 860 jockeys who ride in almost 20,000 races every year in Australia, a massive eighty-nine per cent have had at least one fall that has required medical attention. Find any other profession in modern Australia where that kind of collateral damage to its key workers is acceptable.

There are 2690 race meetings at 370 racetracks – big and small – across Australia every year. At every one, jockeys are putting their lives on the line. For protection they wear just a hardhat and an inflexible vest, which many fear might actually contribute to neck injuries. Jockeys who have ridden in Japan have brought back the flexible Descente vest, but they are still waiting for it to be given the green light for Australian courses.

Despite these concerns, jockeys go out every day, stretching themselves to the limit of their ability, jostling for space, battling to win, on powerful animals that weigh over 500 kilograms and power along in a thundering burst of muscle and sinew at sixty-five kilometres per hour. The jockeys do this perched high in the stirrups, balanced unnaturally in order to maximise the horse's speed. Anything can go wrong – and it frequently does. A rein or stirrup can break, a saddle can come loose, a horse can trip, break a leg or suffer a heart attack. Any of these will send a rider tumbling nose-down into the turf. Almost ten per cent of all jockeys have reported that they have fallen from their mounts more than twenty times.

Ray Silburn is one. He had already ridden over 1000 winners in his career when he turned up to ride Caza Ladron on the first day of the Sayers Black Opal Stakes Carnival in Canberra on 25 February 2005. 'I took a fall on the job,' he said. 'Two hundred metres from the finishing line my horse went down and fell on top of me. The fall left me a C4 quadriplegic. That means I have got no feelings or movement in my legs and limited movement in my arms and no feelings in my hands. My injuries left me with little income. I had no qualifications and not many places to turn to.'[22]

It changed everything. 'You don't realise what a difference one stride of a racehorse can make in your life,' Silburn said just a few months after his injury occurred. 'I haven't seen the fall but I've been told I was unlucky to be caught between two horses at Canberra. One minute you're riding for everybody, the next minute it's taken all away. To be part of something you love and have it taken away is awful.'[23]

Silburn was thirty-eight years old and in the prime of his life, the loving father of two young boys. After the accident he split from his wife, the mother of his sons. Despite fellow jockeys Darren Beadman, Neil Payne and Jim Cassidy and former test cricketer Mark Waugh pitching in to raise $235,000 for him, he fell on increasingly hard times. Silburn turned to the AJC for help.

Its president, Paul Innes, led a campaign for more funds to help jockeys. During the 2008–09 season, the AJA launched a campaign for 'a tiny sliver of the growing pie of race prize money' to be put towards a sensible raft of measures to protect jockeys.[24] It was a compelling argument. The pitch was for just one per cent of prize money to be put into a fund to cover jockeys for a national insurance scheme for accidents and public liability. Given the risks, jockeys' insurance premiums are high; many could not afford the fees and so were racing uninsured and unprotected. Jockeys like Ray Silburn were left exposed when trouble hit.

'Our industry has many stakeholders,' Innes said at the time. 'In a decade of campaigning for a fair go for jockeys, I've witnessed a lot of buck-passing and not a lot of responsibility.'[25] No one in the industry wanted to part with the loot.

Former prime minister Bob Hawke, in his endorsement of the AJA's campaign, said: 'Many in the racing industry would be embarrassed if details about the real working conditions of jockeys were publicly known. Jockeys earn an erratic income; face high risks to their safety; and are not covered by the industrial protections that benefit many other Australian workers. Better welfare programs are urgently needed for Australian jockeys and their families.'[26]

Those interviewed for the campaign revealed the true hardships. Adelaide-based jockey Clare Lindop said: 'I love being a jockey, but it's a tough career. Only one jockey, once a year, wins the Melbourne Cup and the prize money associated with that. For the rest, the job involves hours of unpaid track work to build relationships with trainers, which can mean weeks of work for one ride. If you don't win, you mightn't get another go. We buy our own equipment and pay for our own travel. Most jockeys with families to support find it tough to balance their household budget.'[27]

Newcastle jockey Andrew Gibbons revealed that he, like many others, could not afford personal income insurance. 'In January last year, I fractured some vertebrae and was out for four months. I received workers comp, but it only covered half of what I would usually earn in that time.'[28]

In March 2009, an agreement was reached with the Australian Racing Board that one per cent of prize money would be set aside to fund public liability insurance, personal accident insurance and welfare programs for jockeys. That one per cent represents around $4.5 million a year. Half of that goes towards paying jockeys' insurance, while the other half is held by the state and territory racing authorities and goes towards welfare programs. Innes remains unhappy about that: 'We have no physical control over that money. We would have liked it to go towards the National Jockeys' Trust to support severely injured jockeys or the families of those who have died.'[29]

The trust relies on sponsorship from Jayco on the jockeys' pants and tin-rattling to fund its work, and to provide its member jockeys with access to experts such as sports psychologists.

When the states' half-share of the one per cent was not forthcoming, Innes went cap in hand to the state and territory governments for contributions to a one-off payout of $5 million to secure the future of the jockeys whom the trust was caring for. 'I saw them all, except New South Wales minister for tourism, major events, hospitality and racing, George Souris, who would not see me – I took that as an indication of the lack of regard for jockeys who put their necks on the line,' says Innes. It didn't make any difference – nobody came up with any cash anyway. 'It's pretty poor, considering New South Wales, for example, receives in excess of $200 million from racing, and we were asking for just $1.1 million from them.'[30]

Many jockeys leave school early to take up racing and have little or no further education. It leaves them with few options for another career when they retire. Jockeys are trapped in the saddle. If they cannot ride, they feel worthless. It should come as no surprise, then, that thirty-nine per cent of jockeys have suffered from depression at some time in their career. Many have committed suicide.

'I know of four jockeys in Victoria who committed suicide in the last twelve months,' says Innes.[31] Tony Crisafi, national manager of the National Jockeys' Trust, adds: 'These guys have left school at fourteen or fifteen, and by the time they hit forty and stop riding they are untrained for anything else. Some of the big-time jockeys have spent their careers in the news and lived the high life with plenty of money. When it ends, they hit the ground pretty hard.'[32]

Keith 'Magic' Mahoney was a typical example. People saw him as a perfectly groomed, supremely successful and confident jockey who was always immaculately turned out in purple satin breeches. His Honda Integra had 'Magic' stickers on the doors. But on the inside Mahoney was still the fragile boy who grew up in a Brisbane boys' home.

By the time he turned forty-two and was racing in Townsville, Mahoney's best days on the track were well in the past. It was 2004 and he was slipping. Already appealing a five-week penalty for careless riding, the stewards gave him another one when his horse moved across the path of two others. That meant three months with no pay.

Mahoney went back to his rented unit and packed up his gear. He drove his Integra to an isolated spot near Mingela, almost 100 kilometres inland, and ran a hosepipe from the exhaust into the car. Police found him dead inside the car two days later.

The day after he committed suicide, Mahoney had been due to meet fellow jockey Neil Jolly in Brisbane. Jolly told Richard Guilliatt from *The Australian*: 'Depression is prevalent in the jockeys' ranks.'[33] He listed others who had taken their lives, including former champion Neil Williams and his trackmate Ray Setches, who were dead within a week of each other in 1999, Rodney Smyth, who had committed suicide four months before Mahoney, and popular Sydney hoop Arron Kennedy, who killed himself in 2007 at the age of just thirty-four after suffering problems with drugs.

'All those jockeys – Keith Mahoney, Neil Williams, Arron Kennedy, Rodney Smyth – they suffered the indignity of their careers stagnating after reaching great heights,' Jolly said. 'They had a few personal problems but they never had anyone to turn to.'[34]

A key factor affecting jockeys' mental health is the wasting regime they go through to maintain their weight. Jolly, who retired in 2009 aged thirty-five because of the battering his body had taken from wasting and injury, said: 'I stopped eating on Wednesday and I wouldn't start eating again until Saturday night. That's what you have to put your body through. It plays tricks with your mind.' For jockeys, he said, the pain is worth the rush. 'People have to understand that for a jockey, every ride could be his last. That's a lot of pressure to contend with, but it's like a drug. When you're winning, there is no better feeling in the world. You're out there galloping at 60km/h astride a 500kg thoroughbred horse and you're risking everything to get to the finish line in front. It's an adrenalin rush you can't replicate in day-to-day life.'[35]

But it is getting harder. Back in 2005, trainer and racing commentator Richard Freedman warned: 'The average sixteen-year-old human is thirty per cent bigger than he was fifty years ago. So by comparison to the normal human, the jockey's now smaller than he's ever been. He's more abnormal than he's ever been and it's just not fair on them. We may not have jockeys in this country if they don't start moving the weight scale.'[36]

In the same *60 Minutes* program, champion jockey Darren Beadman, the winner of the 1990 Melbourne Cup on Kingston Rule, also complained about the wasting regime that could see a jockey normally riding at fifty-three kilograms being asked to ride in big races at anything as low as forty-eight kilograms. Reporter Peter Overton asked Beadman if he had ever ridden while zonked out from wasting. 'Yep, yeah,' said Beadman. 'And you'll go there, probably, Melbourne Cup Day, it's very easy to pick a jockey that's been wasting. His eyes are sunken back in his head, he's very, you know, like that.'[37]

Apart from a minuscule rise in the minimum-weight limits – to fifty-four kilograms – nothing much has happened to improve things since then. 'What is worse,' said Innes of the AJA, 'is that the weight for the big handicap races like the Melbourne Cup is still as low as forty-nine kilograms. That is very hard for them to waste down to when they have been riding at fifty-four kilograms all year.'[38]

For years nothing was known about the impacts of such extreme dieting. In 2009, however, a landmark study looked into the traumatic effects of wasting. Jockeys are generally an optimistic bunch who play down what they go through in order to maintain their racing weight. The reality, as a doctoral student at Victoria University in Melbourne discovered, is horrific. If horses were subjected to the same treatment as the jockeys before a race, there would be an enormous hue and cry from animal-rights groups.

Her ground-breaking study was met with a deafening silence.

Racing authorities have kept the blinkers on concerning jockey welfare. Dr Vivienne Sullivan's thesis, titled *Wasting Away: the influences of weight management on jockeys' physical, psychological and social wellbeing*, made disturbing reading. 'Racing is a reputation sport – you don't get rides if you get a bad name – and so I was very grateful to the jockeys who took part in the survey on condition of anonymity,' she said. 'I think that indicates that jockeys were looking for change as well.'[39]

If they were, it did not come, however. 'This was new research, never done before, and it came from some great stuff from the jockeys themselves,' Dr Sullivan said. 'I sent it to the Victorian Racing Commission but I never ever received a reply. I wasn't surprised, because the way jockeys are treated is a product of the system. They are secondary to the horse.'[40]

What the forty-two jockeys who took part in the survey told her was a shocking indictment of the rigours they put their bodies through in order to race. At least half an hour before a race, a jockey has to 'weigh out'. It is not just their body weight that is taken, but also the combined weight of their silks, boots, pants and saddle. They have to 'weigh in' after the race if they are placed or ordered to by the stewards.

Unlike most other athletes, this means that jockeys don't get the chance to eat or drink before competing. It means they race while low on energy and dehydrated. And they often have to do this for several races throughout the day. One industry professional interviewed for Dr Sullivan's research warned just how dangerous this was: 'Ask a drunk if he's a good driver. He's the worst driver in the world, isn't he? I don't think we can see it in ourselves. Other people can see, but you can't see what's happening with yourself. I think we are pretty good liars to ourselves. We think we are all a lot better than we are, especially under certain conditions.'[41]

Another jockey's father was worried that his son would black out while racing. Eight out of ten jockeys said they had difficulty controlling their weight. That's when they turn to short-term wasting techniques such as saunas, hot salt baths, strenuous exercise, diuretics, food and fluid restriction, appetite suppressants, self-induced vomiting and excessive smoking. Others admitted to putting on sweat gear and turning up the heater in the car so that they continue to lose weight while driving to the racecourse, prompting fears that a dehydrated jockey could pass out at the wheel. Appetite suppressants are banned by racing authorities, but that does not stop the jockeys.

In January 2012 two young Queensland jockeys were suspended after they tested positive to the appetite suppressant phentermine. Adrian Coome and Trinity Bannon were suspended for two months and one month, respectively. It was the second such offence for Coome, who admitted that forcing his natural weight of fifty-seven or fifty-eight kilograms down to fifty-five kilograms on a race day was a problem. Naturally, he was worried about the impact of the enforced layoff. 'I'm not too sure what I will do at the moment but I have been offered a job at the mines. That may help to keep my weight down,' he said.[42]

Jockeys who insist that their natural weight is fifty-four kilograms quickly find themselves at sixty kilograms during such a break away from the track. When they come back, they have to waste hard to get back into shape. The physical impact on jockeys is enormous, with many long-term side effects. Eight out of ten jockeys reported that wasting left them regularly fatigued, six out of ten felt dizzy and almost half felt nauseous. Eight out of ten said that wasting left them thinking constantly about food, and three-quarters said they thought constantly about their thirst. One of the ten female jockeys who took part said: 'You can go without food, I reckon, for a fair while but when you're thirsty, it's pretty much all-consuming.'[43]

The wasting regime also takes an enormous mental toll. Eight out of ten jockeys said it made them moody, six out of ten felt depressed and half felt angry. One said: 'Yeah, it gives you mood swings, and you just feel like you're trapped in a corner ... and you think it's just the same thing week in and week out.'[44] Another said it left her feeling out of control of her emotions and described the type of incidents at work that could push her over the edge: 'Anything. I'm usually quite patient with horses, and if they played up, you know, I'd lose my temper pretty easily. If, you know, someone didn't have something ready when it should've been. You know, it's anything, anything just got up my nose. I just wanted to be in and out as quick as possible and, you know, it wasn't as if I knew that, I knew I was being like it, I just couldn't stop myself. I was just so angry at the world pretty much for having to do it, you know.'[45]

Another jockey described receiving the news that he had a light ride: 'As you hear the phone ring you'd be feeling all right, but as soon as you heard it was a light ride your mind would change straight away, you know. I knew that I was a different person. You start feeling a little bit shitty because you know what you've got to do.'[46]

Such mood swings impact directly on jockeys' families and friends. The jockeys are irritable and hard to live with. One father said that when his son was wasting before a race, he only dared communicate with him via text message, for fear of upsetting him. Three-quarters of the jockeys said they had suffered some sort of social impact because of wasting.

One wife of a jockey described their social life: 'Not much of a family life. When he's wasting, and when he gets holidays, he's cranky. The moment he comes back from his holiday he's got to waste a week on the track to get his weight down to where he can ride again.'[47] Christmas is the worst time. One of only two race-free days in Australia during the year, jockeys cannot enjoy themselves because there are race meetings on Boxing Day. They either avoid family functions, attend for only a short time or eat just a few steamed vegetables.

Dr Sullivan said the lack of race-free days meant that jockeys, who were always worried about losing rides, seldom took time off. 'Unlike many other countries, it is entirely possible for Australian jockeys to ride all year without taking a break because they are afraid that if they reject a ride they will lose the support of the owner or trainer,' she wrote.[48] Based on her study, she recommended that jockeys be given one day off a week – possibly making Mondays a race-free day – and that jockeys mandatorily be given four weeks' paid holiday a year. A proper study should be undertaken to set an overall realistic minimum weight for jockeys, she argued, in order to prevent the need for harmful wasting before a race. Each jockey's minimum weight should be set after a medical examination. And minimum weights on races after public holidays such as Boxing Day should be higher, so that jockeys can join in the fun. Counselling and professional help should be available for jockeys, and education and training for trainers and owners.

The chances of that happening are somewhere between Buckley's and none. Paul Innes is another who believes that jockeys remain the forgotten figures of Australian racing; he refers to a recent incident to prove his point. In January 2012, Racing NSW's official magazine ran a photograph of apprentice jockey Tiffany Jeffries coming to grief, with her horse stuck on top of the barrier. Inside, a series of photographs showed the incident in slow motion.

Legendary trainer Gai Waterhouse wrote on her daily blog: 'I look daily at the Racing NSW magazine and see this horrendous photo of a young lady jockey positioned awkwardly on a horse which is straddling the rails at a country meeting. The heading is "Dare Devil Jockey". Does this really have to be the front cover of this publication which is meant to speak positively about racing? We all know accidents happen and to make this the signature photo of the month is crazy thinking.'[49]

Innes was incensed. 'I think it's disgusting. The reality is that these things happen regularly. That trainers like Gai Waterhouse and others who are right at the coalface don't have an understanding of the dangers is almost beyond belief.'[50] He wrote to Racing NSW magazine to applaud the use of the picture to highlight the darker side of racing. 'To maintain the "hidden side" is an attempt to escape the reality of these dangers and an insult to the 840 jockeys in this country who daily put their necks on the line in the interest of the industry, including connections.'[51]

Tiffany Jeffries herself was concerned the photographs would cast her in a bad light. 'Then I thought it is good to show that us jockeys have a really hard time sometimes. Some of the horses we ride, particularly at the barrier trials out in the bush, are a bit greener – they are not like the ones you see on the TV from the meetings in Sydney.'[52]

Tiffany is the daughter of bush jockey Dale Jeffries and trainer Sharon Jeffries, and the granddaughter of three-time Golden Slipper-winning jockey Kevin Langby. Dale was watching when Tiffany's horse mounted the barrier. 'I don't mind when I am riding myself, but when it's your daughter it is a different matter altogether,' he says. 'Her mother broke the 100-metre record to get to her from her seat in the grandstand.' It reminded him of the time when he himself, as a young jockey, had attempted to ride a wild horse that threw him fifteen times. 'Eventually, one of the senior riders told me "stay down, boy".'[53]

Tiffany says she had immediately been able to tell the horse was green and skittish. 'It was a bit exciting. As soon as we got on the track it put its head down between its hooves and started bucking.' The sequence of photographs showed her battling the horse as its hind legs mounted the barrier. 'They show that these things do happen. I thought the photograph showed that we do a good job,' she said.[54]

A female jockey who wasn't so lucky was Lacey Morrison. The 23-year-old was a star jockey with a brimming trophy cabinet, having ridden 250 winners in both country and city races. She was the first female jockey to finish in the top ten of the Brisbane jockeys' premiership, coming sixth in the 2002–03 season, when she rode the female jockeys' record of thirty-seven winners. Turning into the home straight of the Gai Waterhouse Classic on Ipswich Cup Day, 14 June 2008, it all changed.

Morrison's horse, Stella Joy, went down with three others in a high-speed tangle of limbs and flying bodies. Jockey Phillip Wolfgram was behind her on Street Smart. 'Lacey was the first to fall,' he said. 'It looked like someone galloped on her horse's back leg and dragged it down. We couldn't do anything to avoid it.'[55] Wolfgram's horse came crashing down in the carnage, as did Jason Holder on Centinelle. 'I was in the backwash and couldn't avoid the runners that fell in front of me,' Holder said.[56] It was a chain reaction that also brought down Tony Pattillo on Seconde.

Holder and Wolfgram jumped to their feet and rushed to help the other two fallen jockeys. 'Tony [Pattillo] was in a lot of pain but he was conscious,' Holder said. 'Unfortunately, Lacey was unconscious and didn't look too good.'[57]

Pattillo was taken to hospital in a neck brace, but was released after X-rays showed he did not have any fractures. But Morrison's fall left her unable to talk properly – her speech was slurred – and the medical team at Brisbane's Princess Alexandra Hospital had to teach her to use her legs again. And all the time she kept dreaming of getting back in the saddle.

A year after the horror fall, she got back on a horse for a Gold Coast barrier trial. It was a big mistake. 'I should never have tried to ride then,' she said. 'It wasn't a bad fall, but the next day I couldn't walk or speak all over again and I had this throbbing headache that wouldn't go away.'[58]

Morrison took a job as a steward and was very good at it, but it just wasn't enough. In December 2011 two neurosurgeons gave her the green light and she got back in the saddle, starting with trackwork and then barrier trials, before a stint in the bush helped her to get her confidence back. 'You're always aware of the risks,' she told the *Sunday Telegraph* in 2012. 'I know half a dozen jockeys who have broken their necks, but the way I look at it, the excitement and the lifestyle of racing far outweigh the risks. I'd hate to be stuck in a job when I really wanted to do something else, and for me there's nothing to compare with riding fast horses in races.'[59]

Sitting in the Castle Hill offices of the AJA after discussing the courage of jockeys like Lacey Morrison, and the rigours jockeys put themselves through simply to race, Innes shakes his head. 'Really, you know, I don't know why they do it.'[60]

RACE 5

RAPE

The eighteen-year-old female horse strapper believed the six boys when they told her nothing untoward was going to happen. She knew the reputation of the run-down fibro accommodation shack at Perth's Ascot racecourse. But she trusted the boys, all of whom worked with her in the Western Australian racing industry.

It was a big mistake.

Once inside, the boys grabbed her and held her down. They gang-raped her eighteen times. She was smeared in Vaseline, taunted and horsewhipped with a sixty-centimetre jockey's whip. They used the technique to force open the mouth of a horse to make her perform oral sex. One of the boys sat astride her and laughed to his mates that she 'bucks worse than a horse'.[1]

The boys were not laughing when they appeared before Judge Michael Muller in the Western Australian District Court a year later. Unusually for the male-dominated world of racing, this girl, who was in a stable de-facto relationship, was standing up and fighting back.

Neither the teenage girl nor any of the six accused could be identified in the case, which shocked Perth's close-knit racing community. The boys were all from good families, had strong work ethics and promising careers in the industry. One of the young jockeys had a bright future as one of Western Australia's best riding talents. The youngest of the boys was just fourteen years old at the time of the attack. Their defence was that the girl knew exactly what to expect. The fibro shack was known colloquially as 'the Love Shack' or 'the Chop Shop'.

Under cross-examination by Tom Percy QC, the girl admitted that she knew what happened at the Chop Shop. She said a 'chop-up' was: 'Where more than one apprentice goes through a girl, like they all have a turn and what not …'[2] Girls who took part were known as 'chop-up queens'. In her statement to police, she said: 'All the apprentices in Ascot have a reputation for getting a girl to come back to their quarters and getting their friends to have sex with her.'[3] She said it was sometimes consensual – but not always, as the lawyer was suggesting.

The defence counsel argued that jockeys, like footballers, were constantly being stalked by groupies for sex. The boys' defence hinged on the argument that the incident had been consensual; group sex is not a crime. The jury disagreed; gang rape is. The girl had struggled to break free. 'You must have realised that what was happening was not consensual group sex but group rape,' said Justice Muller.[4] The boys, pimply terrified youths in crisp new shirts and ties, bit their lips, went red and cried.

The eldest boy, nineteen years old and just 150 centimetres tall, was sentenced to three and a half years in an adult jail. 'We love you, son,' shouted his mother as he was led away in tears.[5] Two seventeen-year-old jockeys were each given four-year sentences in a juvenile detention centre, and a sixteen-year-old private schoolboy who helped out at the racecourse in the afternoons received three years. Two others, including the fifteen-year-old brother of one of those jailed, were acquitted of rape but found guilty of deprivation of liberty and given twelve-month non-custodial sentences. Justice Muller said the gang rape was depraved, sordid, premeditated and totally appalling.

Outside the court, the brothers' father was furious. He said the Western Australian Turf Club had a lot to answer for and should have defended the boys. 'My two boys find it hard to show remorse for the girl when they are sitting in jail for something they don't believe they did,' he said.[6] He was referring to evidence that the shack had been used for the last seventy years as a venue where jockeys and strappers lured young women to take part in group sex. Seven decades! It was a seedy initiation into the world of racing that racing officials did not see – or had chosen not to see. One former jockey told *The Australian* that the shack had been used for group sex since he was an apprentice in the 1960s. The turf club's boss, Philip Neck, was stung into a response: 'I feel very passionate about it,' he said. 'If it has been the norm, I am certainly not going to stand back, and neither will my committee, and let it continue.'[7]

Clearly, the Australian racing industry's reputation for its treatment of women needed a bit of a lift. In 2001, one of the sport's first female jockeys, Valerie Kost, was awarded the Australian Sports Medal for services to the racing industry. The pioneering Newcastle jockey had ridden her first race when she was seventeen in the 1970s. In thirty rides she'd had four wins, six seconds and nine thirds, but she'd walked away after just three seasons. In order to accept the award, Kost felt she needed to be honest about her experiences as one of the first female jockeys in Australia.

Kost revealed that, from the age of eleven, when she first walked into a racing stable because of her love of horses, until she quit as a jockey eleven years later, she had been repeatedly raped and sexually abused by a string of her racing colleagues. She finished her career early because she felt as though she were dying inside.

At the time, she had been too scared to speak out – something she felt enormous guilt over. She had been a pioneer for women in the racing scene but had failed to warn them about exactly what they should expect once they got there. She had been inspired by the courage of the eighteen-year-old strapper in Perth, however, and was ready to talk.

Kost had also been pack-raped. Her ordeal – at the hands of seven men – had lasted for five hours. 'I was never sure whether the worst thing was the continual abuse over those eleven years or one day with a group of boys – it was premeditated,' she told the ABC's *Lateline* program. 'Um, they laughed about it after and told me.'[8]

The unexpected revelation of systemic abuse – from all levels of the industry over more than a decade – from someone just awarded for her contribution to racing was shocking. 'There was a total of nineteen people that I can recall, over eleven years,' Kost said. 'That was a combination of all trainers, jockeys, apprentice jockeys, stable hands.' She said she did not feel as though she was being picked on because she was a woman; the attitude was far more chilling. 'It was just like an acceptable thing, actually,' she said. 'It's like, "You're there and you're available for use." It was almost like I saw myself being treated as a horse, as in being owned, like I was the property of those people.'[9] Even the racing industry could not ignore this.

Other female jockeys added their horror stories to the growing list of shame. Janette Pearce told *The Australian* how she had been raped by a trainer, a jockey and a stablehand at Warwick Farm in Sydney twenty years earlier. She had been sixteen years old, naive and a virgin. After drinking with the three men – all colleagues from the stables – at the Stardust Hotel in Cabramatta, she had agreed to go with them to their shared house for coffee and to get ready to go straight to work. Instead, they had raped her. She'd complained to police but had dropped her complaint for fear of reprisals. She too had walked away from the industry.

Others, scared of revealing their names for fear of losing work, told how trainers would expose themselves and tell the female jockeys to sexually service them. They said trainers would give female jockeys rides with the clear intention of receiving a different ride in return. Females put up with being touched inappropriately as a routine cost of working in the racing industry. Another sixteen-year-old told how she would be cornered in a stable and attacked. So far, she said, she had managed to break free.

The abuse was not just sexual. A successful female jockey told how, as a seventeen-year-old apprentice, her trainer saw her chatting with someone and asked her what she had been talking about. She said it was nothing and would go back to work the horse. The trainer told her to get back to the stable. 'He pulled the whip out of my hand and just flogged me on the horse,' she said. 'He flogged me, the horse was freaking … he was just flogging me with the stick until I fell off the horse.'[10] A stablehand witnessed the assault but said nothing. She got up and walked away, and everything returned to normal. With that very controlling trainer, however, 'normal' meant being punched, kicked or dragged through the stables by her hair. Fortunately, she did manage to spurn his sexual advances.

It was all too much – something had to be done. In March 2001, New South Wales' gaming and racing minister Richard Face announced that a retired District Court judge, Barrie Thorley, would conduct an independent review of sexual harassment policy and practice in the racing, trotting and greyhound industries in the state. Female jockeys warned that, if the review was to be successful, it would have to become a nationwide inquiry, with the identities of female jockeys protected. The woman who started it all, Valerie Kost, said: 'I'm a bit worried about it. No one will come forward unless their identity can be protected, because the next day they'll need to go back to the track.'[11] The report remained confined to New South Wales, but when it came back four months later, it was damning.

Judge Thorley said his inquiries confirmed that there was 'a bank of unreported cases' of sexual harassment within the racing industry, and that they continued to go unreported.[12] The reasons for that were complex but were not helped by a lack of industry action to encourage reporting offences. Thorley's advertisement calling for people to speak to him had garnered only a minimal response. The responses he did receive, however, left him in no doubt: 'It is, I believe, more than sufficient to assume that there have been and that there are continuing such acts of harassment.'[13]

One young woman who contacted Thorley offered what he described as 'a recount of sexual assault of very serious quality followed by a pattern of completely unacceptable conduct such as forced the complainant out of the industry completely'.[14] The assault had happened in 1995; Thorley asked her why she had not reported it at the time. 'The answer appears to be because of a mixture of reasons,' he reported. 'These include fear, shame, inadequacy from and age and experience and desire to continue in her job.'[15]

She had come forward after reading of Valerie Kost's experiences. She had contacted Kost, who had encouraged her to speak out. Thorley said that when racing officials followed up his visit, however, the girl changed her mind and said she did not wish to pursue her complaints. Kost told the *Newcastle Herald*: 'The two responsible lived nearby.' In case anyone missed the point, she spelled it out: 'She was threatened.'[16]

Thorley's seven recommendations encouraged racing authorities to be proactive in deterring acts of sexual harassment, and to support the reporting of it. Racing minister Richard Face immediately adopted all of them.

One of the review's key recommendations highlighted 'one of the most vulnerable situations', where young apprentice jockeys 'live in' at the trainer's stables.[17] A report in the *Sun-Herald* had already explained exactly what 'living in' meant for some female apprentice jockeys. One sixteen-year-old girl, apprenticed to a prominent trainer, told reporter Johanna Leggatt that she would lie in bed at night holding a stick, braced for a fight, and waiting for her bedroom door to open. A male colleague would come in and try to rape her. If she screamed loudly enough, sometimes another male in an adjacent room would hear and come to her aid.

Eventually, she quit. Her bosses reassured her that the matter would be dealt with internally and there was no need to go to the police. 'I got a letter [from the trainer] saying that the man who did it wasn't sacked because he was a hard worker,' she said. 'This kind of thing is rampant in the industry. It's incredibly sexist and the guys are always trying to corner you in the stables.'[18]

The problem for these young girls is that the system ties them in to a 'master and serf' situation with the powerful trainers. One of the few female trainers, Kim Moore, speaking in 2001 before her marriage to Australian cricketer Mark Waugh, confirmed that racing is a man's world: 'I think the horse racing industry is a tough industry on its own let alone for women. I employ a handful of young women and they're quite shy so I think it's probably a good thing that they can work on a property at my house which is removed from the track.'[19]

The New South Wales government went on the front foot after the release of the Thorley report and announced, amid great fanfare, the appointment of a specialist investigator to look into cases of sexual harassment in the racing industry. Former detective Lynda Summers, one of the state's first female investigators, was given the task of picking up the two cases left unresolved in the Thorley report, and her phone number was publicised so that anyone with a complaint could contact her.

Summers, who was also a lecturer in investigations at Charles Sturt University, received a number of calls from men and women about sexual harassment. They expressed doubt that the system could actually protect them, but they were willing to take a chance. And then the door quietly closed. Summers says: 'I met with the minister Richard Face and his chief of staff and they were really serious about making things happen. They were the only genuine people I met.'[20]

After the initial publicity blitz, Summers received calls from around a dozen individuals and organisations, two-thirds of which were victims of sexual assault or bullying. A couple were young boys who had been bullied. 'They were all very nervous, they didn't have faith in the process,' she says.[21] And with good reason. Summers went to meet the powers that be in what was then the Thoroughbred Racing Board (TRB). 'I really thought they were just paying me lip service. The minister had told them to meet and cooperate with me and they were going through the motions.'[22]

Sure enough, a few weeks later Summers received a letter clarifying the position. The letter said the TRB was really capable of investigating any complaints itself, and that it would request her expert assistance on an 'as needed' basis. She was sidelined, and the posters and channels of reporting that the TRB had set up were deemed to be enough. 'I was supposed to be engaged on some sort of a retainer but that never eventuated,' she says.[23]

Summers was deeply disappointed. Her gut feeling was that there were a lot of unreported sexual harassment problems in the industry. 'A lot of young girls are attracted to the industry and they naturally fall in love with the horses,' she said at the time. 'They are often less sophisticated than some other teenagers and are vulnerable. The issue for me is not so much to investigate matters right through, but to try and ensure the situation of harassment stops so they have a reasonable working environment.'[24]

That was exactly what the minister had intended, of course, but apparently not what the people in charge of racing in New South Wales at the time had in mind.

Have things changed? Racing is clearly still a man's world. In 2001 Gold Coast jockey Kelly Purdy complained about the sexism in the industry. Females were given bad rides and dealt with improper advances from trainers by moving on. 'It makes me so mad, I wish I was a male. It's so wrong,' she said.[25] Female jockeys complained that they were constantly given 'donkeys' to ride; they hated the larrikin punters' trackside mantra: 'If they've got a crack, give 'em the sack.'[26]

Bernadette Cooper was the first female to be named as Queensland's apprentice jockey of the year, with 160 wins under her belt. But when she lost her weight claim – the bonus given to apprentices to help them learn as they ride – she also lost her rides. 'It was shattering, it's as though your whole world is just over,' she said. 'I knew things would drop off, but I didn't think so fast.'[27] Today, there are a lot more women jockeys: nineteen per cent, meaning that one in five jockeys is female.

Riders like Clare Lindop (who in 2003 became the first woman to ride in the Melbourne Cup), Chloe Chatfield, Christine Puls, Kate Dyson and Michelle Payne are all familiar names to students of the form guide in recent years. There is strength in numbers. Paul Innes, chief executive of the AJA, says: 'In some races it is fifty/fifty, male to female, and in some of the country races – one in Braidwood just the other day – the whole card was ridden by female jockeys.'[28]

But that has created another problem: unbelievably, in the second decade of the new millennium, many racetracks still do not have separate changing rooms for women. Innes says: 'We have fought hard for improvements but they are slow in coming. Some of the smaller clubs only have one change room. A lot of the senior male riders are concerned that they could be accused of some kind of sexual assault because they are being forced to change in the same room as the female jockeys.'[29]

And what about the female riders themselves? A September 2010 AJA survey of its members found: 'Female members are skewed younger and encounter all the problems apprentices nominate however in addition to that they have to deal with less support, lower standards of facilities and a male dominated culture. The findings both quantitatively and through the comments highlighted this.'[30]

That male-dominated culture was underscored by a 2009 Victorian report, which said that jockeys felt owners and trainers still behaved in a way that constituted workplace bullying. 'They [trainers and owners] scream in your face and you still have to be polite or risk losing future rides.'[31] Imagine facing that as a sixteen-year-old girl living away from home for the first time, especially as you understand that the angry man screaming spittle into your face has total control of your future.

In the AJA survey five years later, jockeys were asked to provide comments on how they felt things might be improved. Several themes appeared repeatedly. One was: 'Improve conditions – especially for women. Improving workplace conditions – jockeys' rooms, make safe and comfortable. Stricter work place harassment/sexual harassment policies.'[32]

Clearly, things have not improved much. The comments on the worst tracks in the country were telling. 'Every track on the western circuit is terrible for female rooms i.e. showers and food – all shared with males,' said one.[33] Wauchope attracted particular criticism: 'Is the worst track for female jockeys. The female's room is a "spare room" and to use the bathroom facilities we must use the men's room, with the shower not having a door/curtain; hence most of us do not use this facility. Thankfully the track is only used occasionally.'[34]

There were constant complaints that the facilities for women were either non-existent or smaller than and inferior to those for men. Some were worse than others. At Coonabarabran and

Gilgandra, women had to share the showers and jockeys' room with the men. At Parkes, the female jockeys' room was too small to use and the showers were shared. Jockeys complained that at Muswellbrook they: 'Have to walk through the males' room to get to the scales and outside. Female room is too small, people have to sit in the hallway the room barely fits.'[35]

Despite these problems, Paul Innes says: 'I am aware of some male riders making inappropriate sexual comments but I am not aware of any sexual assaults or rape.'[36] Dale Jeffries, whose daughter graced the cover of Racing NSW's magazine, says that when he was riding, girls were a novelty. 'But I think within ten years there will be more girls than boys.' He thinks things have changed. 'Back in the bad old days there were always rumours; you know, a girl who was a bit loose. Certainly, being a male-dominated sport, a girl would have had to have a thick skin for all the comments that flew around. But these days the girls know their rights.' So how does he feel about letting his own daughter join that male-dominated world? 'Well, she has always been with us at our stables,' he explains.[37] Close and safe.

Tiffany adds: 'We are a small stables – there is only me, my mum, dad and cousin, so it's just family there. I have heard stories; it goes on with stablegirls and other jockeys. The girls get a really bad name for themselves.' For her, the problem lies in the entrenched male domination of the industry: 'It is still a bit sexist. Girls get a good go in the country but it is very hard for us to get rides in the city. It is rare for a female to make it there – really, only Kathy O'Hara is getting the regular rides. When we are offered rides, don't you worry, if a boy comes along the trainer will be happy to put him on over me simply because he is a male. They think he is stronger but that doesn't always mean better.'[38]

Her point is underscored by the Leading Group Race Jockeys by Group wins table for the 2010–11 season, which had only one female in the top twenty: Michelle Payne at thirteenth, with two wins and a prize money total of $620,000, a long way short of first-placed Luke Nolen, with $4,512,500 in prize money. The Leading Jockeys by Wins for 2010–11 tells the same story. Kyra Yuill was the only woman in the top twenty, coming in at number ten with 120 first places and prize money totalling $2,682,376.

Other women have left the country to try to get a better chance. Kayla Stra was an top-class jockey in Australia before she left to race in California. She too was frustrated at the sexism in the industry. 'I wish I was a boy,' she told an interviewer in America. 'Seriously, there's been so many times I wished I was a boy, and I really mean it. I love riding horses. I love racing. And the amount of times I could have ridden a horse and I should have ridden a horse and I haven't, it's broken my heart. I work the horses. I know the horses, and I could have just won on so many horses and had so many nice horses and just the fact I was a girl, they don't want to know me. They'll just say, "No." That was the hardest part of going through everything – being a girl. But I don't like to think about it.'[39]

Stra appeared on Animal Planet's reality TV series *Jockeys* but, after encountering the same frustrating sexism in Southern California, she moved north to Golden Gate Fields, where she has at last been accepted. Even then, she has to share her locker room with the track veterinarian and the paddock judge. Clearly, there is a long way to go before true equality comes to the world of horseracing. But is sexism the first step on the road to sexual assault?

Investigator Lynda Summers still wonders what has really been fixed in the last twelve years. 'I suspect the WorkCover laws over the last decade have been really beefed and have provided support to people in the workplace,' she says. 'But I might be being an idealist. Imagine any other industry, the police or prisons or hospitals, where men and women had to change and shower together. Young women are still being made to feel as though they are an outsider, lower in the pecking order and more vulnerable. There is sexism in a lot of male-dominated industries and, for assaults to occur, like bullying, it has to occur in an environment which gives some form of power to one group over another.'[40]

This is a bleak assessment, and it's one that Summers thinks is unlikely to change anytime soon. 'It is leadership that is required,' she says. 'A fish rots at the head. If leadership is not driving the issues then it is very hard to expect any change. I certainly didn't see any of that when I was around.'[41]

In March 2012, successful Caulfield trainer Rick Hore-Lacy, the man who had guided Australia's highest-priced stallion Redoute's Choice to glory, found himself before the Racing Appeals and Disciplinary (RAD) Board. In December 2008, a twenty-year-old woman had finally realised her dream to work with racehorses, joining his outfit as a stablehand. She had only been at the stables for two days when Hore-Lacy tried to kiss her and offered her money for sex. The girl was traumatised.

Unfortunately for the tormenting trainer, she was a member of the Australian Workers' Union (AWU). Its Victorian secretary, Cesar Melhem, said: 'Our young female member had every right to expect to follow her dream of working with horses, without being subjected to sexual overtures and assault by her employer.'[42]

The RAD Board's panel described Hore-Lacy's conduct as 'disgusting and reprehensible' and fined him $5000.[43] A criminal proceeding had earlier ordered him to pay $500 to charity. His career continued, but the girl's didn't. 'She could not go back and work in the industry,' said Melhem. 'The trauma left her with no option but to leave the industry.'[44]

That's justice in racing today – a $5500 financial penalty for the offender, and a destroyed dream and a career in tatters for the innocent victim. 'The trauma she has been through is unbelievable,' said Melham.[45]

More than a decade after Valerie Kost first spoke out about the abuse of women in the racing industry, it is fairly obvious just how much has changed.

RACE 6

THE BIG PLUNGE

The horses leapt out of the barriers for Race One – the Rotary Health Research Handicap – at Rosehill Gardens on 6 May 2006. Interfere, the 6/4 favourite ridden by Jim Cassidy, had a dream run. Through the middle sections, it was made easier when jockeys Hugh Bowman and Dale Spriggs rode their mounts, Admirelle and Throne Inn, very wide. Interfere, a two-year-old filly trained by Tim Martin, sailed home comfortably to win her first race.

The stewards were not happy. One massive punter, Eddie Hayson, was – he had cleaned up on the race. At the time, he owned sixty good-quality horses and regularly bet millions of dollars. Together with his trainer, Tim Martin, he really knew his form. He felt that Interfere had excellent breeding but had been misread by the experts. 'It won a trial in very fast time at

Rose Hill, beat a very smart horse in Tango Fire,' Hayson said. 'And Tango Fire then went and trialled at Canterbury and beat a very good horse, Astounded, by four or five lengths. It looked a very good bet. It looked the best bet we've had in Sydney for a long time,' he said.[1]

Hayson was also the owner of Sydney's biggest upmarket brothel – Stiletto, in Camperdown – and the stewards were unhappy that he had been hosting regular Friday-night meetings in the swanky bordello with a number of top jockeys and trainers (there was no suggestion that Spriggs or Bowman were ever at these meetings). The suspicion was that they were cooking up schemes to nobble races.

It had been done before. In 1995, New South Wales premier Bob Carr reported to parliament the findings of Operation Caribou, the drugs investigation that led to the Jockey Tapes scandal. 'Mr Speaker, on December 10 last year the Federal Police referred 42 tape recordings to NSW Police. The Minister has subsequently informed me that the crime commission found: Numerous instances of jockeys flouting racing rules by manipulating betting arrangements for kickbacks and improper rewards; evidence that jockeys signalled race prospects from restricted areas. They used signs such as touching their cap with their crop or carrying the crop wedged under their arm. Mr Speaker, the commission also heard that a big beaming smile from a jockey signalled a bet should be placed on a particular mount. On one occasion a mistaken smile cost one punter $40,000. Some jockeys may have been riding in concert to fix races and sharing the proceeds of race bets they arrange to be made on their behalf . . .'[2]

With these kind of precedents, it was inevitable that when the stewards found out about the bordello meetings and saw the

Interfere race, an inquiry would be set up. Racing NSW's chief steward, Ray Murrihy, said: 'I think if they're going to profit by orchestrating a race, first of all, [what] you want to do is pick the best horse because it needs least help. We were concerned that there was a lack of pressure put on the horse. Interfere, which was up the front of the field, it led. On the day, we asked some questions of riders that ride what we call on pace runners that normally we might expect to see up there.'[3]

The inquiry called in the jockeys, trainers and Hayson. It looked at phone records, which showed that Hayson had called Cassidy on the morning he rode Interfere to victory. They also revealed that Hugh Bowman, whose horse came in fourth, had called Hayson on each of the three days before the race. Hayson admitted he was friends with the jockeys but denied a plot. 'I might have got their voice-mail or they got mine, but we never actually had a conversation,' he said.[4]

The records also showed several conversations between Hayson and Pat Sexton, head foreman for trainer Gai Waterhouse. Hayson had been asking him about Admirelle, which Bowman had ridden and which the stewards felt had given Interfere such an easy ride. Sexton described any insinuation of wrongdoing as 'seriously crap'.[5] Nevertheless, his five-year friendship with Hayson cost him his job with Waterhouse.

The Racing NSW inquiry confirmed that there had been communication and an exchange of information between the jockeys, trainers and Hayson, but said the evidence fell short of proving there had been any financial advantage to any of those involved. It found that Throne Inn ridden by Spriggs had been trapped wide and restrained early, and that Spriggs had been somewhat restricted in his ability to ride his mount out due to it laying in under pressure. It said Bowman had ridden 'consistent with instructions given' and that while his ride 'lacked initiative in the circumstances it could not be deemed blameworthy.' It also found: 'What the investigation exposed was a worrying feature in the development and nurturing of relationships between punters and licensed persons.'[6]

Murrihy said the inquiry remained open – that there was unfinished business: 'What it has uncovered is, in our view at least, some unhealthy liaison, or communication, between punters and licensed persons. Now we don't see that from an image point of view to start off with [as] particularly appealing. And that is a matter that we intend to continue to pursue.'[7]

One jockey who happily admitted to attending the meetings in Stiletto was champion bush rider Allan Robinson. The rider of more winners than any other jockey in Australia in 1998, Robinson also held the world record for suspensions, with more than 100. His outspoken career has been a running dogfight with the stewards.

Robinson said racing officials had warned him eighteen months earlier to stay away from Hayson's bordello. Happily married, he was quick to point out that he did not go there for the 'Hello Dolly' or to fix races: 'It's a bar to me. I'll go down and we'll have something to eat and drink. There's been plenty of licensed people there. I hate going to Randwick to ride let alone going to Stilettos to talk shit. Three or four other people who think we're going to fix a race up. You know. And fixing races. There might be 10 of us. We fix up eight of them. The other two will beat us home. You know. It's with the fairies, mate. It's with the fairies.'[8]

The fairies had already been pretty active. On 2 March 2006 at Gosford, Robinson was riding a two-year-old called Flying Song. The horse was trained by Tim Martin and part-owned by Hayson. Stewards were unhappy with Robinson's ride on the odds-on favourite, which came in second to Down The Wicket. Robinson and Martin were subsequently cleared of any wrong-doing, but the stewards were unhappy that Hayson had used a betting commission agent, Steve Fletcher, to back Flying Song on Betfair.

Betfair was the Australian racing authorities' worst nightmare. They had fought a long campaign to keep the betting agencies out of Australia. Betfair allowed punters to back a horse to lose, which the authorities felt played straight into the nobblers' hands, since it's much easier to make a horse go slow and lose than it is to make one go faster and win. The next step would be exotic bets. 'I have concerns about it,' said the chairman of the AJA, Ross Inglis, when that prospect arose a few years later. 'Say they have a who-can-run-last bet and there'd be three jockeys seeing who could apply the brakes the hardest.'[9]

In 2006, Tasmania struck out on its own and gave British-based Betfair, in a joint venture with the Packer family's Publishing and Broadcasting Ltd (PBL), the foothold they needed to enter the Australian market. All bets were on. Hayson was the first owner to be charged under the new rule AR175B(1)(b), which stated that 'no owner who has a horse engaged in any race in Australia shall place or have placed on his behalf a transaction with a betting exchange on any horse in such race'.[10] Fair enough, and clear enough – except that Hayson had already sold the horse. Apparently, Martin had informed Racing NSW's officials but the details had not been updated in the race book. Hayson was let off with a reprimand.

Stewards are also good students of form. And in the combination of Hayson and agent Steve Fletcher, they had plenty of previous form to study. This dynamic duo had cleaned up almost $1 million from the bookies with a plunge on an obscure greyhound called Lucy's Light at a Gold Coast race in December 2005. Lucy's Light was paying as little as $1.10 on UNITAB – the South Australian TAB. Hayson put two bets of $60,000 on Lucy's Light, one with South Australian bookie Curly Seal, who paid punters UNITAB dividends on certain races. With moments to go before the beginning of the race, Fletcher put $16,000 on each of the other five runners, blowing out the UNITAB price from $1.30 to $13. It was a classic sting. Seal refused to pay up, but eventually he and Hayson settled out of court.

Fletcher had also been banned in 2011 for a year by Racing Queensland after the investigation into his association with jockey Bobby El-Issa and the Bold Glance affair.

Hayson was also being looked at closely for a number of plunges on the National Rugby League. He had reportedly asked Fletcher to place bets against the Newcastle Knights in 2006, when they were hot favourites to beat the vastly inferior and unfavoured New Zealand Warriors. It turned out to be a good bet as star playmaker Andrew Johns hurt his neck doing weights in the gym on the Thursday night before the Sunday game and couldn't play. Hayson denied any prior knowledge of this and, despite the business relationship between Hayson and Andrew and Matthew Johns, there is no evidence to suggest otherwise.[11]

That denial came two weeks after Hayson was forced to deny being behind a $200,000 plunge, again by Fletcher, betting on the St George Illawarra Dragons to beat the highly favoured Knights. 'A fluctuation like that on the day of the game hugely indicates that it is fuelled by informed money,' Sportingbet's Michael Sullivan was reported as saying.[12] David Castor, a spokesman for bookmaker Col Tidy, agreed: 'Someone must have known something.'[13]

Meanwhile, back with the fairies ... In 2006 they sprinkled a lot of magic dust on Hayson's favourite jockey, Allan Robinson. He reclaimed the record for the most wins in a season. 'My word there is a feeling of achievement,' he said after topping Greg Ryan's 2002–03 record of 216 wins in a season.[14]

But even as Robinson celebrated his record-breaking win – on Princess Pedrille, trained by Tim Martin, in the 1400-metre Grafton Print Fillies and Mares Class One Handicap – the stewards were circling to spoil the party. They announced that they would be examining his ride on ZouZou in Grafton the day before.

Robinson had initially led the Ron Skinner Dixon Mowers Maiden Plate (1200 metres) on the Craig Martin-trained ZouZou, before his tactics in the middle of the race led to the horse weakening and finishing unplaced. The race was won by Second Choice, trained by Craig Martin's brother – and Robinson's regular employer – Tim Martin. After the race, the disappointed owners transferred ZouZou to Rosehill trainer Chris Waller, and she won her first race in his care.

The stewards were already looking at Robinson's ride on Silent Song at Rosehill on 17 June 2006. In the Bamford Associates Lawyers Handicap, over 1400 metres, Robinson took the John Hawkes-trained Silent Song into the lead at the 600-metre mark and then kept him there. The horse faded at the finish to allow Contrast, also trained by Hawkes, with Darren Beadman in the saddle, to claim victory. At the inquiry, chief steward Ray Murrihy suggested that Robinson had 'set the horse alight' in order to assist the backmarkers – effectively a charge of team riding, which Robinson strongly denied.[15] Asked later on Channel Nine whether he had pulled the horse up, he said: 'No. I pulled it up after the winning post because I had to come back to the enclosure. But no pulling up horses. Because they know I won't help them. I wouldn't do anything wrong. Honest Al, the punter's pal, they call me.'[16]

That inquiry also quizzed Honest Al about calls he made to Hayson's brothel. On more than one occasion, he explained, the phone had been answered by a female employee who was interested in buying one of the three units Robinson was building at Tea Gardens on the north coast of New South Wales.

Later, both Robinson and Hayson told Channel Nine reporter Adam Shand that there had been no conspiracy. Hayson said: 'The betting supervisor, Terry Griffen, thought I'd backed the horse in six or seven places. They handed me a letter – a note saying, "These are all your bets" and they were all completely wrong. None of them were my bets at all.'[17] He told the inquiry: 'My name's getting dragged through the mud because I'm a big punter,' and said that he would hand over no more phone records without a court order.[18]

The stewards were unhappy because they felt they could see a common thread. They were also looking at Robinson's victory on Typhoon Zed at Canterbury in June. In that race, the riding of Clang Fashion by up-and-coming star jockey Zac Purton was called into question. Purton was second in the New South Wales jockeys' premiership when he got stuck on the inside and finished fourth. Typhoon Zed, trained by Tim Martin and with Robinson in the saddle, was backed in from $17 to $8.50. He led all the way to win the 1100-metre race.

Hayson had backed Typhoon Zed for a big win, but not to the tune of $500,000, as some excited newspaper reports claimed at the time. Clang Fashion's trainer, Matthew Smith, was furious: 'I read the papers, I know what's going on,' he fumed at the young hoop after the race.[19]

'You are reading too much into it,' said Purton.[20]

But Smith was concerned – he knew he could lose both the horse and his licence if he were dragged into a fix. Purton, he said, was on his own.

It got dirty. During the inquiry, the jockey accused Smith of lying about the pre-race instructions he had issued. Purton said he was only told to stay away from the fence in the straight.

Smith's foreman, Scott Cameron, who strapped the horse on the day of the race, disagreed: 'When Matthew legged Zac on the horses I heard him say "remember to stay away from the fence".'[21]

Others were unhappy with Purton's ride too. Marcus Corban, manager of the Cambridge Stud in New Zealand, got on the blower to the inquiry. He managed the Australasian racing interests of Clang Fashion's Hong Kong owner, Dr Gene Tsoi, and said he had expected the horse to make a wide late run – just as he had when he'd won his previous race, at Wyong. In case anyone missed his point, Corban added: 'I was disgusted with the ride, I thought it was totally incompetent.'[22]

Purton received a two-month ban, which was reduced to one month on appeal.

The stewards were also looking closely at the links between Hayson, Robinson, Gai Waterhouse's head foreman, Pat Sexton, and jockeys' agent and Ingham employee Peter Barrett. According to Hayson, they were barking up the wrong tree. He pointed to a race at Rosehill on 3 June 2006 – all the same players were involved but no one was asking to look at the phone records of that time.

'I backed Canyonville that day, had three times as much on it as I had on Contrast,' Hayson said. 'The same set of connections were involved. John Hawkes trains Canyonville, Allan Robinson rode the favourite [Throne Inn] and rode it a treat, and Gai Waterhouse won the event with Certain Magic.'[23]

So why weren't the phone records examined, he demanded? He would have spoken to the same group of friends, after all. 'Why was nothing said? Because the horse lost. It appears it's only when I back a winner that suddenly these phone conversations are so important.'[24] Robinson was given a three-month ban for the ZouZou incident and a month for Silent Song. He accused the stewards – chief steward Ray Murrihy, in particular – of having a vendetta against him, and he unsuccessfully lobbied jockeys to support a no-confidence motion against the senior stipe.

Two years later, the officials were still on the case. An investigation was launched into the activities of Robinson and fellow jockey Dale Spriggs. An anonymous punter was alleged to have made a fortune betting on country races. Stewards looked at two months of betting activity – from June to August 2008 – after officials at the Hunter and North West Racing Association raised the alarm over the handling of a horse called Shyspin in a race at Gunnedah. They were convinced the fix was in.

The stewards reported: 'What was established during the investigation was that the person operating a betting account (not being the account holder or a licensed person) was involved in a series of wagering activities between 20 June 2008 and 15 August 2008 which indicated a distinct bias towards horses ridden by licensed jockeys Allan Robinson and Dale Spriggs, with such offers to wager being at odds well in excess of what was generally available in the betting market for the particular race.'[25]

Once again, the stewards were satisfied that there was a relationship between the jockeys and the punter. But they did not have enough evidence to prove that information had been given by the jockeys in return for monetary or any other consideration. The investigators were not helped because the punter, who had spoken to the inquiry by telephone from his lawyer's office, subsequently refused to help.

Despite this finding, Robinson was still given a three-month ban for his ride on Kwila's Law in the John Cobcroft Tribute Rating 62 Handicap, over 1200 metres, at Quirindi on 1 May 2009. It was a classic of its kind. Starting out of barrier twelve, at the halfway mark the four-year-old gelding was sitting on the heels of the eventual winner, Tomino, perfectly placed to follow the same line into the home straight. Instead, Robinson allowed Kwila's Law to be pushed wide by Storm Falcon. The long-striding gelding now had more ground to cover over the second half of the race.

Rather than capitalising on that open run, Robinson allowed Kwila's Law to drift inside of Storm Falcon and Tomino, and to drop in behind Eagle Juan. With 300 metres to run, Robinson could be seen looking to the inside and then turning his body inside, removing any urgency or vigour from his ride. There were clear opportunities for Kwila's Law to push either side of Eagle Juan, and at 150 metres Kwila's Law, in his first start in twelve months, was improving and appeared set to push up alongside Tomino. Instead of taking up the challenge, Robinson allowed the gelding to remain firmly seated on the heels of Eagle Juan. It eventually drifted past the post in fourth place.

Robinson later conceded that it had been a lazy ride. The stewards argued that it was in breach of rule AR135(b), 'namely, having failed to take all reasonable and permissible measures throughout the race to ensure his horse was given full opportunity to win or finish in the best possible placing'.[26]

Dismissing Robinson's appeal against the finding and the ban, the Racing Appeals Tribunal noted: 'It is highly unusual to find a rider so frequently in breach of this rule, especially finding four of those breaches occurring in the last four years.' The ride was in the worst category of breaching the rule. 'It was a culpable ride for its lack of intention, purpose and vigour,' said the panel. 'Indeed, there was such a lack of professionalism about the ride that it presented a picture to the wagering public of indifference bordering on the uncaring.'[27]

In this, the ride went to the very heart of the integrity of racing: 'Unless there is compliance with this rule allowing the betting public to invest on the basis that every horse will be given a full and fair opportunity to win or obtain the best possible place, the industry as a whole will suffer.'[28] One punter may have been happy, but a lot of others who study form and follow successful jockeys would have been very disappointed.

After serving his ban, Robinson was not back in the saddle for long. His colourful career finally appeared to have come to an end after a fall at Cessnock in 2010 that left him with nerve damage in his skull. He suffered vomiting and dizziness if he stood up quickly. His surgeon told him to take six months off and said that it might take surgery to try to improve things. 'That is not a great prospect so I have to be prepared for the reality that I might not ride again,' Robinson said.[29] Honest Al, the punters' pal, was out of the stewards' hair for good.

'Fast Eddie' Hayson's headline-grabbing fun with the gee-gees was also running into difficulties. The punting wasn't paying – he was on a killer losing streak. In 2008 Hayson was sued for $431,590 in bad debts by betting agency Betstar, which is owned by Michael Eskander and his son Alan. Financial records filed with Melbourne's County Court showed that Hayson's account with Betstar had a turnover of $1.914 million over just six betting sessions. In a rare win, he had betted on the NRL, picking up $191,000 for punting $100,000 on the Knights to beat the Eels.

Hayson had also invested in the US Masters and US Seniors golf tournaments and, of course, in the horses. In a five-hour splurge betting on races at Rosehill and Morphettville on 12 April 2008, he lost ten straight bets, the biggest being $30,000 on No Wine No Song. He lost $163,800 on the day. He racked up further losses of $320,000 in just five days during August 2008, and then he stopped betting with Betstar.

The agency hit him with a $30,000 late-payment fee. Hayson sold twenty-four thoroughbreds at the Gold Coast Magic Millions for $1.9 million, and a Cremorne apartment block for $16 million, to put his finances back on track. The ticklish problem with the Eskanders was sorted out by October, but Fast Eddie was still losing cash fast.

From October 2008 to March 2009 he managed to clock up more than $1 million in bad debts with Sydney bookmaker Tom Waterhouse. In taking on Hayson, young Tom was following in the footsteps of his legendary grandfather Bill, whose long career as a bookie had featured well-publicised betting battles with gamblers such as The Filipino Fireball and Frank Duvall.

In 2007 Tom Waterhouse took Hayson on and was quickly down $500,000. But, under the guidance of his grandfather Bill and his infamous bookie father, Robbie, Tom knew the money would come back. By October 2008 Hayson owed him $8500. By the time the Spring Carnival was over and six months had rolled around, Hayson owed $1,005,038. Waterhouse charged the gambler $55,000 in interest and claimed that Hayson had placed a lien over one of his properties to cover the debt.

Clearly, things were bad. A few weeks after that story came reports that Hayson had offered ownership of his last horse, a $1-million colt called Wanted, to Sportsbet in the Northern Territory. In April 2012 the North Sydney Local Court heard that Tom Waterhouse had placed a caveat over the Stiletto brothel as security for the gambling debts. Betstar was also chasing Hayson through the courts in Victoria for $181,150 of bad gambling bets.

Hayson was ordered to pay $100,000 to society architect Nick Tobias for work on his Cremorne property, and another legal action was looming. Then his former partner Sascha Fletcher took out an apprehended violence order against him. Apparently, among many other things, she objected to being called a 'dumb loudmouth stupid slut' who should go and hang herself.[30] Not the best sentiments to commit to a phone text. It seemed that Fast Eddie's luck was really running out.

Meanwhile, Tom Waterhouse went on to become the biggest on-course bookie in Australia. His online betting platform, www.tomwaterhouse.com, even came to the rescue of punters left in the lurch by the voluntary liquidation of betting provider Sports Alive. He is polite, professional, doesn't drink and, like his grandfather, is always prepared to take on the big bet.

Even so, Waterhouse ended up chasing in court an anonymous Victorian punter who ran up a debt of $400,000 after a betting spree went bad at the end of 2011. The punter had won

$300,000, which the bookie had paid immediately. Knowing he had the money, Waterhouse had allowed the man to bet again, only to find that when the punter lost he went to ground. It's a tough business.

Waterhouse allowed the *Daily Telegraph*'s Andrew Webster into his betting control room and told him about the first big lesson he had learned as a bookie. A new client had lost $1.2 million to him. Waterhouse had reduced the risk by laying off $800,000 with other bookies. 'At the end of the day, I thought, "I've won $400,000. Gosh, I'll have to buy a car or go on a holiday",' he said. 'I was in my 20s. I was thinking the world was an amazing place. Then the punter left me in the lurch. That was a devastating time. To think I'd won that money, then to find out I'd sent the whole thing into an absolute mess. I saw a little bit of the money a year and a half later. Then he lost a little bit more and left me completely in the hole. There's been a couple of people I've played big since, but having that lesson was invaluable.'[31]

Tom's grandfather once had an equally bruising time with a giant Australian punter – Kerry Packer. Bill Waterhouse took on the media mogul under a special arrangement in 1976. Waterhouse had long given up off-course SP bookmaking, but Kerry, settling up after a bad day, asked for an off-course telephone number to try to get square. Waterhouse broke all his own rules, he said, because this was one punter he thought could 'take the knock' – that is, Packer could afford to lose.[32]

In his 2009 autobiography, *What Are the Odds?*, Waterhouse said Packer tried the 'martingale' – chasing losing bets with more money – and then welshed on the bill. One Saturday Waterhouse left his secretary and another to take Packer's bets. They were inexperienced, and Waterhouse felt that the media magnate had tried to take advantage. Packer began with small bets in the thousands in Sydney, Melbourne and Brisbane but only picked one winner – Arctic Flash, on which he bet $25,000 at 11/4 – and had one successful place bet. Packer increased his bets as the day wore on but kept losing, to the tune of more than $1 million. From an outlay of $1,131,000 he won $123,750 and lost $1,007,250. That's a lot of money to lose in one day today, and it was a hell of a lot in 1976.

'I phoned Kerry on the Monday,' Waterhouse wrote. 'He was sore at himself for losing so badly but acknowledged the bets and the amount owed. He asked for a short time to settle as he was in a temporary bind, and he said he was finished with betting. As you would expect, a short time became a long time.'[33] Waterhouse knew it was a ticklish situation, since the off-course bets were illegal and therefore unenforceable.

Years passed, and eventually the bookie saw an opportunity to get his cash. His son Robbie was working the trots, and Packer agreed to an arrangement betting with him: he would collect his winnings and pay his debts, unless it was a big win, which would see some money paid off his outstanding debt of more than $1 million. Eventually, following the known criminal George Freeman's tips, Packer landed the big one: he took $100,000 to $10,000 each way on the winner of the Inter Dominion final, Koala King at 10/1.

Waterhouse expected to see Packer use some of his $125,000 in winnings to pay off his outstanding $1 million debt. Yet Packer, Australia's richest man, had no intention of doing so; he now insisted the bets were separate. It was an impasse: Waterhouse was not going to pay Packer's winnings until something was paid off the bigger figure. Waterhouse wrote: 'Kerry could see the position was not going to change, and, very coldly and deliberately, he said, "Anyhow, you've been talking to people about our debt. You can go and get fucked and whistle for it. You'll get nothing from me." With that he slammed down the phone.'[34]

Waterhouse maintains that he had told no one about the debt, and concedes he was at fault in allowing Packer to bet off-course. Yet he never forgave Packer or spoke to him again. 'Kerry was my biggest ever defaulter, but the most galling thing was that I had lost him as a future marvellous punter,' he said.[35] In fact, he lost him to a bookmaker who retired on Packer's money, Bruce McHugh.

McHugh recalled Packer striding through the betting ring at Rosehill and offering former Melbourne bookmaker Mark Read $40,000 to $20,000 about a horse in the opening hurdles race in Melbourne. Read declined the bet but McHugh took it, and so began an astonishingly massive five-year punting dual with 'the Big Fella'. Within weeks of that first encounter, they were turning over $10 million a day.

It was crippling. McHugh told him: 'Kerry, I'm going to go broke or you're going to have a heart attack. Let's put a limit on bets that only allows you to back one to win $2 million.' Packer agreed, and on the first race at Flemington had $2 million to $500,000, in Brisbane $2 million to $600,000, and in Adelaide an even $1 million on the favourite. 'After they went down,' McHugh said, 'Kerry came over to me ... it was ... rather daunting ... seeing this huge man looking down over his glasses and saying, "This is no fucking fun anymore, I'm changing the rules and I want an even $6 million on the next favourite in Melbourne".'[36]

The punting hit its peak at the start of the 1990s. In just three days of the 1991 Australian Jockey Club's Easter Racing

Carnival, McHugh took on Packer and reportedly won to the tune of a whopping $55 million. McHugh handed in his licence two days later, and steadfastly refused to divulge the details of one of the greatest betting splurges in Australian racing history.

In 2011 McHugh appeared in the Federal Court to mount a challenge on the ban on artificial insemination in the thoroughbred industry. During the arguments, it was put to him that his sudden retirement was timed to protect his massive payday against the chance of Packer returning to the track and trying to win back the cash. McHugh denied that and refused to talk about the splurge, saying he had an agreement with the mogul never to talk about it – even if it amounted to contempt of court: 'The fact that he is dead now, that doesn't give me the right not to honour that pledge.'[37]

Bill Waterhouse and Bruce McHugh are not the only bookies who have had trouble turning down a punt. Simon Beasley, a former Footscray footballer and one of Victoria's biggest bookmakers, got into trouble for exactly that in April 2009. His defence counsel, Damian Sheales, told the Victorian Racing Appeals and Disciplinary Board: 'He is a person who just can't seem to say no to people.'[38]

Racing Victoria's investigators had found that on no less than 954 separate occasions, Beasley had been unable to say no to music promoter Andrew McManus. The regular at the Spring Racing Carnival had punted a total of $1.78 million with Beasley, on the condition that his bets remained secret. And that's just not allowed. McManus, who brought artists such as Diana Ross and The Who to Australia, had done nothing wrong; he said he simply enjoyed the discretion he got with Beasley's secret book.

So did plenty of others. Terry Forrest QC, acting for Racing Victoria's stewards, said Beasley had run a 'massive hidden book'.[39] For example, the Hong Kong punter Keith Lim had bet almost $1.8 million with Beasley in just six weeks in the middle of 2007, and no one was any the wiser. 'It is critical to the survival and success of the industry that bookmakers' activities be totally transparent,' said Forrest.[40]

In fact, Beasley's 'off book', which detailed the bets that had bypassed the authorities, became totally transparent only when it was mistakenly emailed to them by one of Beasley's trusted staffers; it showed $3.5 million in undeclared bets over a two-year period. Whoops. The Australian Tax Office was delighted to hear about that. The mistake cost Beasley a $50,000 fine and a four-year disqualification. And as bookmakers are not allowed to take bets from a disqualified person, this also prevented Beasley from having a bet as a punter. The board's chairman, Judge Russell Lewis, said Beasley's actions were motivated purely to maximise his profits, and that his lack of contrition and his destruction of thousands of files stored on a computer in his South Yarra office was 'disgraceful'.[41]

Beasley's continual denials and attempts to destroy the evidence weighed heavily against him. Judge Lewis said that even 'your counsel, Mr Sheales, seldom lost for words, contented himself with describing your involvement in the shredding exercise as "headless"'. Many of Beasley's supporters came forward to describe him as an honest, trustworthy man of integrity. 'The Board is unable to embrace any of these opinions,' Judge Lewis observed drily.[42]

Another bookmaker having problems with his punters was Mark Read, whose online betting company, International All Sports (IAS), was taken to court by the Commonwealth

Bank in 2004. It seems that, over five years, the bank's branch manager in Karratha, Western Australia, stole $19 million for a punt on the horses. Kim Faithfull was eventually identified as a pathological gambler and sentenced to five years' jail for the fraud.

Before he was caught, however, Read's agency had sent him lavish gifts, including two cases of Penfolds Grange, delivered directly to the branch, and invited him to the Melbourne Cup as Read's personal guest. After all, he was providing the agency with sixty-five per cent of its annual revenue.

The bank lodged a claim for $17 million in compensation in the Federal Court, claiming that IAS had 'wilfully shut its eyes to Faithfull's fraud, or consciously refrained from inquiry'.[43] The matter was eventually settled with no fanfare on the last trading day before Christmas 2006, with IAS paying the bank $7 million but with no admission of liability.

Read was no stranger to publicity. This was the bookmaker who, five minutes before the start of the race, took $1 million from Kerry Packer on Saintly to win the 1996 Melbourne Cup. It was a good bet – Read had already backed the horse himself. 'I put it straight on the NSW tote, via the Northern Territory, they'd just arranged an agreement to co-mingle,' he said.[44] Saintly won, and so did Read.

That shouldn't be a surprise, when you consider that his mother was famous flame-haired punter Mabel Reed. When her husband, bookmaker Jack Read, died, she remarried a respected jockey and trackman, Lal Reed. In 1966 Lal told her he fancied a horse called Galilee. She successfully backed him for the Caulfield and Melbourne Cups double with bookmaker Albert Smith, to the tune of $200,000 – or $6 million in today's money. Clearly, betting big runs in the family. Years later,

Mark Read would pull off one of the biggest betting plunges in modern racing history.

Read owned an unknown three-year-old colt called Getting Closer that had failed in its previous two starts in Melbourne in November 1981. Michael Fraser, stable foreman to the horse's trainer, Henry Davis, said they decided to bring the horse to Sydney and give it a crack at winning a bush maiden. No one recognised it during trackwork in Sydney, and so when the betting opened for the 1250-metre Domain Stakes at Canterbury in January 1982, the horse's odds were high. One experienced rails bookmaker, Digger Lobb, opened Getting Closer at 200/1. 'They came at me straight away, it was the perfect old fashioned plunge,' he told the *Sun-Herald* afterwards. 'I soon got rid of the 200-1 but I consistently took wagers at 50-1 and more. I was taken several times for $20,000 to $400 and $10,000 to $200.' Read himself conceded that his Getting Closer co-owners 'do like a bet'.[45]

Years later, at an after-lunch speech, jockey Malcolm Johnston recalled the trainer's instructions. 'Henry came out and said "he's a real lazy horse and when he jumps, make sure you put one around his arse and get him outside the leader". He said "he goes all right this horse, don't take any notice of his form; he'll really be hard to beat".' One look at the tote board as the horse walked around the enclosure showed Johnston that he was paying $87 and that 'Henry has gone [expletive] mad'.[46]

As the horse cantered around to the barriers, Johnston wondered, 'What the hell am I doing riding 100-1 chances? It drew barrier three and I thought I'll keep mad Henry happy, so the barriers opened and I went whack, whack, with the stick and sat him outside the leader. Anyway, we got to the corner and I thought I'll give this thing a kick in the guts – and he won by about three [lengths]. I pulled him up and I thought you're not that [expletive] mad Henry after all. I came back in, looked over at the tote board and it was paying $2.90 and I thought [expletive] me! I checked my saddlecloth number again. I brought him to the winners stall and there's media blokes running around saying did you know anything about it [the plunge]. Do you know it was backed from 100-1 into 5-2? They said a bloke [named] Mark Read organised it.'[47]

Johnston received a $10,000 sling for the ride. Others were not so lucky. 'They hit me for $60,000 to $6000 and $10,000 to $200 in separate bets. It was unbelievable,' said bookie Robbie Waterhouse. 'I cannot remember a plunge to equal this.'[48] The stewards had no thought of an inquiry, suggesting that it would be a matter for the stewards who had seen Getting Closer's previous two starts in Victoria. The bookies lost $1 million and Mark Read was pictured in the paper with a great big smile on his face.

All of that pales in comparison with the performance of the world's biggest punter, Tasmanian-born Zeljko Ranogajec. This is a man so clever that he worked out a system to make a profit from losing bets. No, really. And boy, is he rich – Ranogajec apparently punts $1 billion on racing every year. Yet, until recently, very little was known about the fifty-year-old son of Croatian immigrants. He has never given an interview or posed for photographs. *The Australian* managed to get a photograph of him at Balmoral Beach near his Mosman home on Sydney's leafy north shore after the *Daily Telegraph* outed him a couple of years ago, asking him whether he was the world's biggest gambler. It was a notion he denied. 'I'm not interested in talking to a reporter … no offence but it doesn't do any good at all,' he said, very politely.[49]

He was spotted at the opening of the Museum of Old and New Art (MONA), on the bank of the Derwent River in Hobart. That appearance can be explained by his friendship with the museum's eccentric owner, David Walsh. The two became mates as card-counting teenagers, beating the blackjack tables at the Wrest Point Casino thirty years ago. Walsh wrote in his book on the museum, *Monanisms*: 'I got the money [for the museum] mainly by gambling the odds in my favour and borrowing off an extremely loyal rich mate.'[50] That was Ranogajec, and Walsh wasn't kidding. Walsh went on to describe how he had used his mate's gambling system as a money mine, and said he was using the cash to pay for the museum and pull in the chicks. He knew all about Ranogajec but wasn't spilling the beans.

For years, muttered rumours speculated about the highly secretive gambling operation that Ranogajec runs from the top floor of the NSW Tabcorp offices in Pyrmont, Sydney. How did he win? Were there really up to 100 people employed to analyse form for his punting on races all over the world? Ranogajec said nothing, and neither did his friends. He used a *nom de plume*, John Wilson, and registered his luxury properties under the name of his wife and first love, Shelley Wilson.

In 2008, however, Ranogajec took his former bookmaker, Karl O'Farrell, to the Federal Magistrates Court in Sydney to try to recover $2.5 million he said he was owed, and in doing so Ranogajec helpfully explained the whole story. The case passed unnoticed at the time, but four years later Angus Grigg of the *Australian Financial Review* got hold of the transcripts and Ranogajec's secrets were laid bare. For punters looking for a share of the prize money, and for members of the racing community who rely on gambling money to keep the industry afloat, his operation is a very scary one.

Ranogajec has persuaded totes all over the world to give him massive rebates – unavailable to the average punter – on all his bets. He has convinced them to do this simply because of the sheer amount of cash he punches through. The totes want the turnover, but the scale of the rebates means that Ranogajec always wins, even on a losing bet. In fact, as he told the court: 'You bet to lose, so that you actually turn over more money and the win comes from the rebates.'[51]

He explained how the system works by referring to his US operation. In three and a half years, and from an outlay of just US$200,000, he had earned $44 million. Just fifteen per cent of that, or $8 million, came from picking the right horses. Totes around the world take out fifteen to twenty per cent of all the money wagered and put it back into the racing industry. Over a long period of time, most mathematicians believe, the removal of this money means that the average punter cannot ever come out on top. Unless, of course, you have the Ranogajec edge.

Once he'd persuaded the US totes to give him a rebate of thirteen per cent on every losing bet, he was set for success. 'If you bet $100 and lost $5, but you get a 10 per cent rebate, you still make 5 per cent,' he told the court.[52] Brilliant. With his system, he would back a horse and lay horses for every possible combination so that, regardless of which horse came first, second and third, he would lose no money. The money was in the rebate – the more money he turned over, the more cash he would rake in.

Ranogajec had 300 people in offices in Sydney and Hobart crunching algorithms to place millions of dollars with totes moments before the barriers opened in the United States, Australia, England, Hong Kong and Japan. Ker-ching!

In the United States, bets were placed by bookmaker Karl O'Farrell's ACT-based company, Capital Play. When he didn't pass on $8.5 million worth of rebates that Ranogajec felt were owed to him, the heavy-hitting punter called in a $2.5 million loan, launched his court case and bankrupted O'Farrell.

The US operations of so-called rebate shops such as O'Farrell's Capital Play had been highlighted in a report commissioned in 2008 by New York's governor, Eliot Spitzer. 'Rebate shops have for some time been associated with illegal activities such as race fixing, money laundering and tax evasion,' it said.[53] The New York Racing Association pulled the pin on Capital Play's punting activities at the Aqueduct, Belmont Park and Saratoga, and Keeneland Race Course in Kentucky followed suit. Capital Play was toast.

Ranogajec turned his attention to the TABs in Australia. In the four years to 2011, TOTE Tasmania (TT) almost tripled its turnover to $937 million. Yet in 2011 it only made $1.5 million profit. That's because, according to a Macquarie Equities report, it was aggressively rebating to big punters like Ranogajec, at an average of 10.5 per cent. A source told the *Australian Financial Review* that TT had forked out $45 million in rebates in the previous financial year, most of which would have gone to Ranogajec. TT was sold for a tiny $103 million in December 2011 to the Tatts Group, which operates the tote in Queensland, South Australia and the Northern Territory. Chief executive Dick McIlwain told the newspaper that the heavy rebating 'became a race to the bottom'.[54]

Other TABs across the country have followed suit, giving the big punters hefty rebates. That means the massive turnover of rebated gamblers like Ranogajec has flattened the odds and reduced the wins enjoyed by the average punter. 'The recreational gambler is losing their money faster,' McIlwain said. At the beginning of 2012, he worried that this, in turn, would result in punters losing interest in racing and less money flowing into the industry. He called rebating a disease and blamed the TABs in Western Australia, New South Wales and Victoria for continuing the disastrous strategy. 'They are giving money back in rebates to punters so they can screw over the betting pools,' he said.[55]

As with all systems and fixes in racing, there is only one big winner. In this instance, Ranogajec is that man. But there are losers too: you. 'The ordinary punter is subsidising these guys,' said McIlwain.[56]

Even the taxman is getting in on the action. In 2012 Ranogajec and his mates were being targeted for a whopping $900 million in unpaid tax. David Walsh proved very chatty in resisting his own $37 million bill. Walsh explained how he and Ranogajec upped the ante during the 2009 Melbourne Cup to fund his Museum of Old and New Art. They 'went crazy on the cup' and scooped a cool $17 million to pay the builders and keep the project on track.[57] The punters insist this is just a sideline. The taxman takes the view that a punting operation with a $2.4 billion turnover that has 300 employees working on analysis and form is something more than a hobby – and wants a cut.

Of course, no matter what the authorities try, there will always be a punter with a system, or a group looking to make a killing. Punters such as the Australian Alan Woods, who, according to Max Presnell in the *Sydney Morning Herald*, used a computer system to net almost $1 billion. This money he lavished on his favourite pastimes: the party drug ecstasy and Filipino bar girls.[58] In 2007, the year before Woods died, he splashed out $500 million in bets to recoup a profit of $40 million. The folding stuff dreams are made of.

In May 2010, Adelaide jockeys Chad Lever and three-time premiership rider Paul Gatt, along with Sam Kavanagh, the son of trainer Mark Kavanagh, were among six people spoken to by stewards after a suspicious plunge at Morphettville. Lever had been the short-priced favourite to win the Adelaide Jockeys Challenge and had several promising rides on the day. Suddenly, bookies noticed that Gatt, the underdog, was being backed in from $21 to $2.40 to win the challenge. As luck would have it, Lever called in sick and Gatt was given his rides. He duly raced home first in one race and second in the other.[59]

Nice work if you can get it.

RACE 7
THE FIX

Crystal Lily only entered the 2010 Golden Slipper at Rosehill Racecourse in Sydney when owner David Moodie forked out the $150,000 late-entry fee. He was inspired by her win in the Sweet Embrace Stakes at Randwick a few weeks before. In the Slipper, the horse drew a barrier on the inside rails and looked good from the outset, with Hong Kong-based jockey Brett Prebble in the saddle. In the final 200 metres, she piled on the power in the world's richest dash for cash for two-year-olds.

The 'wrong way' bias forced the filly to veer out noticeably in the final erratic burst for the line. Prebble was literally just along for the ride. 'I couldn't even ride her out,' he said after crossing the line in first place. 'I just had to sit there and keep her straight.'[1]

The late fee turned out to be a great investment for Moodie. The total prize money for the Slipper was $3.5 million, and

Crystal Lily's $2 million share took her winnings – for four wins from seven starts – to more than $2.2 million. 'She's got untapped ability,' enthused Prebble.[2]

Less than a year and a half later, she was dead.

In September 2011, jockey Glen Boss – a legend for his three consecutive Melbourne Cup victories on Makybe Diva – was riding trackwork on Crystal Lily at Flemington when the four-year-old filly began to fail, collapsed underneath him and died. Boss took the brunt of the impact from the fall on his left shoulder, which was fractured and put him out of action.

Co-trainer Mark Zahra was watching from the stands. 'She was probably halfway through the trial and started to drop out suddenly and then collapsed to the ground,' he said. It appeared the champion filly had suffered a massive heart attack. 'She's never had any issues in her whole life, from day one,' said Zahra. 'It's an unfortunate incident.'[3]

The Victoria Racing Club's chief executive, Dale Monteith, joined in: 'It's a shame when a horse of the calibre of Crystal Lily drops dead on the track.'[4] Proud owner David Moodie was too upset to talk about it. But plenty of other people were prepared to speculate, and they raised a lot of nasty questions.

Crystal Lily was in fact the fifth horse to die suddenly in Victoria in a matter of months. In May, eight-year-old jumper Zendi had begun the trend when he dropped dead after training in Ballarat two weeks after winning the Galleywood Hurdle. Trainer Damien Hunter was preparing him for the $200,000 Grand National Hurdle at Sandown. 'He just trotted and cantered yesterday and when I got him back to the stable he suddenly got distressed and collapsed,' Hunter said of the horse's suspected heart attack.[5]

In August, Cedarberg, a highly rated contender for the

upcoming Caulfield and Melbourne Cups, collapsed and fell through the running rail towards the end of a routine 1600-metre run at Moonee Valley. Jockey Rhys McLeod escaped without injury. Cedarberg had already brought home $1.5 million in prize money, including a Group 1 win in the weight-for-age BMW at Rosehill on Golden Slipper day. After the horse died, trainer Pat Carey speculated: 'From what I would think, usually it would be something like a ruptured aorta but the horse will have a post-mortem on him and time will tell.'[6]

The next month, promising three-year-old Delago's Lad dropped dead, also after trackwork. Trainer John McArdle's wife, Bernadette, was riding the gelding during the training run and was uninjured. The gallop was the final test to see whether he was ready to travel to Sydney for the $1-million Group 1 Golden Rose. Three days later, Tasmanian champion Conquering dropped dead in front of the grandstand at the Hobart racecourse after finishing last in the Members Sprint Handicap.

All were healthy horses with runs on the board. Racing Victoria's chief steward, Terry Bailey, while waiting for autopsy results to see if the deaths were linked, conceded that they did look bad for racing. 'It seems to me that it looks more than coincidental, but that would be just pure speculation,' Bailey said. 'It's extremely concerning. Darren Gauci almost lost his life when one died underneath him and who's to say one won't bring a field down.'[7]

An anonymous leading trainer confided to the *Herald Sun* that the deaths were bizarre: 'Yet there would seem no real reason [for them]. These have all been fit, healthy horses who'd proven through longevity that they were healthy. And in most cases, they were not extending themselves.'[8] From his hospital bed, jockey Glen Boss added: 'There's been a few, hasn't there?'

He quietly drew attention to the glaringly obvious: 'It's been a hell of a lot in a short period of time.'[9]

He was not the only one concerned – when horses fall, the jockeys suffer. Over in Sydney, radio 2GB shock-jock Alan Jones was setting the airwaves alight. The deaths suggested that 'something odd was going on in Victorian racing', he said. The 'gossip is that the deaths are induced by drugs'. The horses' health was being put at risk 'to improve performance'. In characteristically bombastic fashion, Jones challenged Racing Victoria 'to clean the joint out if it needs to be cleaned out'.[10]

Racing Victoria's response to this verbal barrage was the equivalent of thrashing him with a feather. Chief executive Rob Hines said: 'He made a point of saying "if" and so on, but the comments are disappointing, especially given tests taken from the dead horses had not yet yielded results.' So there would be no legal action taken against Jones for the allegations. Hines said the horses' deaths were being scrutinised, and if the autopsy results showed they were more than a coincidence, they would be investigated. What's more, the results would be frozen for testing in the future – that is, for substances not currently known to the authorities. 'If there is a substance that comes up through these autopsies that we can't currently test for, then we want to have them until we can,' he said.[11]

The trainers in question were unimpressed, suggesting that the racing official's response was actually fuelling further speculation. Mat Ellerton, co-trainer of Crystal Lily, said Hines' comments almost made it sound like he agreed with Jones. Pat Carey said all the trainers involved were cleanskins who had never turned in a positive drug test.

But Jones had gone a step further in his blistering attack on racing in Victoria, having dared to describe the amazingly successful run of trainer Peter Moody as 'freakish'. He stopped short of linking the trainer of Black Caviar – Australia's most popular horse since Phar Lap – with the mysterious deaths and gossip, but the damage was done.

Black Caviar won at her first twenty-two starts, making her the World Thoroughbred Racing Rankings' top sprinter. The Australian public loved her. Damn, she was quick. In one section of the Lightning Stakes at Flemington, she was motoring at an astonishing twenty metres per second – that's seventy-two kilometres per hour. Glyn Schofield, rider of the not inconsiderably talented Hay List, was 1.8 lengths behind her at the finish. Black Caviar's effort was even more impressive because she was backing up from a longer 1400-metre race the week before. 'I've never been in a sprint race like it,' said Schofield. "There was a suggestion Black Caviar may be vulnerable coming back to 1000 metres but horses don't run that fast and record those sectionals if they are. She is honestly a freak.'[12]

There is certainly no suggestion that Black Caviar is anything other than an absolutely astonishing racehorse. But Peter Moody could have done without Alan Jones's comments, which came following his galloper Lethal Arrow returning a positive drugs test after winning at Pakenham in May 2011, a few months earlier. A post-race urine sample had registered positive for the banned drug Oripavine, a narcotic analgesic that can act as a stimulant in horses. Stewards conducted extensive investigations into feed samples at Moody's Caulfield stables before issuing him with the charge in July. Rumours abounded that there were a total of forty positive tests under investigation.

The speculation was quashed by Racing Victoria's chairman of stewards, Terry Bailey. Finally, in October 2011, Moody faced the Victorian Racing Appeals and Disciplinary Board. It emerged that fifty horses had been tested at his stables, with a further three showing slight traces of the drug. Moody, the winner of the Melbourne Trainers' Championship for the past two seasons, represented himself at the hearing and pleaded guilty to presenting Lethal Arrow to race with a prohibited substance.

Board chairman Russell Lewis let him off with a warning. He disqualified Lethal Arrow from winning but rejected the stewards' call for a fine. The stewards could not tell whether the drug had been ingested through contaminated feed or deliberately administered. The board decided it had come from contaminated feed – possibly poppy seeds – although no one could explain how they'd got there. Afterwards, Moody said: 'This is a greater issue to the industry. This has happened once and I am worried it could happen again with a more public horse.'[13] And boy, did he have a more public horse!

Of course, Moody was not the first or the last top trainer with a championship-winning horse to come under a cloud of suspicion because of drugs. Takeover Target has been described as the best $1375 his trainer – a former taxi driver, Joe Janiak – ever spent. He picked up the bay gelding with bad knees and a terrible temper at a dispersal sale in Sydney. Takeover Target went on to race all over the world, winning twenty of his forty-one starts in a six-season career that netted over $6 million in prize money.

In December 2006, Takeover Target was aimed at the $2.5-million payday of the Hong Kong Group One 1200-metre sprint at Sha Tin. He was the hot favourite, coming off the back of a globe-trotting run that had seen him win the King's Stand Stakes at Royal Ascot and the Sprinters' Stakes in Japan. He was tested on arrival in Hong Kong in October and came up positive for 17-alpha-hydroxyprogesterone hexanoate, a hormone/steroid that reduces stress and can build muscle. He was tested again five more times, each time coming up positive, before being scratched just hours before the big race. Janiak was fined HK$200,000, but the fifty-three points the remarkable horse already had in the bag saw him crowned the Global Sprint Challenge Champion for 2006 without even leaving his stable in Hong Kong.

When Takeover Target returned to Royal Ascot in the United Kingdom two years later, the doping scandal was keenly remembered. Scottish trainer Mark Johnston, a straight-talker who contemporaries say could start an argument in an empty room, immediately came to the point. A qualified veterinary surgeon, Johnston labelled the champion sprinter 'the drug runner from Down Under'. He pulled no punches. 'As I understand the rules of racing in this country on drug use, it is an offence to administer a prohibited substance to a horse with intent to affect the racing performance,' he told *The Times* in London. 'It strikes me that Mr Janiak is guilty under those rules and that if I was to admit administering anabolic steroids to one of my horses I would be liable to have my licence to train withdrawn. I cannot, therefore, understand how a horse which has previously tested positive for a prohibited substance and whose trainer has freely admitted administering the drug, can be invited to participate in a race in this country.'[14]

Janiak had not actually done anything wrong by Australian standards – the steroid was permitted at the time because of its calming effect on horses, and he'd administered it to help Takeover Target travel. The Australian Racing Board did subsequently ban the drug because of what had happened in Hong Kong.

Back in the United Kingdom, it fell to fellow Australian Peter Moody, whose horse Magnus was contesting the Kings Stand with Takeover Target, to spring to Janiak's defence: 'We [Australians] have far more stricter drugs rules than they could ever dream of having here in England. Everyone, myself included, try and give our horses every advantage but at the same time try and work within the rules and this particular drug wasn't against the rules of racing … It was only banned in Australia in February and everyone was given sufficient warning and stopped using it. Have a look at this horse's current form since he's been off this so-called wonder drug.'[15]

Commentators in England said Moody's view was cynical and obeyed the letter of the law while sticking two fingers up to its spirit. Greg Wood in *The Guardian* wrote: 'It is also poisonous. Moody denies ever having given steroids to Magnus but the simple suggestion that there are trainers out there who have been testing the limits with anabolic steroids can only make others ponder whether they should do the same. And before long, everyone just assumes that they are all at it, and the innocent – men and horses both – are condemned along with the guilty.'[16]

In Australia to race his horses Fox Hunt and Jukebox Jury in the 2011 Melbourne Cup, Mark Johnston did not resile from his earlier comments. He maintained that Australian horses were winning because they were boosted up on steroids. Cheating, in other words. The regulations allow that 'a horse can have a preparation and then a spell and during that spell it can be given anabolic steroids', he said. 'Joe Janiak said he gives them to him to help them travel. So there was no denying that horses in Australia regularly use anabolic steroids. In Britain there's almost none, and it's strictly against the rules. If I was to stand up and say I give Fox Hunt anabolic steroids to help him travel, well, I'm going to be banned for life.'[17]

Just how fair is it for a horse to be built up on steroids and for the trainer to be able to work on that extra muscle long after the drug has been flushed from the system? Particularly when others are sticking to the rules?

Perhaps the answers lie overseas. Racing in America is in a mess because of drugs. It has the most races in the world; Australia is second and could learn a lot by taking a good look at the world leader. On average, twenty-four horses die every week on American racetracks.

At Ruidoso Downs in New Mexico, champion jockey Jacky Martin was sent crashing into the dirt after crossing the finishing line fourth in September 2011. His terrified horse, its leg broken, was lying next to him. The horse was euthanased on the track. Martin's neck was broken in three places, and he now faces the rest of his life on a respirator. Another horse collapsed in almost the same spot on the Ruidoso Downs course the next day. After that, two terrified jockeys refused to get on their rides. They no longer trusted the trainers to be fielding fit horses that were safe to race.

America banned anabolic steroids after a horse called Eight Belles broke both its ankles in front of millions on live television during the 2008 Kentucky Derby. But horses are being fielded every day that are pumped full of painkillers, which keep them running harder than they should, long after they should have stopped.

'This is just a recipe for disaster,' former Louisiana Racing Commission chief veterinarian Dr Tom David told a *New York Times* investigation into the carnage on American tracks. 'Inflamed joints, muscles and mild lameness are masked by medication and therefore undetectable to the examining veterinarian.'[18] The *New York Times* team crunched the numbers from 150,000 races and found that, since 2009, a massive 6600 horses had broken down or shown signs of injury. 'It's hard to justify how many horses we go through,' said Dr Rick Arthur, the equine medical director for the California Racing Board.[19]

No wonder jockeys are worried. Trainers were caught drugging their horses 3800 times, but the real figure is far greater because only a tiny percentage of horses are ever tested. In most cases, the trainers of drugged horses that won kept the prize money. And, just like in Australia, the US authorities lag a long way behind when it comes to detecting the newest high-performance drugs. Meanwhile, trainers experiment with anything and everything that might give them a winning edge: the sexual wonder-drug Viagra, cobra venom, stimulants, cancer drugs, blood-doping agents and the chemicals used to bulk up pigs and cows before they are slaughtered. Try testing for that lot.

Proof that doping horses to mask their pain can result in dead jockeys – if any were needed – came in Perth in 2002. Jason Oliver was riding unraced two-year-old Savage Cabbage during a 400-metre trial at Belmont when the horse broke its foreleg. The 33-year-old jockey went over the front of the horse, which then skidded along the track with him trapped underneath. He was flown to Royal Perth Hospital and died having never regained consciousness. As previously described, his death received an enormous amount of media coverage because his brother Damien went on to ride Media Puzzle to victory in the Melbourne Cup a week later.

What has been far less widely publicised is the two-year suspension Savage Cabbage's trainer Steve Wolfe initially received after pleading guilty to allowing the horse to trial with a prohibited substance in its system. The WA Turf Club's chief steward, John Zucal, said stewards had evidence that Savage Cabbage was suffering from dorsal metacarpal disease, commonly known as shin soreness, when he contested the trial. 'Veterinary researchers have established that gallopers are more susceptible to leg fractures when they are shinsore,' Mr Zucal said.[20]

Wolfe said the colt had a swollen leg from kicking a side rail, so five days before the trial he had told his partner, Maureen Kaye, to give Savage Cabbage twenty millilitres of phenylbutazone. The drug is commonly used to reduce swelling in horses but they are not allowed to compete with it in their systems. Experts from the Australian Racing Forensic Laboratory contradicted Wolfe's timeline, saying the drug had been given to the horse just two days before the trial.

Wolfe was devastated at the hearing. 'Jason Oliver and I were close friends for 15 years,' he said. Wiping tears from his eyes, he added: 'His death has had an effect worse than anything else in my life. We were more than a trainer-jockey team. Jason often discussed his life in our conversations.'[21]

A year later, Wolfe's appeal against the two-year ban was upheld by the Racing Penalties Appeal Tribunal, which found there was no causal link between administering the drug too close to a race and Oliver's death. The tribunal said the penalty was excessive. Afterwards, Wolfe said: 'I'm a professional horse trainer and if you speak to any horse trainer in Australia they've all used therapeutic drugs at different stages of their career. We've got a petition that's been signed by 140 trainers in Sydney stating that.'[22]

One wonders how reassuring that statement was to the jockeys who ride those 140 trainers' horses for a living.

Students of Australian racing history are not surprised at the lengths to which a trainer will go to ensure that his horse is first past the post. Or last, depending on the sting.

Legend has long had it that the nation's greatest racehorse, Phar Lap, died in the United States in 1932 from a build-up or an overdose of arsenic. He was in top form at the time of his death: two weeks earlier he had won the world's richest race, the Agua Caliente Handicap. The diary of Phar Lap's trainer, Harry Telford, contains recipes for horse tonics that include cocaine, morphine and the poisons strychnine and arsenic. In small doses, the poisons were considered a great pick-me-up, giving a horse a great appetite and a lustrous coat, but they took a long time to clear the system, hence the suggestion that arsenic might have built to dangerous levels in Phar Lap.

In 2006 American scientists tested hide from Phar Lap's skin, preserved in the Melbourne Museum, and concluded that he had ingested a large dose of arsenic thirty-five hours before his death. This fuelled speculation that he was 'rubbed out' on the orders of the American mob. It does not tally with an interview given by Phar Lap's loyal strapper, Tommy Woodcock, to Hobart newspaper *The Mercury* in 1936, four years after the champion racehorse died in his arms. 'At first I used to argue that [a] horse like Phar Lap did not want a tonic, but as time went on I adopted tactics,' Woodcock said. 'To please Telford I would take the bottle and pour a quantity down the drain each day so that he would think I was carrying out his instructions.'[23]

The mystery endures, as does the belief that the old remedies contained in the arsenic-based tonics of the day, such as Fowler's Solution, are still valid. The 2011 Melbourne Spring Carnival was rocked by the revelation that an unnamed horse in a Moonee Valley race on the eve of the AFL Grand Final had tested positive for arsenic. The trainer could not be named either, as the stewards had not yet charged him.

Racing Victoria's chief steward, Terry Bailey, said that swab samples had been sent to Hong Kong after the race. Anecdotal evidence had indicated that a new French-made performance-enhancing wonder drug, known as ITTP, was in circulation; Hong Kong had the most sensitive testing equipment to find it. There was no sign of the new drug but the laboratory did unexpectedly turn up the trace of arsenic. The poison is still a tonic in small doses and a go-slow in larger doses, making it perfect for fixing races or giving tired horses wings.

Hong Kong is the only place in the world that tests for arsenic, which presented a problem: how could they have the B sample independently tested to double-check the finding? Stewards froze the prize money and got the second sample checked out by an independent French analyst in Hong Kong. That turned up positive too. However, it was outside the specified procedure, and five months later, as stewards dithered over whether to charge him, the trainer demanded the prize money.

The bad old ways have obviously not been forgotten. Another trick is to give a horse a teaspoon of baking soda after training. 'Bicarb – or baking soda – has been used by trainers for many years but the whole perspective of that changed some years ago when there was evidence that people were using large quantities of it with the intent of trying to have some effect on performance,' Racing Victoria's chief veterinary surgeon, Dr John McCaffrey, said in 2004.[24]

He was speaking after trainer Rick Hore-Lacy was called before the stewards at Sandown. His horse Oddball had returned positive pre-race tests for elevated levels of bicarbonate. The trainer confessed to drenching the stomachs of four of his horses with bicarb the day before, in an attempt to emulate the winning streak of his rivals. Bicarbonate of soda occurs naturally in horses and is allowed as a recovery treatment during rest periods, so if any officials appear at the stables and see it there, it's not a problem. It's cheap and easy to get hold of, and it mops up the lactic acid produced by exercising, thus speeding up a horse's recovery and giving it a dramatic edge in endurance racing.

'It does not make the horse run faster,' said McCaffrey. 'It basically means the horse can perform at the same level for longer.'[25] Because bicarbonate is produced naturally, it cannot be banned completely, but there is a natural limit and tests pick up levels that exceed this. Oddball was scratched as a result of the finding.

Legendary trainer Tommy Smith also had his problems with the drug tsars in racing. In 1950 he was found to have failed to have taken the proper precautions to prevent a two-year-old called Sunshine Express from being doped with go-faster drugs. Australia's first full-time drug tester, Jean Kimble, had found traces of drugs from the morphine group in the horse after she won the Maltine Stakes in Randwick. Stewards gave Smith a five-year ban. He sought legal representation from Jack Cassidy QC and appealed.

The ban was turned into a severe reprimand when Smith's stablehand Moree Ryan was held responsible. He had been heard boasting that he was going to make money on the race. Jockey Ted Kremmer was called to give evidence. In 2011 he told the ABC: 'And I told the AJC board and everything, I said, "Look, Moree does this every week. He wouldn't know how to dope a horse. He doesn't know anything about dopin' horses. That's the way he talks." But he got put out for flamin' 10 years or something.'[26]

Kremmer's son Christopher, inspired by his father's stories from the underbelly of racing, researched the industry and spoke to Jean Kimble as he wrote a novel. He said that what happened to Moree Ryan set a precedent. 'There was a pattern that was then established in these cases where the lowliest people on the food chain in racing were the ones who got drummed out.'[27]

History often repeats itself. Smith's daughter, the hugely successful Sydney trainer Gai Waterhouse, had an equally fortunate experience with the stipes when a horse of hers tested positive for cocaine in 2005. Three-year-old filly Love You Honey tested positive for benzoylecgonine (BZE), a metabolite of cocaine, after competing in Race Seven of the Neild & Co Fillies and Mares Class 2 Handicap at Gosford on 25 April. Waterhouse at first pleaded guilty and was fined $15,000, before changing her plea and mounting an extraordinary defence.

Cocaine use, she said, was an 'epidemic I didn't know existed'. Why, even her children, socialite Kate and bookmaker Tom, saw people 'snorting all around them' when they went out to Sydney nightclubs. Waterhouse strongly denied administering cocaine to the horse. Instead, she pointed the finger at the 'known drug den' the Regent Hotel, which is close to her Randwick stables.[28]

One of her stablehands, Roy Storch, then stepped up to say that, yes, he had indeed been to the Regent Hotel the night before Love You Honey's Anzac Day race, and he could well have come into contact with cocaine. In fact, he went on to confess, he had even used cocaine himself – not then, but twice before, in November 2004 and May 2005. Afterwards, he said: 'Anything I may have done in my personal time away from Mrs Waterhouse's stables that could have caused the contamination … I am deeply sorry. I'll never take drugs again.'[29]

But how had Storch passed it on to the horse? From under his fingernails? Veterinarian Craig Suann and analyst Allen Stenhouse said that the small amount of cocaine found in Love You Honey's system could have come from human contact with the horse's mucous membranes. Not the kind of snorting normally associated with a horse's nostrils.

Then a bloke known only as Peter came forward to give closed evidence that stitched up the stablehand good and proper. He detailed Storch's alleged drug use on the night before the race. Chief steward Ray Murrihy noted that Peter was unimpressive and very unreliable, and counselled that no weight should be given to his evidence.

Meanwhile, Waterhouse's lawyer, Clive Jeffreys, produced several scientific tracts about how cocaine was appearing on everyday items like banknotes. It seemed to be everywhere. In September, the Racing NSW Appeals Panel noted Waterhouse's outstanding record of compliance with the drug rules, and how things at her stables had been tightened up since this all happened. 'This is an exceptional case. The trainer had no personal involvement in it at all,' it concluded. 'The panel has weighed all the circumstances of this case and considers that the appropriate course to take is to impose no penalty at all: no reprimand, no fine, no suspension or disqualification.'[30] The fine was quashed but the conviction of presenting a horse with a banned substance in its system stood.

Three years later, a routine urine test of the Waterhouse-trained filly Perfectly Poised, which had just come second in a race at Canterbury, returned a positive result for significant levels of the synthetic anabolic steroid boldenone. So convinced was Waterhouse of her innocence that she secured a deferral to enable testing of Perfectly Poised's hair and mane in Kentucky. Numbered but unnamed samples were sent from Perfectly Poised and three other test horses.

When the results came back, Perfectly Poised was clean but samples from a gelding, Wizard, one of the racing authority's test horses, were positive. The horse had no history of having been given the steroid. It could have been a mix-up in the lab; either way, a central plank of Waterhouse's defence was undermined, because the samples were now considered unreliable. Waterhouse said she had only paid the huge cost of getting the testing done in America because she knew she was innocent: 'If I knew I wasn't 100 per cent innocent I would not have done so. It would have come back and bitten me on the … toe.'[31] She copped a $10,000 fine.

Clearly, even the most squeaky-clean trainers can become caught up through no fault of their own. Others are just working up the next best way to beat the system. Stewards have a full-time job just trying to keep ahead of what's out there. And there is plenty to go at.

In 2004, Dr McCaffrey, speaking from the authority of his position as Racing Victoria's chief veterinary surgeon, was confident that the performance-enhancing drug EPO had not been detected in Australian racing. He told *The Age*: 'To my knowledge, we've never had a positive in horse racing and we've got such a good screening test for it now that we can tell it's been used some weeks before a horse races. But there is evidence that EPO actually causes a side effect of anaemia, from which horses do not recover, so it's a huge risk to take.'[32]

He did not have to wait long. Out-of-competition samples from two horses trained by the father and son team Bevan and Richard Laming tested positive for EPO in 2009. The results were confirmed by the Hong Kong testing laboratory, and entries for the two horses to race that weekend were immediately rejected by Racing Victoria.

The Lamings went to the Victorian Supreme Court in a bid to allow Benelli to run in the Group Two J. J. Liston Stakes at

Caulfield, and War Dancer to run the next day in the Crisp Steeplechase at Sandown. Opposing their action, Racing Victoria's barrister, Terry Forrest QC, said: 'These are, I think, the first positive tests that have been conducted in thoroughbred racing.' And he added: 'It is of great concern to authorities.'[33] The Victorian Supreme Court's Justice Elizabeth Hollingworth said the stewards had not acted unfairly and dismissed the Lamings' application.

The discovery was of great concern to jockey Craig Williams. Benelli had won at Sandown in June and at Caulfield in July. If those wins were scratched, Williams' share of the 2008–09 Melbourne jockeys' premiership title – for which he was then tied with Damien Oliver – would be in jeopardy.

In the end, Williams was safe but the Lamings were not. EPO is used for treating anaemia in humans; in horses, it increases the supply of oxygen to the muscles and can add a crucial couple of seconds to a horse's time over the course of a race. The side-effect, an increase in blood pressure, can also kill the horse.

Richard Laming eventually pleaded guilty to seven charges of having unregistered drugs at the family's Clyde training complex. He was disqualified for three years and fined $3250, and his father, Bevan, was fined $1000. The Racing Appeals and Disciplinary Board's chairman, Judge Russell Lewis, said that the use of EPO 'tarnishes the image of racing'; as a result, 'nothing less than a lengthy term of disqualification is warranted.'[34]

Go-fast drugs that have catastrophic effects on horses are nothing new. The big one is etorphine, known at the track as elephant juice. Although it's used as a tranquilliser on large animals such as elephants, if administered in the right way to horses it can act as an incredible stimulant.

Elephant juice first hit the headlines in Western Australia in the 1980s. Back then, racing in Perth was known colloquially as the wild, wild west – thanks in no small part to the antics of exuberant cavalier banker Laurie Connell. He already had form: in 1975 he was banned for two years for a dodgy deal that became known as 'the Kalgoorlie Sting'.

Connell knew that the race call from Melbourne to Kalgoorlie was delayed by the relay station in Perth. He waited in Kalgoorlie, and once he got the tip from his Melbourne offsider he put his money on His Worship to win, knowing full well he was backing the victor. Unfortunately for him, he only managed to bet $790 of his planned $8000 as the price firmed. Then the stewards started looking into it and he was banned. The stewards suspected, but could not prove, that he had done it before. Connell didn't care – he just wanted to win.

In 1983 Connell fixed the AHA Cup at Bunbury. He paid jockey Danny Hobby to jump off the favourite, Strike Softly, and leave the way open for the horse Connell had heavily backed, Saratoga Express. An unrepentant Danny Hobby explained to the ABC years later why he had taken Connell's $5000 to leap off the horse at the start of the race: 'Sometimes the money's better if you get beaten than what it is if you win. If you see in my case for Strike Softly I was going to get two hundred dollars to win that race and five thousand to lose it. So that the choice, for me, was obvious. There was no argument for me or, no, there was no battle of conscience for me in it. The choice was there and the choice was obvious. I mean, we didn't realise that we were actually breaking a law when we did it because we were doing it all the time and other people were doing it.'[35]

That race did not go too well for Connell, either: the riderless Strike Softly obstructed Saratoga Express, leaving the way clear for a 6/1 shot, Rowella, to romp home. Hobby got a two-year ban, and then Connell paid for him to go overseas for eight years on an all-expenses-paid trip, in order to keep him out of the clutches of the other investigators nipping at Connell's heels.

'He was the best travel agent I'd ever dealt with,' said Hobby. 'I mean, I used to ring from somewhere – I'd be sitting in London, lying in bed still, and I decided . . . I might go to France or Switzerland. So I'd pack my case and make a phone call and by the time I got to the airport there'd be a ticket there waiting for me. I mean . . . you couldn't ask for better.'[36] The cost of Hobby's enforced holiday was put at more than $1 million. Eventually, he came home to face the music. He was jailed for three years and warned off racecourses for seventeen years.

Meanwhile, Connell moved on from paying off jockeys to fixing the horses and winning, thanks to the crooked joys of elephant juice. One of his trainers at the time was George Way. They had a winner with Brash Son at Ascot in Perth in January 1987. It tested positive for etorphine and Way was banned for twenty years.

Shortly after, Connell had the favourite in the 1987 Perth Cup, Rocket Racer, trained by Buster O'Malley. Connell reportedly had at least $500,000 riding on the 2/1 favourite, plus the $210,000 prize money. He boasted that some of the bets had been put on eight weeks previously, when the horse had been priced at 50/1. Top hoop John Miller wasted six kilos below his normal fifty-four-kilogram riding weight to pilot Rocket Racer in the race. He had nothing to do. Rocket Racer absolutely flew home – in front from the start and over the finish line nine lengths ahead of its nearest rival. Immediately the cry of 'Elephant juice!' went up.

Connell shouted the members' stand to drinks for the rest of

Black Caviar at Ascot in England in June 2012. She claimed her historic twenty-second straight win by a nose, and jockey Luke Nolan, in trademark salmon silks, came in for ferocious criticism for allowing the mighty mare to cruise in the final stretch. It later emerged she was carrying an injury. (Action Plus Sports Images / Alamy)

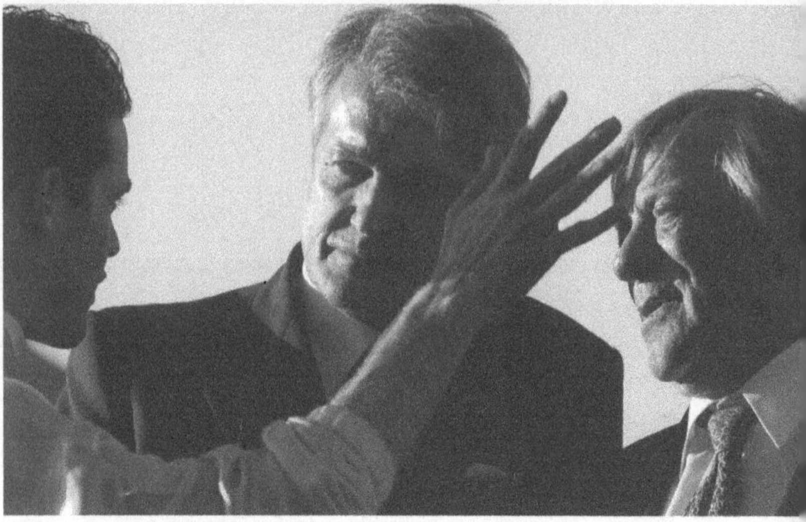

Les Samba (centre) speaks to his future son-in-law, Danny Nikolic, and trainer Bobby Thompson on Stradbroke Cup race day at Eagle Farm in Brisbane in 2004. Those were the halcyon days. Samba would die in a hail of bullets, Nikolic's marriage to Victoria Samba would end in divorce, and the jockey would be mired in the Smoking Aces corruption allegations. (Andy Zakeli / Fairfax Syndication)

Self-made mining magnate Nathan Tinkler at Randwick Racecourse in September 2008. He came into racing like a whale, splashing big. But by the middle of 2012 he was reportedly unsuccessfully trying to sell his racing empire to Qatari royal Sheikh Fahad Al Thani for $200 million – $100 million less than he had paid to build it up; and was being accused by many contractors of not paying his bills, and by his Patinack workers of not paying their superannuation. Eventually, in May 2013, he sold off the Patinack Farm stable in a series of Magic Millions sales. (Nic Walker / Fairfax Media)

Delighted trainer Gai Waterhouse celebrates the Jupiters Magic Millions victory of Dance Hero in Queensland with jockey Chris Munce in January 2004. Munce would go on to export his successful career to Hong Kong. And get greedy. He was jailed for thirty months after Hong Kong's Independent Commission Against Corruption caught him swapping tips for bets. (Andy Zakeli / Fairfax Media)

'Ring-a-ding-ding, the Pumper is king.' Controversial jockey Jim Cassidy celebrates in typically flamboyant style after riding Maluckyday to victory in the Victoria Derby Lexus Stakes in 2010. He is less forthcoming when questioned about being caught on tape taking money for tips. (Paul Rovere / Fairfax Media)

Everybody loved jockey Stathi Katsidis, pictured here after coming second in Race 5 at Turf Club Racing at Eagle Farm, Brisbane, in May 2004. He said he had put his wild ways behind him, but just five days before he was due to ride Shoot Out in the 2010 Cox Plate, he was found dead on his living-room floor after a twelve-hour drink and drug binge. (Andy Zakeli / Fairfax Media)

Damien Oliver celebrates his 2002 Melbourne Cup victory on Media Puzzle just days after his brother Jason died in a horrific fall during a trial at Belmont. 'As soon as I crossed that line, I looked up to the sky and it was almost as if he was there with me and it was a great tribute to my brother,' he said afterwards. (Sharon Smith / Fairfax Media)

Trainer Rick Hore-Lacy at Flemington in 2011. Two days after a twenty-year-old female stablehand joined his outfit, he tried to kiss her and offered her money for sex. The Racing Appeals and Disciplinary Board described his behaviour as 'disgusting and reprehensible' and fined him $5000. His career carried on but the traumatised girl left the industry. (Michael Dodge / Newspix)

Pioneering female jockey Valerie Kost. In thirty rides she had four wins, six seconds and nine thirds. She later revealed that she quit her career after three seasons because of repeated sexual abuse, including a five-hour pack rape by seven men in the racing industry. She spoke out when other women told of similar abuse by male colleagues. (Anita Jones / Fairfax Media)

Sydney brothel owner Eddie Hayson arriving at Racing NSW's Mascot headquarters in 2006 for an inquiry into the win of previously unraced two-year-old Interfere. Stewards were apparently unhappy that he was hosting regular Friday night meetings for jockeys and trainers at his swanky Stiletto bordello in Camperdown. (Brett Costello / Newspix)

Professional punter Stephen Fletcher checking the form during a break in the 2011 Racing Queensland inquiry into his punting activities. He was banned for a year for his role in jockey Bobby El-Issa's questionable ride on Bold Glance, but was subsequently cleared of the charges on appeal. (Jono Searle / Newspix)

DRUGS IN SPORT...
JUST SAY NEIGH.
Wilcox

A rare shot of publicity-shy Zeljko Ranogajec, one of the world's biggest punters. He and his mates worked out a system so good that one of them, David Walsh, funded the Tasmanian Museum of Old and New Art on the back of it. Unfortunately in 2012 the taxman came looking for a $900 million slice of the action. (Craig Greenhill / Newspix)

Underworld boss Tony Mokbel enjoys a chuckle with bookmaker Frank Hudson during Oaks Day at Flemington Racecourse in 2004. Publication of this picture incensed authorities – Mokbel bragged he had just won $400,000 on the Melbourne Cup, while his assets were frozen by police. New laws giving police the power to ban known criminals from racetracks were passed the following year. (Craig Borrow / Newspix)

The Galleywood Hurdle at Warrnambool in May 2010. Sirrocean Storm broke his leg at the third hurdle. As the other horses thundered round for the second time, the jockey and track workers desperately attempted to get the horse to stand on its three good legs and clear the track. The horse stood – and fell – time after time, before he was finally destroyed on the edge of the track. (Pat Scala / Fairfax Media)

'You'd have to say you could do with less excitement, but it was a hell of a spectacle,' said Racing Victoria's chief executive, Rob Hines. At the 2011 Warrnambool Grand Annual Steeple, riderless horse Banna Strand jumped a high-brush fence, which it mistook for a steeple, and landed in a crowd of spectators. Seven spectators, including an eighty-year-old woman and a two-year-old boy, were taken to hospital. (Sharon Lee Chapman)

Blue Magic. Victorian trainer Rod Weightman outside the stewards' room at Moonee Valley Racecourse in 2004. His astonishing success rate with broken-down old racehorses that had been picked up for just a few thousand dollars was eventually attributed to the stamina-enhancing drug propantheline bromide, known colloquially as 'blue magic'. (Jon Hargest / Newspix)

Queensland trainer Hayden Haitana with Australia's most infamous racehorse, Fine Cotton, at his stables in Brisbane in 1984. Haitana was jailed for his part in the ring-in. He claimed he was left in no doubt what would happen to him if he did not take part. 'Oh, they just told me I'd end up like [murdered trainer] George Brown, you know. Um, there's always those threats involved; there's guys walking around the stables carrying guns and stuff, pistols,' he said. (News Ltd Archive / Newspix)

Bill and Robbie Waterhouse at their 1984 Australian Jockey Club appeal hearing, as the Fine Cotton scandal rumbled on. The clumsy swap of picnic racer Fine Cotton for a horse called Bold Glance is Australia's most famous fix and demolished the Waterhouses' grip on the nation's betting industry. They still protest their innocence. (Ian Mainsbridge / Newspix)

Melbourne Cup-winning jockey Darren Beadman falls from Pembleton at Randwick in December 2000. Like all jockeys Beadman has had a number of accidents, but a horror fall during a barrier trial at Sha Tin in Hong Kong in 2012 effectively ended his career. 'Mate, my last ride [in a race] was a winner, that was where I was at. I'm just glad I've had my day in the sun,' he said. (Simon Alekna / Fairfax Media)

The Sheriff. Chief Steward John Schreck, scourge of racing cheats everywhere. Pictured here in 2004 giving the official word on the suspensions of jockeys Jim Cassidy and Kevin Moses at the conclusion of that race-fixing inquiry. (Jeff Herbert / Newspix)

the afternoon, while Rocket Racer continued running around the track. When he was eventually stopped and brought to the scale, both jockey and horse were in a pitiful state – Miller because of the extreme wasting and Rocket Racer because he had run himself into the ground. The horse was staggering around the mounting yard.

Chief steward John Mahoney ordered him to be taken to his stall for emergency treatment – a saline drench. The horse was considered too ill for a swab to be taken, and so the suspicion of elephant juice was never proved. The distressing images of the shattered horse being manhandled off the track played across the national news that evening, confirming for the Australian public what they had long suspected – that racing in Perth at the time was rotten.

Still Connell didn't care – he was too busy celebrating at his swanky restaurant, The Mediterranean. Rocket Racer recovered and raced once more, a month later. He came fourth and then died in mysterious circumstances while spelling after that race.

Connell's antics off the course with his collapsed Rothwells Merchant Bank eventually led to the WA Inc. Royal Commission and the jailing of both Connell and former premier Brian Burke. In 1996, Connell died of a heart attack at the age of forty-nine in his luxurious Peppermint Grove apartment with less than $2000 cash to his name.

Stewards are constantly looking for suspicious activity or anything that smacks of a fix to improve a horse's performance. If the stipes are clamping down on horses going quicker, the obvious thing is to make them go slower. As we have seen, there is big money to be made when the favourite does not come home first.

And, of course, there's a drug for that. Dr McCaffrey told *The Age*: 'A beta blocker called Timolol hit Sydney racing some years ago. Beta blockers were the ones the shooters used to slow their heart rate down so their hand doesn't move while they are shooting. In horses, they would appear normal, but the heart wouldn't go any faster so the horses would just stop.'[37]

Three horses from prominent stables were nobbled in Sydney at the start of 1990: Consort, trained by Dr Geoff Chapman, The Oval, trained by Bart Cummings, and Signal, trained by Vic Thompson. All three tested positive for Timolol. The stewards called in twelve bookmakers to be quizzed behind closed doors and then passed on the names of a 'handful of heavies' to the Gaming Squad of the New South Wales Police. Nothing came of that and no one was charged.[38]

But there was plenty of Timolol around, and a year later trainers were being warned to be on the lookout for nobblers. In the 1900-metre Sports Cricket Club Plate at Canterbury, the heavily favoured Sir Tito showed all the signs of being a Timolol horse. It did not just get beaten, it got distanced – by twenty-two lengths – by the strongly backed Red Taipan.

Jockey Shane Dye told stewards that his horse was 'terribly beaten' at the 1000-metre mark. 'Going to the barrier he dipped, favouring his off-side but I can't use that as an excuse. He was beaten 300 yards,' said Dye. 'He was wandering around like a drunken sailor.'[39] Sir Tito's trainer was Dr Chapman. He was nonplussed by the performance of a horse that had recently won at Randwick.

The AJC's chief steward, John Schreck, was forthright: 'There are some very ordinary people who live under rocks but come out at carnival time.' And he warned: 'While trainers should always be aware of their responsibilities when it comes to security, they should be even more so now.'[40]

Naturally, those with money don't need to cheat with drugs

– or so it would seem. In 2009 the International Equestrian Federation found that an endurance racehorse, Tahhan – owned by Sheikh Mohammed bin Rashid Al Maktoum, the ruler of Dubai and the world's most powerful racehorse owner – had tested positive for two banned substances, including the steroid stanozolol, in two competitions. Trainer Abdullah bin Huzaim, no doubt trembling at the time, admitted to doping the horse without the Sheikh's knowledge and copped a one-year ban.

In endurance racing, however, it is the rider who is held primarily responsible for the horse's condition, so all the Sheikh received was a six-month ban and a fine of 4500 Swiss francs. His wife, Princess Haya of Jordan, was the president of the International Equestrian Foundation and was leading a clean-sport campaign at the time.

Ah, racing – you couldn't make it up.

RACE 8

RAMPANT

The South African voice on the other end of licensed Victorian rails bookmaker Rod Cleary's telephone line was familiar. During two days of the 2007 Spring Racing Carnival, a man called Jack Hinden had placed five bets, the biggest of which was $100 each way. The only problem was that 'Jack Hinden' was not actually Jack Hinden. He was Stephen Allanson, at the time the chief executive officer of Racing Victoria, and he was calling from racing HQ's very own committee room.

While committee members entertained distinguished guests under Carl Kahler's famous 1887 paintings of the Flemington Spring Carnival, the 47-year-old chief executive was a having a sneaky punt on the blower. After a lifetime in racing, twenty-one years of which were with Racing Victoria, Allanson should have known that placing a bet under a false name was against the rules of racing.

And even if that had slipped his memory, one of his staff, bookmakers' supervisor Anthony O'Connell, had reminded him. A member of O'Connell's team had picked up Allanson's betting activities on 17 October and 26 October that year. Allanson's South African accent was easily recognisable to the staff who routinely monitored bookies' betting tapes. O'Connell confronted his boss on 12 November and was heartily reassured that Allanson had not broken any rules and that it would not happen again.

Then the wheels came off. On 8 January 2008 an anonymous punter tipped off Racing Victoria investigator Jim Monaghan, and two days later the chief steward, Des Gleeson, launched an inquiry. It was all very hush-hush, and anyway, as Allanson reassured them, he had only placed five bets. Even the board was kept in the dark.

At that stage, Racing Victoria's chairman, Michael Duffy, should have looked into the *nom de plume* Allanson chose for his irregular punting activities. The real Jack Hinden was a South African hero of the Boer War, lionised for his destructive talent against British railways. Allanson would prove to have an equally destructive power over the cosy silence that shrouded much of what went on in Victorian racing on his watch.

On Monday 11 February 2008, the ten-member board of Racing Victoria gathered for a regular meeting. The chief executive and the chairman, Allanson and Duffy, did not feel the need to inform the other eight members about the ongoing inquiry. It might be fair to assume, however, that the board members would have appreciated a heads-up about Des Gleeson's quizzing of bookmaker Rod Cleary the Saturday before

– particularly given that the five bets he was asking about had been placed by the man Gleeson would be reporting back to.

It did not matter. The next day, the board members learned of the investigation for the first time – it had been leaked to *The Australian*. Allanson started to panic. He spoke to O'Connell and was alarmed to hear that all betting transactions were archived for seven years.

On Wednesday 13 February, Allanson attempted to pressure O'Connell into getting more involved in the investigation and interceding on his behalf. Allanson wanted him to prevent the archived records from being retrieved. O'Connell refused, unswayed by his boss's pleading.

No wonder Allanson was worried. The archives revealed that he had placed a further thirty-seven bets between January and September of 2007. Allanson had lied. He fell on his sword. In a prepared statement, he said: 'After spending a lifetime in thoroughbred racing administration, I have an appreciation of the critical importance of integrity in the conduct of racing.' And he continued: 'While the recent events concerning my actions in betting under a nom de plume were not a breach of the rules, it is clear the action was inappropriate and a serious mistake. For that, I am deeply sorry.'[1] Incredibly, although betting under a false name *is* against the rules, it is not actually a punishable offence to do so.

So basically, Allanson had done nothing illegal, although it certainly appeared unethical. Newspapers at the time suggested that perhaps Cleary was offering him a better price – an accusation that was never substantiated. But the bookie had broken the rules by taking the bets under a false name. Cleary was reminded of his obligations to make sure he had the right name in future and let off with a warning.

Allanson's mistake was that he lied – and got caught. But the handling of the whole sorry affair raised more serious questions. Opposition racing spokesman Denis Napthine went after the chairman of Racing Victoria like a terrier. 'I think Michael Duffy has got a lot to answer [for] here in that he has been involved in a secret arrangement, a cover-up, that has been exposed by good media investigation,' he said. 'He was trying to keep a lid on the whole thing, trying to shut it down, keep people in the dark and protect Stephen Allanson.'[2]

Clearly, a full inquiry was required. The rules for punters to disclose their identity were put in place in order to prevent criminals from using bookies to launder money. Of all people, Allanson should have known just how important those rules were. His gambling had started a chain reaction that would really prove the point.

Allanson went home to become a full-time dad. He had indeed spent a lifetime in racing. His father, Don, was a jockey and later chief starter in the KwaZulu-Natal province of South Africa. At thirteen, Allanson had joined the Durban Turf Club as a casual totalisator technician, before migrating in 1987 to Australia, where he joined the Victoria Racing Club as the bookmakers' supervisor. He progressed through the jobs of manager (betting services), general manager (technology, planning and development) and director of racing operations, before in 2006 becoming chief executive. At home with his four children, he said: 'I made a foolish decision to put the bets in a false name because I didn't want my staff to know my bets. In hindsight it was a silly thing to do and I regret it ... The biggest regret is that I didn't openly and immediately tell the chairman [the full story].'[3]

The full story, when the official report was handed to the

Office of Gaming and Racing in March 2008, was that Allanson had used an alias to place 692 bets with bookmaker Rod Cleary in 500 phone calls over a five-year period. For a man who was the boss of racing in Victoria, he did not prove to be a very good measure of horseflesh – he was down $7000.

The inquiry conducted by the stewards, Pricewaterhouse-Coopers and investigator Calibre International found that his bets ranged from $20 to $400. Embarrassingly, the report was finished before Des Gleeson thought to enquire whether Allanson had also been placing bets with the big corporate bookmakers. He gave Darwin-based Sportsbet just two days to check its records to see whether the former chief executive had any accounts with them.

Even then, Gleeson was only prodded into action when Sportsbet chief executive Matt Tripp questioned the thoroughness of the inquiry in the *Herald Sun*. 'No one asked to look at our books,' Tripp told the newspaper. 'And representatives of the Northern Territory Racing Commission have told me they believed no other company's books have been examined. Just how fair dinkum are they?'[4]

Victoria's racing minister, Rob Hulls, swung into action, appointing a retired judge, Gordon Lewis, to examine integrity in the Victorian racing industry. The can of worms was about to open.

Judge Lewis called on Victoria Police's organised crime squad, the Purana Taskforce, and the Australian Crime Commission for help. They briefed him fully, as he later revealed in his report: 'The further I probed, particularly about allegations of criminal involvement, and certainly after submissions from and subsequent discussions with the Purana Taskforce, I was satisfied that the racing industry was affected by a more serious blight than had been suggested by the isolated matter of Allanson. Access to an anonymised Australian Crime Commission (ACC) report, sourced to me by Victoria Police, convinced me that criminal activity in the industry was rampant.'[5]

Rampant! The strong word upset quite a few in Victorian racing, although it was, it seems, totally justified. The Purana Taskforce had been set up to investigate organised crime, following a spate of gangland killings that were immortalised in all their blood-soaked glory in Channel Nine's *Underbelly* television series. The taskforce eventually brought to an end the tit-for-tat shootings that left most of the Moran clan dead and Carl Williams bashed to death inside Barwon Prison. A by-product was that it also tracked a lot of the people the crooks were dealing with.

'Accordingly a large number of persons associated with the racing industry, including bookmakers, trainers, jockeys, commission agents and racetrack identities have come to the attention of police, as having improper associations with known criminals,' wrote Judge Lewis. Oh dear. He continued: 'Available information suggests a culture of tolerating criminality within the racing industry, whereby funds suspected of being illicitly attained are widely accepted by industry participants including bookmakers, trainers and horse owners.'[6]

So, dodgy money in the industry was acceptable. And what about dodgy people? 'A number of industry and non-industry representatives knowingly engaged in betting activity with suspicious persons. It appears many horse racing industry participants were not concerned with whether or not funds used to engage in betting were legitimately attained. Participants typically took the position that persons subject to criminal charges and likely to be betting with illicitly attained funds were "innocent until proven guilty" and welcome to continue betting.'[7] Translation: Your money's good with me, guv.

A lot of the information on people in racing circles came up circumstantially as the police attempted to get the dirt on one man in particular: Tony Mokbel. The Ferrari-driving underworld boss behind the Victorian amphetamines trade hit the headlines when he was investigated over several killings in the Melbourne gangland wars and did a runner to Greece. He was extradited to face the music in 2008.

But before all that became public knowledge, Tony Mokbel had made a lot of friends in the racing industry. Judge Lewis reported: 'A major focus of Purana has been the investigation of a well-known criminal and his direct associates who, despite the best efforts of [Racing Victoria Ltd] stewards, had long been suspected of laundering the proceeds of large-scale drug trafficking and other organised crime, through the thoroughbred racing industry. It was acknowledged that, while some emphasis had been given to his name in respect of dealings with bookmakers and trainers, he did not enjoy a monopoly over these illicit activities attributed to him.'[8]

The ACC investigation, upon which Judge Lewis relied, had taken secret evidence from a number of racing identities, including bookmakers Alan Eskander, Frank Hudson and Simon Beasley, jockeys Danny Nikolic and Jim Cassidy, and trainers Jim Conlan and Brendan McCarthy. They were not treated as suspects but as witnesses in the ACC's joint efforts with the Purana Taskforce to disrupt the activities of Victoria's established criminal networks – and specifically Mokbel's.

Just who was this one-man army of corruption?

Tony Mokbel was born in Kuwait in 1965 to Lebanese parents, and grew up in the Melbourne suburbs of Coburg and Brunswick.

Largely uneducated, he bumped along with menial jobs, including waiting tables and washing dishes. But Tony had rat cunning and ambition. He started off with a few cannabis deals, moved into speed with brother Horty, and then hit the big time when ecstasy became the drug of choice for young clubbers.

Mokbel disguised his dirty deals with a cover as a genial entrepreneur, beginning with a milk bar he and wife Carmel bought when they were in their early twenties. As his drug business blossomed, it was concealed behind a network of legitimate investments in property, fashion labels, brothels, coal and oil companies. They were all fronts. An in-joke was the name of one of his fashion houses – Love of Style and Design, or LSD for short.

More than anything, however, Fat Tony loved the gee-gees. The turnover of his drug-dealing empire was estimated to be $180 million in the decade leading up to his arrest, and a vast amount of that was laundered through thoroughbred horse-racing in Victoria.

Tony first came to the attention of racing authorities in the 1990s, when he organised a group of punters to coordinate betting plunges on racetracks in Victoria, New South Wales and Queensland. The lurid gear they wore to the tracks earned them the nickname 'the Tracksuit Gang'. One of their late plunges, just before the start of the race, won the gang a cool $500,000. Naturally, they demanded to be paid in fresh green hundred-dollar bills rather than the old ones they had used to place the bet. Observers later noted that this was among the purest forms of money laundering.

For Mokbel, this was the beginning of a long and dirty involvement with racing in Victoria, which was thoroughly exposed by *The Age*'s dogged investigative reporter Nick McKenzie in 2008.

Mokbel became a player in the racing world in the early 1990s when he bought Doug Laversha's 200-acre property 'Somerset', in Kilmore, north of Melbourne. Now Mokbel was not just another punter – he was part of the racing pack. He hired Caulfield trainer John Salanitri and cheekily named his horses after slang terms in the drug trade, such as Frosty the Snowman and My Cook. Salanitri introduced Mokbel to jockey Danny Nikolic before deciding that he did not want to work at Kilmore.

By the time Queensland jockey Gavan Duffy decided to try his hand at training and moved his family to the property, it was in need of a bit of work. But there was plenty of money. Duffy bought a string of horses for Mokbel: Randy's Rancher, Supposing, Panet D'Or, Perennials, Scotch Gambit, Galatee and Solo Version. All were purchased in Duffy's name and ranged in price from a few thousand dollars up to almost $30,000. Many were also registered in the names of Mokbel's friends and family. Scotch Gambit was registered under the name of Duffy, Carmel Mokbel, and Tony's pal and next-door neighbour Paul Howden.

In 1997, however, Howden kicked over a tin of solvent at his home, sparking a chemical fire. Firemen attending the chemical blaze discovered a $78-million amphetamine factory, and police arrested the badly burned Howden at the Alfred Hospital shortly after. He took the rap and spent four years in the big house.

Two weeks after the fire, detectives raided 'Somerset'. The penny finally dropped for trainer Duffy, who realised where his boss was getting his money from. He promptly took his family back to the safety of northern Queensland. Undeterred, Mokbel drew on the knowledge of his mate Nikolic; on his recommendation, he hired another Caulfield-based trainer, Brendan McCarthy.

McCarthy's appointment coincided with Mokbel being jailed for drug trafficking; he then had that conviction overturned on appeal. McCarthy spent his time buying Fat Tony some more horseflesh. First off the auctioneer's block were Yamemma and Randy's Rancher, which McCarthy continued to train when he became a tenant at 'Somerset' in 2000. Meanwhile the drug-factory fire and Mokbel's overturned incarceration had alerted racing stewards to the likelihood that drug money was being laundered through the races. They talked to the police but got little help. Chief Victorian steward Des Gleeson told Nick McKenzie: 'From 1998 to 2005, there was a void there where we didn't get any information [from the police] basically at all.'[9]

Racing officials looked into the Mokbels' horse ownership, which at one stage involved offering the gift of a horse for the wife of a top hoop. They concluded that the Mokbels were crooked and dangerous, and passed on their report to police. Three weeks later, one of the officials involved in the confidential report was threatened by a member of the Mokbel family. Clearly, the crime clan had good contacts.

On 16 April 1999, racing officials announced that Tony and Carmel Mokbel were banned from owning racehorses. It made absolutely no difference. A horse for which Tony Mokbel had paid $100,000 at the Easter Yearling Sales in Sydney two weeks before the ban was simply transferred into the names of his old friend Jack Doumani and fellow horse owner Mark Kassis from Sydney.

Not only was he still owning horses through third parties, he was breeding them as well. Records showed that he was the breeder of two horses, Cyar and Echuca Beauty, from the brood-mare Yamemma – which he had just been banned from owning!

Some trainers were doing a lot more than just training Mokbel's horses. They were giving him tips as well. There is nothing wrong with a trainer providing tips – unless he or she is doing it in return for cash. Mokbel was offering the trainers a percentage of his winnings, which were not inconsiderable.

Judge Lewis quoted from the ACC report: 'Industry representatives admitted to accepting "slings" [payments for tips on winning horses]. Payments of up to $50,000 had been accepted from suspicious persons who were later revealed to be involved in criminal activity from which substantial amounts of illicit funds were derived. It is suspected such persons were not only approaching trainers with slings, but also their support staff.' It added that the dirty dealings did not stop there: '... material alleges that owner/punters regularly "sling" for access to information on "pot" horses [horses that are not raced at their full capability out of the carnival season in preparation for the larger prize-winning opportunities during carnival].'[10]

In 2002, respected trainer Peter Moody took over Jim Conlan's Caulfield stables and began paying rent to Mokbel's brother Horty. One of the horses Moody had under his wing in the stable was Pillar of Hercules, a great stallion that had stormed to victory in the 2007 Norman Robinson Stakes at Caulfield. The victory was part of the three-year-old's preparation for the $1-million Victoria Derby a few weeks later.

Then the police swooped. The Supreme Court granted a restraining order over seventy-five per cent of the horse, which was registered in the name of Irene Meletsis, amid suspicions that Horty Mokbel was the silent owner. If proved, the seventy-five per cent share could be confiscated as the proceeds of crime.

At that stage, Horty was banged up and facing charges of trafficking $40 million worth of amphetamines. Peter Moody, who had bought the horse at the Easter sales for $475,000 and registered the remaining twenty-five per cent in his wife Sarah's name, was shocked. 'To the best of my knowledge, neither myself, my wife Sarah, or Moody Racing or any of my staff have at any time had any dealings with, or association with, any person known to have criminal record or criminal ties,' he said in a statement.[11] But a police affidavit suggested that the horse had been paid for with drug money as part of a money-laundering operation, that Irene Meletsis knew nothing about horseracing, and that they had intercepted phone calls and SMS messages between Horty Mokbel and Moody discussing what to call the horse. Pillar of Hercules was sold for $1.8 million at a hastily convened auction, and the new owners kept Moody on as the trainer.

It's all very well having tips from trainers, but what a clever dirty punter really needs are the jockeys. Judge Lewis observed: 'Of concern also, are examples of well-known criminal identities offering to pay both trainers and jockeys for tips in races, in which they are participating. With a relationship of that kind having been established, it seems to be a small step before that same criminal identity is in a position to offer a cash payment to achieve the poor performance of a horse. It is more difficult to make a horse go faster by unlawful means and remain undetected, than to make it go slower and not be detected.'[12]

Police phone taps picked up Mokbel's regular chats with three leading jockeys. Racing officials were already concerned. One trainer had called Des Gleeson to complain about the behaviour of champion jockey Damien Oliver, who was getting very close to the gangster. The stewards gave him a warning in no uncertain terms and he backed off sharpish. Danny Nikolic's association with Mokbel was well known – he rode at least five of his horses in the early 2000s. 'When I was told by the stewards not to associate with him, I took their advice,' said Nikolic, who insisted he did not tip horses to Mokbel.[13]

But the third jockey, Jim Cassidy, affectionately known to fans as 'the Pumper' because of his riding action (when he won a race he would say: 'Ring-a-ding-ding, the Pumper is king!'), told stewards he 'had nothing but respect' for the crook, who at that stage was on the run.[14] Police information showed that Cassidy had taken money from Mokbel, in return for tips about races he was riding in. This was a decade after the Jockey Tapes affair, when Cassidy had been caught doing exactly the same thing. He was thought to have begun passing tips in 1997, the year he won the Melbourne Cup. One tip was Bezeal Bay, which Cassidy rode in a race at the Geelong Cup Carnival in the same year.

Such payments are a clear breach of the rules of racing. Racing NSW's chief steward, Ray Murrihy, said he had requested assistance from the ACC, Victoria Police and the New South Wales government; nothing had been forthcoming. 'We went down every avenue possible and we would still be interested if information held by authorities was passed to Racing NSW,' Murrihy said.[15]

As is the way with misdemeanours in racing, all was quickly forgotten. Cassidy was one of the three jockey poster boys for the 2012 Sydney Autumn Carnival, replacing the usual glamorous ambassadors such as Miss Universe Australia winners Rachael Finch and Laura Dundovic and model Erika Heynatz. This was the same Jim Cassidy who, when asked by a Fairfax reporter about taking cash for winning tips just four years before, had replied as any racing ambassador would: 'Your paper can go fuck themselves. And so can you.'[16]

The problem with Tony Mokbel, or at least one of the problems with him, was that he loved to rub the racing officials' noses in it. In 2004 he was photographed by the *Herald Sun* at Oaks Day, at Flemington, laughing with bookmaker Frank Hudson in the members' enclosure. He bragged that he had won $400,000 on the Melbourne Cup a couple of days earlier and had just backed three winners in a row, including the appropriately named Hollow Bullet. This came at a time when $20 million of his assets had been frozen by police.

The authorities were incensed, and the next year new laws were passed giving the Victoria Police the power to ban suspected gangsters and organised crime figures from racetracks. Mokbel was one of the first names on the list. He had already been banned from Crown Casino. His close links with bookies had long been a source of consternation and frustration.

Judge Lewis noted that bookies were the key to successfully laundering money on the racetracks: 'Available information suggests a widespread culture within the horse racing industry of tolerating criminality with respect to the laundering of illicitly attained funds. This culture extends from bookmakers to betting agents, horse trainers and their support staff. Rogue bookmakers are able to facilitate corrupt betting practices through actively breaching protocols and knowingly operating outside existing legislation.'[17]

Lewis found that bookmakers were employing a range of tactics to allow known crooks to keep on betting, usually because they knew the gangsters would make extravagant bets and leave the bookmaker with a substantial profit. What the crooks wanted was that big winning ticket that would show they had made their money legitimately.

This nexus saw bookies setting up accounts in the names of third parties whom they knew were betting for known criminals, and paying out cheques in the names of people who were not the betting account holders. One bookie told the ACC that he had opened a ghost betting account to allow Mokbel to bet under another man's name. In just one week of the 2002 Spring Racing Carnival, the account turned over $445,000. The name on the account was Emido Navarolli, the man who thoughtfully dropped Mokbel's $500,000 Mercedes back at the car yard two weeks after he fled to Greece.

Other bookmakers told reporters from *The Age* how Mokbel's erratic gambling had clocked up massive losses. One said he had cleared $6 million over a number of years. Another explained how he met Mokbel at a Port Melbourne coffee shop to pick up $80,000 he was owed. Mokbel took him to his car and collected the cash from a stack of notes totalling at least $300,000 that he had stashed in the glove box.

The figures involved were often large, and bookies and crooks colluded to break up big bets into several smaller ones in order to avoid the $10,000 reporting threshold put in place by AUSTRAC, Australia's anti-money laundering and counter-terrorism regulator. Accordingly, a $10,000 bet would be broken up into several smaller bets of $3000 or $4000 so it could fly under the authorities' radar.

The ACC report quoted by Judge Lewis said: 'One bookmaker issued winning cheques for non-existent bets after the relevant race and testified that no payment was received for this. However, they did take the opportunity to record the loss for taxation purposes. One industry participant had successfully exchanged cash for a winning cheque from a bookmaker.'[18]

There was also a pattern of gangsters failing to honour their debts, and bookies not chasing the money because they were intimidated or simply wanted to keep the underworld figure's business. In the early 1990s, bookie Rick Macciotta was an unhappy early victim of Tony Mokbel's punting. 'Another bookie and I were owed half a million and we only got paid a small percentage,' he said.[19]

Judge Lewis reported a 'disturbing' trick employed by bookmakers for a 'potentially simple method of money laundering'.[20] Essentially, bookmakers were waiting until a race had been run, winding the clocks back on their laptops and then issuing the crooked punter with a winning ticket. Cash for tickets – trebles all round. In fact, it would be a double win for the bookies, since resistance would presumably have been unwise.

Bookmakers called to face the ACC investigation as witnesses did not fare too well afterwards. As we have seen, Simon Beasley, one of Australia's biggest bookmakers with a turnover of more than $60 million a year, came unstuck when one of his staff accidentally emailed his secret spreadsheet to racing officials.

Frank Hudson got into trouble during a day out with friends at the Carioca Bar at Warwick Farm in Sydney in October 2004. He was not licensed in New South Wales and had gone through an elaborate process to rendezvous with Hass Taiba and Michael Khodr, two Melbourne commission agents who'd had associations with Mokbel. Commission agents are unlicensed and so don't have to use licensed telephones, as bookmakers do. They are therefore entirely unmonitored – racing officials have no jurisdiction over their actions. But Taiba and Khodr sure looked suspicious.

Robert Nicholson, Racing NSW's chief racecourse inspector, watched as Hudson, Taiba and Khodr moved from the table to check out the TV monitors and then return to make notes on white sheets of A4 paper, all the while making regular use of their mobile phones. Sure enough, when the officials pounced later that afternoon and seized the papers, they found lists of horses and monetary figures. Clearly, the three were running an unlicensed betting operation. Tallies of the bets listed on the A4 sheets totalled almost half a million dollars. Not bad for an afternoon at the races.

The stewards quizzed Hudson that afternoon on exactly what he was doing. 'Well, I'm here. I'm chasing a punter who bet with me about four, five months ago and hasn't paid me,' he explained. But as the questions got tougher, his answers got shorter.

In frustration, the chairman asked: 'Why can't you assist us now by just telling us what these notations are? What if I was to put to you that on face value they look like a running sheet and they're bets?'

Hudson said: 'I have no comment.'[21]

The discussion moved to punter 'TC'.

Hudson said: 'You're welcome to see if I've got a punter "TC" because I don't think I have.'

The chairman then hit the nail on the head: 'Maybe "TC" might be a person who bets with Mr Taiba with you. "TC Restless Wind $8,000". When we look at the sheet you have here, Sydney Race 2, No. 1, which correlates with Restless Wind $8,000 at $2.40, losing $8,000. Race 2, TC $10,000 No Penalty. Sydney Race 3, No. 5, $10,000 at $2 plus $10. Do they all relate to the same thing?'

Hudson replied, naturally: 'I've got no comment.'[22]

Why so reticent, Mr Hudson? Could it be because 'TC' was actually Victoria's biggest drug dealer and tough guy, Tony Mokbel? The New South Wales stewards correctly concluded that this was a significant, highly organised operation between an unlicensed bookmaker and a punter.

Keeping mum on the identity of 'TC' and of anything else, Hudson took the fall – a $50,000 fine and one-year ban from bookmaking. Khodr was fined $15,000; Taiba did not even get a slap on the wrist.

Frank Hudson was in close. Tony Mokbel was known to never forget a friend – or an enemy. In the year before he fled overseas, Mokbel was living in an apartment owned by Hudson, but he was not paying rent. He was sharing it with his girlfriend, Danielle Maguire, the mother of his small child and former lover of standover man Mark Moran. Mokbel was later found not guilty of financing the murder of Mark's father, Lewis Moran. That kind of thing can play on your mind.

Mokbel reportedly spent $100,000 renovating the apartment while he was staying there. He then fled the country in early 2006 during his trial in the Victorian Supreme Court for importing cocaine. He hid out, under a very bad Beatles-style wig, in Athens and attempted to chase up $1 million, which he felt, rightly or wrongly, that Hudson owed him in relation to the apartment. Mokbel was arrested in Greece carrying a false passport and driver's licence, and was extradited to Australia in 2008. He pleaded guilty to drug charges. Despite an attempt to change his plea and a minor heart attack, on 3 July 2012 the Victorian Supreme Court sentenced him to 30 years, with a minimum term of 22 years, for drug trafficking. Naturally he appealed, arguing the toss because of ill-health and earlier arrangements, but however it worked out, he was facing an awfully long time in the slammer.

Judge Lewis made a raft of suggestions to clean up the Victorian racing industry. His sixty-three recommendations across seven areas included giving the police more coercive powers to investigate criminal links within racing, and reinstating the specialist Victorian police racing desk. Halfway through the review, he still had hopes that changes could be effected without the creation of another layer of red tape and bureaucracy. 'However, in the light of the many integrity issues raised before me, particularly the evidence of criminal activities detailed in this report, that has not proved possible,' he said.[23]

Racing in Victoria was just too dirty for the existing systems to cope with it: 'The present disciplinary procedures are unacceptable, and require revision. In addition, there is a demonstrated need for the appointment of a Racing Integrity Commissioner, who will have an overview of the industry as a whole, be responsible for cooperation with Victoria Police and be answerable to the Minister for Racing.'[24]

That man, when he was appointed by Victoria's racing minister, Rob Hulls, two years later, in March 2010, was Sal Perna. He was the perfect untouchable for the job. Perna was a twenty-year police veteran and the former head of corporate security with Australia Post and Telstra, and he had developed an anti-corruption program for Tennis Australia and served as a consultant to the AFL.

He got straight to work. In his first year he investigated forty-two complaints across all the racing bodies, more than half of which were integrity-related. 'There are aspects of money laundering, illegal betting and criminal activity within the industry,' Perna said in 2011. 'It is important for stewards to know [the difference] between right and wrong.'[25] And he did not shy away from controversy in his first annual report, calling for more coordination of stewards to eliminate the doping of horses, and naming jockey Danny Nikolic as the focus of one of his investigations. Tony Mokbel might have been in jail but his old jockey mate was still at the centre of controversy.

Nikolic had caught the stewards' attention when an odds-on favourite he was riding, Finishing Card, was beaten by three-quarters of a length by New Venture at Mornington on 8 January 2010. The stewards spoke to him at the end of the 1210-metre maiden, and in their report on the day said: 'D. Nikolic explained that after jumping from a wide barrier and being caught wide he would have had to restrain to the rear of the field to find cover and therefore allowed the gelding to stride forward.'[26] The *Herald Sun* described the race succinctly: 'The Clinton McDonald-trained Finishing Card drew barrier 13, covered plenty of extra ground and flew home late. New Venture enjoyed a perfect run behind the leader and took advantage of a rails run to win.'[27]

The subsequent investigation became known as the Finishing Card Inquiry. Integrity officers with Betfair had picked up unusual betting patterns on the horse. The licensing of Tasmanian-based Betfair had been resisted for the very reason that it allows punters to bet on a horse to lose.

With the microscope on Nikolic's activities, the investigation widened to include several more of his rides, and also horses trained by his brother John Nikolic in Queensland. One inquiry focused on the short-priced favourite Baby Boom, which jockey John Keating rode into fourth place on the Sunshine Coast on 3 January 2010.

The issue was Nikolic's friendship with professional punter Neville Clements, an old family friend, who had placed a string of bets on the jockey's mounts to lose. Stewards looked at twenty-one of Nikolic's rides and identified eleven that were questionable. According to Betfair records, Clements had gambled on all of them to lose. They were:

Horse	Date	Track	Bet	Profit/ loss
Hot Danish	3 October 2009	Flemington	$10,876	$6373
Farasi	15 October 2009	Cranbourne	$1323	$700
Midnight Wine	13 November 2009	Moonee Valley	$20,152	$7822

Horse	Date	Track	Bet	Profit/ loss
Rachine	13 November 2009	Moonee Valley	$6316	–$6316 (finished second)
Moorunda Lass	20 November 2009	Moonee Valley	$1383	$276
Buddy Amazing	18 December 2009	Moonee Valley	$17,691 $9721	$1592 $3660
Ruby Slippers	13 January 2010	Sandown	$26,965	$7304
Retrieve	11 February 2010	Ballarat	$4058	$391

All in all, Clements risked a total of $98,485 to make a profit of just $28,118. No wonder the stewards and Betfair watchdogs were suspicious. Their logic was that you would only risk that kind of exposure if you knew you were going to win. Clements also laid Baby Boom in Queensland at $1.80 to $1.89, risking $56,400 and winning $45,424.

Betfair bets by two other Queenslanders, long-term Nikolic family friend Alessandro Alaimo and his mate Kevin McFarland, were also examined. They too risked a lot to make a little. Alaimo risked $2838 on Imprudence on 22 December 2009 at Seymour to make a $169 profit, and $6112 on Summarise on 24 January 2010 at Ballarat to make a $583 profit. McFarland put $15,717 on Finishing Card to gain $11,969 in profit and $3537 on Summarise to make just $324. All very whiffy.

Nikolic confirmed that, since returning from riding in Mauritius in the middle of 2009, he had been in regular contact with Clements to discuss form. Essentially, he was tapping in to Clements' expert analysis of the factors in the race such as form, race tempo, barriers, the racing patterns of other horses and the things to watch out for. Senior riders often consult form analysts and pay for the privilege, but Nikolic enjoyed the service free of charge.

He told stewards he had discussed a couple of the horses he was riding with Clements, but they were not on the suspicious list. He also denied any knowledge of the Baby Boom episode, saying he had spoken to his brother John but neither had spoken to Clements before the race. Clements himself said he had slapped the $56,400 down 'on a whim'. 'The Board has reservations as to Nikolic's evidence relating to Baby Boom,' the final decision noted drily.[28]

Neville Clements was 'bloody annoyed and frustrated' by the whole thing. Not only that, but his Betfair account was suspended. He explained the nature of his seven-year friendship with Danny Nikolic to the the *Herald Sun*. 'Danny rings me, obviously. And he rings me for guidance as in pace in races and the hardest horses for him to beat.'[29]

Nikolic was also being investigated for using his phone to call Clements from the Flemington racecourse on 1 January 2010 without the stewards' permission. On that day he had ridden Atlantic Air to victory. Clements said that Nikolic's call was purely to make sure that he should push his horse forward; anyway, Clements said, he had not bet on the race. But he refused to hand over his phone records, and the Racing Appeals and Disciplinary Board warned him off. That was overturned on appeal by the Victorian Civil and Administrative Tribunal.

At the end of the day, the Racing Appeals and Disciplinary Board found that the stewards' circumstantial evidence was not enough to prove that Nikolic had communicated the chances of his mounts, and so the charges against the jockey were dismissed. Some minor charges about turning up to the course late – with less than forty-five minutes to the start – were upheld.

Nevertheless, Nikolic was unhappy about how the investigation had been handled. He particularly questioned how information about it was leaked to *The Australian* newspaper. He also complained about being issued with non-raceday charges during a race meeting. Racing Integrity Commissioner Sal Perna's report, which named Nikolic, was viewed as a win-win by both sides. Perna said the stewards were justified in checking out the irregularities; after all, that was their job. And he said that jockeys should not be issued with non-raceday charges during a race meeting, and that legal advice should be sought before those charges were laid. These were hailed as victories for all jockeys by Nikolic's legal team.

The removal of the punting CEO Stephen Allanson certainly had aired Racing Victoria's dirty laundry. And it wasn't dirty washing that the bookies were laundering. The new chief executive tasked with the unenviable job of cleaning it all up was Rob Hines, a racing cleanskin who had fallen in love with the sport of kings as a boy while watching the great Lestor Piggott ride in Ireland. Hines was appointed in July 2008 and came in with a fresh approach that was music to the ears of punters. 'I haven't been an owner,' he said. 'I don't know that much about that side of the business but I don't think it would do racing any harm to have a stronger customer focus anyway.'[30] He also acknowledged the money-laundering problem. 'This crime was rampant and that's not to say it doesn't still exist,' he admitted.[31]

He was right. In 2010, veteran Victorian bookmaker Peter Coster was charged with laundering drug money for a crime syndicate. The charges came after police taped a phone call in which drug trafficker Danny Mark Mousley made arrangements to launder money with the help of an accomplice named Chris Costelloe. Police swooped after Mousley gave Costelloe

$89,900 wrapped in a white towel. They also found forged betting tickets issued by Coster's Doublebet agency. The case once again caused problems for Racing Victoria, because a legal loophole meant it was powerless to stop Coster from continuing to run Doublebet while the case went ahead.

That case came after one of Mokbel's old Tracksuit Gang reappeared at Flemington to work on a licensed bookmaker's stand. Vincent Panuccio, known as 'Big Nose Vinnie', had previously spent four years inside for trafficking methamphetamine. The authorities were powerless to stop him working because he was not the licensed bookmaker. The Victorian government was once again having to play catch-up with its own laws.

Judge Lewis revealed that criminal activity was rampant within thoroughbred racing in Victoria. Even though the authorities had moved to act, it seems as though someone forgot to tell the crooks.

RACE 9

BIG HURDLES

Horses, unless they have names like Black Caviar or Takeover Target, are all too often the forgotten casualties of the racing industry. In March 2012, jockey Jason Warrington had been smoking marijuana and had failed a urine test. Two separate inquiries were launched by Racing Queensland's stewards, following a bad ride on the Gold Coast on 21 January. During the race, Warrington had allowed his mount, Dwan, to shift out while not clear of Carlson's Gold. The horse had clipped Dwan's heels and fallen, throwing jockey Tegan Harrison to the turf and placing several others at risk.

Warrington was given a three-year ban for his third offence of having cannabis in his system. This was the same jockey who in 2007 had been caught with a sex toy concealed in his pants, which he was using to produce clean urine in a bid to deceive drug testers. The Queensland stewards could find no positive link between the cannabis in his system and the reckless riding, for which he also received a three-month ban. Carlson's Gold was euthanased after the race. Three years for smoking dope, three months for actions that killed a horse.

Establishing exactly how many racehorses die in the course of a year is not easy. Racing authorities don't like to spoil the party with too much blood-and-guts reality. In the 2010–11 season, 31,181 horses took part in almost 19,000 races across Australia. The racing season ends on 31 July and starts again the next day, with just two days off a year. Over the course of 2641 race meetings there were 190,258 starters. So it probably should not be a surprise that some of those horses don't make it to the finish line.

Most horse deaths at the track go unreported. Champion jockey Damien Oliver's horror fall at Moonee Valley in March 2012 received extensive coverage at the time. Mostly this was because he was discharged from Epworth Hospital in time to ride the former Irish stayer Drunken Sailor to victory at Flemington the next day. The night before, Oliver had been riding Like An Eagle through the pack when an incident dislodged the 39-year-old and put him in hospital. 'I was on my way to the front and hadn't quite got there, but if it had been another 50 metres the whole field would have gone over the top of me,' he said. 'I had no warning at all. I did roll a lot and that probably helped me.' He added: 'I was lucky last night.'[1]

Not so lucky was Like An Eagle, which snapped both forelegs. Another death on the racetrack that would have gone unrecorded were it not for Oliver's miraculous return from his hospital bed to the winners' circle in a matter of hours.

Many thoroughbreds are euthanased on the track as their legs or hearts give out. One of the few official studies into horse deaths at the track was conducted by Dr Lisa Boden and examined fatalities in Victoria. Called 'Risk Factors Associated with Racetrack Casualties in Thoroughbreds', the 2008 report is probably the most comprehensive available.

It looked at archived veterinary reports in Victoria, finding there had been 514 fatalities from 743,552 starts over the fifteen years to 2004. In the three years from 2001 to 2004, there were 180 deaths during racing or training in Victoria. That's more than one racehorse dying on a racetrack every single week of the year in Victoria alone. Of these, almost three-quarters (134) were trackside mercy killings after catastrophic musculoskeletal injuries. The remaining twenty-four per cent were a result of sudden death. Multiply that across the states, and it is clear a lot of racehorses die in agony on the racetrack.

On Saturday, 19 May 2012, the racing at Flemington left two horses dead, two broken down and a jockey in hospital. Trainer Danny O'Brien ended up in the stewards' room for questioning the condition of the track. He later tweeted: 'Two horses break legs at Flemington after the track cored two days before the races. Why?'[2]

In the first race, Absolute Spirit, with Danny Nikolic in the saddle, broke a sesamoid bone after finishing fifth. It was put down. In the third race, Sparks Burn broke his foreleg 250 metres from the finishing post. He was also put down. Fortunately jockey Mark Zahra was unscathed. In the Andrew Ramsden Stakes, Mr Riggs bowed a tendon. In the seventh race, Deliver The Dream fell, sending gifted apprentice Katelyn Mallyon crashing into the turf. She was knocked unconscious and rushed to hospital with a broken T6 vertebra and facial fractures. Deliver The Dream was taken from the course in a horse ambulance.

O'Brien was furious. 'The track is thirty metres wide and all the jockeys are looking to ride on a five-metre strip, which causes tightening. It's about making sure the winners don't come down the same section of the track as they did at the previous meeting,' he said. 'The track is a disgrace. There's no kikuyu grass and horses are slipping. It's not up to standard.'[3] And when things go wrong, it is the horses and jockeys who pay the price.

Although it's hard to get an Australia-wide figure for horseracing casualties, a website honour roll of Australia's fallen racehorses lists the largely unreported casualties and asks for extra information from readers to update the list. It is a racing website, not a flag-waver for animal-rights campaigners. And it makes horrifying reading for anyone involved in racing.

The honour roll does not claim to be a comprehensive list and it cannot be verified – the very reason why it exists – but in 2010 it listed eighty-three racecourse or training deaths; and in 2009 it listed a further 133. The worst year was 2008, when there were a staggering 586 racehorse deaths, January being a month of carnage on the racetrack with 174 deaths. The sparse details are a litany of broken limbs, severed spinal cords and sudden collapses. They include the Gai Waterhouse-trained colt Meurice. Darley Stud had just paid $12 million for his breeding rights, following his win of the Group 1 Champagne Stakes at Randwick. He broke his shoulder during trackwork at Randwick and had to be euthanased.

Clearly, no one likes to see horses die – they cost a lot of money and to lose one is tragic. But it is happening all too regularly. One of the reasons why Australian racehorses are dying is because we race them too young, according to some veterinary experts. The RSPCA staunchly opposes the racing of two-year-olds. It argues that the immature horses are still growing, and are only being pushed into racing because greedy owners want to capitalise on their investment sooner. 'The evidence indicates that low-grade injuries and disease occur at a high rate during the training and racing of two-year-olds in Australia, with 85 per cent of horses suffering at least one incident of injury or disease,' says the animal-rights charity. 'Shin soreness or DMD (dorsal metacarpal disease) is the most common cause of lameness in two-year-old horses.'[4]

Legendary vet Percy Sykes, who founded the Randwick Equine Centre and had long associations with trainers Bart Cummings, T. J. Smith and his daughter, Gai Waterhouse, was strongly against racing two-year-olds, saying in 1990: 'I think there's probably a much stronger tendency to have two year old racing nowadays than there used to be … and the lure of prize money. There's a great incentive to race their horses too young too immature. In the old days, you bought your yearlings, you broke them in, you castrated them, you turned them out. You didn't think about them until late two year old and mostly three year olds. The big money came with three-year-old racing. The current owners want two-year-old racing and I think it's a pity. I think it's a pity because it certainly does cause the breakdown of a lot of two year olds.' His words were jumped on by anti-horseracing campaigners.[5]

Yet the 92-year-old has since qualified that statement, referring to the introduction of modern training techniques. 'That was the original thinking but exercise has changed a lot in the last twenty years, and people are able to manage their two-year-olds a lot better,' he says. 'The improvement in training, feeding and breeding techniques means that it is as safe training a two-year-old today as it was training a three-year-old thirty or forty years ago.' What's more, only suitably developed two-year-olds are selected for racing. He answers the RSPCA's point with the admission that two-year-olds do go lame: 'They are like footballers – they go sore, but there are very few that are incurable.'[6]

The most likely time that an Australian racehorse is going to find itself in an 'incurable' position is if it has been entered into a jumps race. Jumps racing is exciting, dramatic and dangerous. Dr Boden's Victorian study found that the likelihood of a horse dying in a jumps race was twenty times greater than in a flat race. Her statistics showed that the chance of a fatality in flat racing was 0.44 per 1000 starts, compared with 8.3 per 1000 jump starts.

The New South Wales government banned jumps racing in 1997, while Tasmania cancelled it through lack of interest in 2007. Today, hurdles and steeplechasing only exist in Victoria and South Australia, where they are as big a part of the animal-rights campaigners' calendar as they are of the racegoers'.

When jumps racing goes wrong, it is high-profile and horrific. Sirrocean Storm was a case in point. The veteran jumper, trained by John Wheeler, sprawled over the third obstacle in the $101,000 Galleywood Hurdle at Warrnambool on 5 May 2010. The gelding's offside cannon bone was broken after he hit the jump. That forced his hind leg into a sickening U-shape, with his hoof bent upwards and pointing at the sky.

The whole incident was captured on film and uploaded onto YouTube. It makes horrific viewing. Jockey Gavin Bedggood was unhurt and can be seen frantically trying to control the stricken horse, making it walk in tight circles around him. But the race was still going on and the pack was thundering around the course for a second lap; Sirrocean Storm was in its path.

Experienced barrier stall worker Andrew Duff rushed onto

the track and attempted to lead Sirrocean Storm to the side. The horse struggled to stand on its three legs, only to fall down again. It is heartbreaking to watch. Sirrocean Storm had to be moved. Duff forced him to his feet but the horse could not move quickly enough and collapsed again. He was forced up again, his broken leg flapping. Down he crashed. Another few metres – that hideously deformed leg uselessly dangling.

Next, the attendants appeared, with green screens to shield this macabre spectacle from the public gaze. As the screens went up, Sirrocean Storm made one last terrorised, frantic bid to escape. Finally, the vet administered an injection to end Sirrocean Storm's last terrified moments of anguish and panic.

Racing Victoria's chief executive, Rob Hines, said the incident was 'most unfortunate'. It was the only fatality during the three-day carnival, which he said showed that the new French jumps were a big improvement on the old ones: 'It's very disappointing, but accidents will happen. I still think the new jumps are performing well. The tempo of the racing has improved and the horses are jumping the new jumps better than they did last year.'[7]

Not everyone saw it that way. The RSPCA, a long-time opponent to jumps racing, launched a case of animal cruelty against the 46-year-old horseman Duff, ignoring the racing officials and holding him solely responsible. If found guilty, he faced a year in prison or a $14,000 fine, plus a decade-long ban from working with horses. Overnight, he became the targeted poster boy for animal rights campaigners. This was a bitter pill for a man described by friends as a lover of horses who had been attempting to avert a disaster on the track. It was a nasty fight. Despite promising to help, Racing Victoria refused to hand over documents it had compiled relating to the investigation of the incident.

For its part, the RSPCA struggled to find a vet prepared to go on the record and support its claim of animal cruelty. Eventually, it drew on the expertise of Dr Paul McGreevy, a riding instructor and veterinarian from the Faculty of Veterinary Science at the University of Sydney who had written six books on equine behaviour. The RSPCA anticipated trouble. 'Given Dr McGreevy's extensive research into the use of whips within horse-racing, the RSPCA did understand that there would be stakeholders within the industry looking to discredit his views,' it said in a statement posted on its website after withdrawing from the prosecution two years later.[8]

The charges were dropped in the Warrnambool Magistrates Court after three industry veterinarians offered their expert opinion to Duff's defence team free of charge. According to a report in *The Age*, their evidence was in direct conflict to that of McGreevy. 'It was not heard in court and I have not been able to present my evidence,' McGreevy fumes. 'The journalist did not approach me and the presentation of this matter was clearly an attempt to discredit me. The jockey was using a technique called circling to control the horse that was far more effective than the one subsequently used by the fellow in question.'[9]

McGreevy had contended that the race should have been diverted away from the stricken horse. But the racing industry vets for the defence disagreed. Thirty-year race-day veterinarian Ray Hutchinson felt that Duff's actions were appropriate, given the dangerous situation. Equine surgeon Glenn Robertson-Smith said: 'In my assessment Mr Duff did a good job and was at significant risk to himself trying to control an agitated, unbalanced racehorse with a serious fracture.'[10]

Forty-year veteran veterinarian Dr Paul Kavenagh agreed: 'If the horse did not want to follow because of pain or fear, then it is my opinion and experience that there would be no way it would follow the direction.' What it would do, he said, would be to follow its hot-blooded racehorse temperament and try to join the pack of horses when they came round again. 'Consequently, it would have been most likely that other horses racing past would have been distracted or spooked with the possibility of causing further accidental injury.'[11] What's more, Kavenagh said, the injured leg would have had no blood supply and badly damaged or severed nerves, so there would have been no pain in the broken leg anyway.

'Wow,' says McGreevy, upon hearing those claims. 'I wouldn't want to be one of his patients.'[12] Jumps racing clearly gets people's blood boiling.

And it divides opinion. A survey conducted by Footprints Market Research for the RSPCA found that seventy-six per cent of females and seventy-four per cent of people aged eighteen to thirty-four wanted jumps racing banned. Despite this, the Victorian government pumped an extra $2 million into the sport – an act that was only slightly marred when gelding Casa Boy crashed heavily in a maiden hurdle, breaking an elbow and having to be put down just forty minutes into the 2011 season.

A lot of horses die during the jumps racing season – thirteen in 2008, thirteen in 2009 and another five in 2010. In the 2011 Warrnambool Grand Annual Steeple, disaster struck when a riderless horse, Banna Strand, jumped a high brush fence, which it mistook for a steeple, and landed in a crowd of spectators. This time, the horse was all right but seven spectators, including an eighty-year-old woman and a two-year-old boy, were taken to hospital. The thirty-three-hurdle race was chaos, with five other horses falling and losing their jockeys and only two of the eight entrants managing to finish. Banna

Strand was chased by a police car before being caught at the main entrance.

Racing Victoria's chief executive, Rob Hines, said: 'You'd have to say you could do with less excitement, but it was a hell of a spectacle. Everybody got around safely, but we're concerned about the spectators ... but I don't know what we could have done.' He added that the incident would have no impact on the future of the sport: 'We've said the sport is a dangerous sport and is not risk-free, and if you look at what happened ... there wasn't too much wrong with the race itself.'[13]

Hines was right about one thing: racing is a dangerous sport. Dangerous for horses, dangerous for spectators and very dangerous for jockeys.

Just ask Leigh Woodgate. She was the pin-up girl for jumps racing – a bush jockey, beautiful and talented, who attracted enormous attention as one of the first female jumps jockeys. She won her first three races hands down. On 1 July 1994 she was on her ninth ride at Hamilton Park in Victoria, the top-weighted Winter Coal, on which she had won before. It had been raining and the going was heavy. Woodgate was near the front and close to home.

'And he tired, and I can remember taking off and going over, and then he buckled on landing and I fell off. I've never seen the footage of my race fall, but I know I went head first into the ground,' she told the the ABC's *Australian Story*.[14] She was thrown over the fence into a blind spot for the following jockeys.

Racing commentator Bryan Martin said: 'And I still see it. It was terribly graphic and disturbing, but her body actually lifted off the ground as the horse collected her – she was lifted probably one and a half feet or something off the ground and then dumped again, so when you watched it you thought, well, it's impossible for her to survive that. The horse that Leigh came off, Winter Coal, escaped injury.'[15]

Unconscious, Woodgate was airlifted to Melbourne with severe brain injuries, broken shoulders, punctured lungs, her jaw broken in four places, bottom teeth that needed to be wired in, five broken ribs, a broken left hip and a dead third optic nerve. She was in a coma for seventeen days, and experts told her parents that she was likely to be a vegetable.

'Being in a coma was like I was underwater,' Woodgate said. 'It was like that I was being sucked down. Every single cell in my body was screaming out for breath, and my brain couldn't tell my body how to breathe, and I felt like I was drowning. I was being sucked down into a deep dark hole.'[16]

When she came round, her tough, beloved father – who had taught her to ride as an equal with the men – told her: 'Your life is finished.'[17] That just made this tough jockey fight harder. She fought back, operation by operation, step by agonising step, slowly and determinedly, year after year.

Seventeen years after the accident, she was back. 'Riding trackwork first thing in the morning when the sun's coming up … there is only you and the horse and you're in sync with one another. There's no better feeling.'[18]

Jockeys clearly love their horses. That's one of the reasons why the use of the whip in horseracing is such a contentious issue. Once again, the RSPCA is leading the campaign for the whip to be banned; it cites whip-free racing in Norway as an example of how unnecessary it is to strike a horse to make it go faster. The Australian racing industry has signed up to international guidelines that prevent a horse being whipped on the sensitive flank or abdomen.

An RSPCA study undertaken by Paul McGreevy looked at fifteen races over two days at the Gosford racecourse, north of Sydney. Stewards found one infraction of the whip rules; using slow-motion replays, however, Dr McGreevy found twenty-eight, including thirteen in which the whip hit the horse's head. Three-quarters of whip strikes were on the sensitive abdomen rather than the fleshier hindquarters. 'If this wasn't taking place on a racecourse it would be a prosecutable offence. It would be an act of cruelty,' McGreevy told *Lateline*. Despite being padded, the whips left indentations in the horses' skin, he said.[19]

Andrew Harding, CEO of the Australian Racing Board, was dismissive. 'Our stewards and veterinarians have professional, ethical responsibilities: examine the horse immediately post-race, and they examine them to determine if there are any markings, and to see if the horses are sound in every other respect,' he said. 'If there are any markings, they are reported, and the evidence clearly is that the horses are not being marked in the fashion that's being suggested by the RSPCA.'[20] Forehand-style whipping is limited from the start of a race, while jockeys are allowed to whip at their own discretion for the last 100 metres. A 2011 RSPCA study found that whipping a horse did not increase its chances of winning a race, and that ninety-eight per cent of horses were being whipped with no influence on the outcome of the race.

After the last RSPCA report, Racing NSW's chief steward, Ray Murrihy, indicated that this was clearly going to be a long-running battle. 'We are not going to regulate on the run just because of one study by one [group],' he blasted.[21] But the day after the release of the report, he took objection to jockey Nash Rawiller's use of the whip at Broadmeadow. 'He looked like he was felling a tree,' said Murrihy. 'The well-being of the thoroughbred is paramount. The use of the whip has been cut down by 50 per cent since 2009.'[22]

In the old days, horses were zapped with a jigger. Known as 'batteries', 'jacks' or 'harps', these were handheld devices that could give a horse a nasty jolt of electricity to speed it up. A former jockey wrote to the *Sydney Morning Herald* racing writer Max Presnell to explain how they worked: 'All apprentices (no exceptions) at some time were given a hand jigger at trackwork and told to give the horse a prod down the neck as soon as they straightened up. About the size of a matchbox and with an elastic band to twine through your fingers, it generally had a retractable contact when pressed against the horse's neck.'[23]

These handheld jiggers were soon replaced with electric saddles, which could give a jolt of electricity down both saddle flaps in the home straight. Jiggers were generally used in trackwork; the policing of the sport meant they could be too easily discovered if they were used in a race. Nevertheless, some have tried. One popular urban myth told of a jockey who, apparently exhausted, slipped from his mount at the end of the race into the arms of a primed and ready trackhand, who calmly palmed the battery and apparatus before the jockey weighed in.

Many horses react badly to being electrocuted. Those that respond to the electric jolts by speeding up, however, are embraced by trainers looking for an edge. In the actual race, jockeys would give a loud roar and jab the butt of the whip – in the old days it would have a shoeing nail tacked into it – into the horse's neck to replicate the bolt of electricity.

Jockey Jim Cassidy was suspended for a month in March 1998, after stewards observed him jabbing the butt of his whip into the neck of Filante as it straightened up in the final stages of the Group 1 1600-metre Chipping Norton Stakes at Warwick Farm.

'The Pumper' claimed it was his normal pumping action and that the whip had got tangled in the horse's mane. Immediately after the race, Ray Murrihy said the clear connotation of Cassidy's action was that a jigger could have been used during trackwork and the jockey was replicating the action. Of course, no one would resort to such barbaric actions just to win a race these days …

In 2007, Victorian trainer Paul Preusker was banned for four years after an undercover Racing Victoria investigation team conducted a raid during trackwork at the Horsham racecourse. His partner, jockey and trackwork rider Holly McKechnie, was caught holding a jigger that could zap 700 volts into a horse's neck.

The deputy chairman of the Racing Appeals and Disciplinary Board, Brian Forrest, said: 'Preusker played the dominant role in the enterprise and remorse was not evidenced.' He said the use of jiggers cut right to the heart of racing: 'The use of electrical devices on horses is an abhorrent practice and tarnishes the image of the racing industry.'[24]

An emotional McKechnie apologised for her actions and was stood down for three years. Owner/trainer Nicole Boyd was also stood down for three years after investigators found her in possession of a cattle prod in the same raid.

According to some, however, getting hit with a whip or zapped with a jigger is the last thing a racehorse needs to be worried about. When Sirrocean Storm's agonised death on the track caused an uproar from animal-rights campaigners, racing commentator Brendan Cormick wrote in the *Weekend Australian*: 'Rest assured, his life would have been a lot shorter as a slow racehorse had he not been able to turn to jumping where life was prolonged and enriched.'[25]

He was right. In the racing industry they call it 'wastage'.

Cormick wrote: 'At a recent horse sale in Adelaide, 130 lots went under the hammer and 20 per cent of those were taken away to the abattoir. Not much love and attention there.'[26]

Horseracing has a massive turnover of horses – the ones that die on the track are just the tip of the iceberg. A 2004 survey of trainers found that almost forty per cent of thoroughbreds were lost to the industry every year through poor performance, behavioural problems or breakdowns.[27] That's almost 125,000 horses. At least 7500 go straight to the knackery. Many more end up there via the auctions.

Studies have found that one of the biggest reasons for the 'premature retirement' of a horse is a lack of winnings. Fifty per cent of racehorses earn less than $500 in their first years of racing, and forty per cent earn nothing at all.[28] Keeping and training a thoroughbred costs about $10,000 in the first year, which rises to $28,000 by the third year – and that is just for the training. Food, shelter and transport come on top.

Eventually, for some owners it becomes a commercial reality that slow horses must go to the knacker's yard. The $500 that the owner pockets from the glue maker is often the only money they make from their investment in thoroughbred racing.

Meanwhile, the lucky breeders cash in on the next big thing. For every 1000 pregnancies to thoroughbred mares, only 300 foals actually go on to race. Of those, just ten per cent ever make it into the winners' circle. The others are farmed out to various other parts of the equine industry – such as riding schools and private enthusiasts – while the highly strung and the very slow end up as pet food in Australia and as meat in the lion and tiger enclosures in Japanese zoos.

According to the Rural Industries Research and Development Corporation, between 30,000 and 40,000 horses are slaughtered in Australia annually for pet and human consumption. That's right, food for humans. Horsemeat cannot be sold in Australia for human consumption but it is a big part of Australia's export trade. Countries like Japan, Russia, Switzerland, Belgium and France consider Australian horsemeat a delicacy. Abattoirs prefer young, well-muscled racehorses to tired old nags.

A 2008 study of horsemeat in one of only two Australian abattoirs licensed to export it for human consumption found that just over half of all horses slaughtered there had come from the racing industry.[29] The Coalition for the Protection of Racehorses estimates that 18,000 of the horses slaughtered annually are racehorses. Every year around 2000 tonnes of horsemeat is exported from Australia to feed people in places such as the Hot Horse Burger Bar in Park Tivoli, Ljubljana, Slovenia.

Things are no better across the Tasman. A recent investigation by New Zealand's *Herald on Sunday* spoke to six transport operators who truck slow, expensive and unloved thoroughbreds to slaughter at the Clover Export Ltd abattoir in Gore. Putting a horse out to clover in New Zealand has a very different connotation – it generally means the animal will end up on a dining table in Russia, Belgium or Switzerland.

Long-term South Island-based horse transporter Bernie Hutton told reporter Sally Webster that business is booming. 'Yes, they are often slaughtered very young due to the nature of the industry – but the other side of that is that young thoroughbreds do provide excellent meat for export,' he said. 'And frankly, the way some of them are neglected, it seems a better fate for them.'[30]

But when mum and dad trainers are struggling, putting down a horse costs money too: a $100 council fee, $200 for a digger to dig the grave and $100 for the vet. That's why many see getting $200 for putting the horse out to Clover as a good deal.

Filly SL 7/8 is a case in point. Born at Soliloquy Lodge at Karaka as the seventh foal in 2008, sired by Russian Hero out of Heatherton, she initially looked healthy. But as she grew, it became apparent that she had bent legs. Owner David Moore originally hoped she would be the next Culminate, his champion which had brought home $800,000 in prize money. She wasn't.

'We kept her for more than two years to see if she would mature, if the legs would straighten,' he told Webster. 'And when it was clear she wouldn't improve, we tried to get some trainers to take her. But the reality is that no one wants a racehorse like that, unfortunately. The feed and stable bills keep coming in and this becomes too expensive to support really ... so we sold her directly from here to Clover.'[31] She never raced and never had a proper name. SL 7/8 went straight from the stable to the table.

The horses are transported to the abattoir, often with other animals, including sheep and llamas, for days at a time. They wait in the paddock until Thursday, when the Ministry of Agriculture and Forestry inspector comes, and they then get a bolt shot between the eyes. The horses' meat is butchered, frozen and shipped out of Port Otago, often to Queensland, where Clover's owner, Meramist Pty Ltd, is based. The whole kit and caboodle is in turn owned by Belgian meat goliath Benimpex Nv.

Belgium has imported more than 1000 tonnes of New Zealand horsemeat over the last ten years. Much of it has ended up on the tables of restaurants such as T Peerd (The Horse) in Antwerp. Owner M. De Ley told the *Herald* that he buys his horsemeat from an Australian company. He has delicacies such as carpaccio of horse fillet with celery, truffle oil and pecorino cheese, and Rossini fillet with sautéed Strasbourg foie gras. 'But my favourite dish is simple – horsesteak Crosse & Blackwell,' De Ley said. After years of sampling, he believes the English pickle is the perfect accompaniment to horsemeat. 'The sourness of the pickle lifts the horsemeat, you see – a meat that is pretty sweet compared to others.'[32]

Thoroughbred racehorses have a lot to contend with. Studies have found that nine out of ten suffer from gastric ulcers because their training and diet leaves them without food for long periods of time. The lack of saliva generated by chewing leads to the stomach ulcers. Almost half of all racehorses have been found to have blood in their windpipes after races, and ninety per cent have blood deeper in their lungs. This is on top of the steady build-up of bone damage to their legs from training, which eventually leads to breakdown on the track.

Then there are the tricks trainers use to keep their horses going, including tongue ties, which lash the tongue to the lower jaw to stop the horse from swallowing it, and the tall chain. This is a chain attached to the horse's tail and then inserted up its rectum to stop air entering, which supposedly affects the horse's speed. 'Although I fail to see how sticking a chain up it makes the horse's arse airtight,' says Dr McGreevy.[33]

And you have the actions taken by the unscrupulous to make money from the horses in their care. This is not just doping to make the horses quicker or slower – there's always the insurance money to think of too.

Horse insurers are not keen to go on the record to discuss horse-insurance fraud in Australia. 'I think it does occur,' says one, on condition of anonymity. 'I mean, you would be mad not to think so, but it's not as prevalent as people think. With a horse, all you have got to do is not get the vet there for twenty-four hours and you can claim your money. However, it would be wrong to suggest that it is common in the racing industry. Ninety per cent of the industry loves their horses and would do anything to save them.'[34]

Richard Logan, managing director of Logans Horse Insurance, said the insurers had built in failsafe methods to prevent fraud: 'The horse is insured for its value at the time of the loss. That is a fraud-prevention measure which allows underwriters the option to lower the value on the claim.'[35] So if a champion hits a losing streak, you can't simply knock it off and make a claim based on its former glory.

Logan, together with a lot of the other equine insurers in Australia, did however get stung by Mark O'Reilly in Nowra, on the south coast of New South Wales. O'Reilly was running a stud called Ylliero – his name spelled backwards – which at its peak had four stallions and 300 horses. In 1993 he got into financial difficulty and took out multiple insurance claims on thirteen horses and foals that later died in his care.

Among them was the foal of Rise n Shine and Regal, which had to be killed by a vet after it was found with a broken leg three weeks after its birth. O'Reilly had it insured for $25,000 – twice. Another mare, killed because of cardiovascular failure, had been insured four times for a total of $15,000. O'Reilly's well-insured horses died from broken spines, broken legs, snake bites, acute gastric torsion, lung infection, colonic torsion, septicaemia and pneumonia. Ylliero was not a good place to be a valuable racehorse – especially if you had more than one fraudulent insurance policy on your head. O'Reilly pleaded guilty to obtaining almost $180,000 by deception and was placed on a $1000 three-year good-behaviour bond.

Despite all these problems, there can be no doubt that everyone involved in horseracing loves horses. Champions such as Makybe Diva are the pin-ups of the industry. When Glen Boss rode her to her third Melbourne Cup win and took her career earnings to an all-time record of $14.5 million, everyone understood what horseracing was about. Trainer Lee Freedman and owner Tony Santic immediately decided to retire the legendary racer. Freedman then uttered the legendary and oft-quoted line: 'Go and find the smallest child on the course, because they will be the only person here who might see something like this again.'[36]

Then again, for every superstar horse that makes the back pages of the newspapers, there are many more with behavioural problems and issues brought on as a result of breeding and training. That need not be the case, according to Andrew McLean, an honorary associate of the University of Sydney and founder of the Australian Equine Behaviour Centre. He argued that ninety-nine per cent of horses with behavioural problems could be rehabilitated, and pointed to many failed racehorses that have proven to be medal-winners at Olympic equestrian events, which include dressage, cross-country and show jumping.

McLean condemned a lot of the techniques used by trainers as 'medieval'. 'I would like to see the horse industry move into the twenty-first century and use effective training techniques that appeal to the way horses learn, their mental capacity and their natural behaviours,' he said. Better-educated trainers and owners would mean 'horses would get a better deal'.[37]

Sadly, such concerns have come too late for a chestnut gelding called Jotilla, who on 21 March was the first horse to die during the 2012 Victorian jumps racing season. Jotilla clipped the top of the second-last steeple in the 'Like Sportingbet Park on Facebook Steeplechase' at Sandown. Jockey Rowan Waymouth was not injured. 'He just clipped the top of the jump,' said Waymouth. 'I thought he'll get up, he'll be right. I thought he just corked himself, I can't believe the outcome.'[38]

It was the first race on the first day of the season.

RACE 10

RED HOTS

It certainly raised a few eyebrows. Steward Matthew Bentley had started turning up for work at Harness Racing NSW in Armani suits. Expensive Armani suits. Not bad for a 24-year-old who was studying law part-time and earned $85,000 a year. Then there were his regular forays to the Star City Casino where he happily bet thousands of dollars in a session. 'People were starting to take notice of Matthew. I suppose there were alarm bells ringing,' a Harness Racing NSW board member told reporters from the *Sydney Morning Herald*.[1] Yet a check of his phone records and those of his 47-year-old fellow steward Paul O'Toole came up with nothing. No collusion between the stewards or any improper contact with trainers, drivers or owners.

Harness racing had been dodgy for as long as anyone could remember. The internet was full of blog postings from punters warning against getting stung at trots tracks across the country. Honest players in the industry were concerned; some were downright unhappy.

Emilio Rosati is a sponsor, breeder and owner. He and his wife, Maria, adore harness racing. They have a string of horses and sponsor the New South Wales Oaks. But at the start of 2011 he was prepared to walk away from the sport he loved. 'I was going out and paying for the best yearlings in Australia, New Zealand and the US and then someone would bring something with no form from New Zealand and beat me,' Rosati told Chris Roots of the *Sydney Morning Herald*. 'That happens in racing but these things were winning four, five, six in a row.'[2] Rosati had champions such as Excel Stride, which had won the New South Wales Derby and the Newcastle Derby, and Lilac Stride, which won her division of the Breeders Crown. But week in, week out at local races, his expensive horses were getting whooped by nags that he described as 'things that would jump out of the ground'.

Rosati is a man not without contacts and influence in the world of harness racing. He made his own inquiries into these new wonder-horses. 'They were there paying only $12,000 for them, so I went over and asked a few questions and got told the horse couldn't run two minutes over [in New Zealand] and they were coming and running 1:54 at Menangle,' he said. 'That doesn't happen. The bottle was ruling again and the enjoyment of the sport was gone for me and my wife.'[3] All he wanted, he told the bosses of the sport, was a level playing field. He was leaving. They begged him to hang on; something was in the pipeline.

Rosati had walked away from harness racing before, at a dirty time when hopeless horses suddenly came out of nowhere and the plunges were so big that even some of the bookies were leaving the game. King of the hill was 'the Colgate Kid', top reinsman Christopher Gleeson, with his trademark white smile.

In 1995 Gleeson pulled up the firm favourite, Coloresque, in the Australia Post Superfecta Pace at Harold Park in Sydney because of broken gear. It subsequently emerged that the hopples on the horse had been deliberately cut. More tellingly, Gleeson's brother Matthew had placed a $22,700 winning bet on the race. His winning supertrifecta ticket had left Coloresque out of the first six places, a decision described in parliament by New South Wales' racing and gaming minister, Richard Face, as 'inconceivable'. Gleeson was banned for life – a decision that was then reconsidered fourteen years later, leaving him free to reapply for his licence. That was 2010, the year before Rosati considered walking away again.

What Rosati did not know was that a whistleblower had come forward to explain what was really going on in harness racing in New South Wales. And it wasn't pretty. In fact, it was far worse than anything uncovered in the Gleeson era and dragged the sport right back to the days when harness racers were known as 'crims on rims'.

Former chief steward Michael Beattie had been trying to piece it all together. For eight months he had endeavoured to prove allegations that steward Paul O'Toole had been taking bribes. Then a person licensed by Harness Racing NSW – meaning they were either an owner, trainer or driver – blew the whistle. The *Herald*'s source on the investigation described this person as 'a rainmaker'. 'This person had been part of the inner sanctum of the rort and they were able to provide us with detailed information and join up the dots,' said the source.[4]

No wonder the check of phone records had come up blank – it emerged that both stewards were using second phones to arrange meetings and pass on information. The two dirty stewards would meet with punters, drivers and trainers at the Crown Hotel in Camden, close to the Menangle Park Paceway in Sydney's south, and decide which horses would not be swabbed for drugs. The stewards would receive payments of up to $1000 for every horse that was guaranteed a green light, clear from the testers.

Harness racing is a big business. Each year punters spend over $2.2 billion betting on the 'red hots'. A few were being given really good information and cleaning up the pot from the rest of the mugs, who were getting anything other than a fair go. The knowledge that their horses would not be tested gave trainers a clear path to pump them full of as much go-fast juice as they liked and then orchestrate the betting plunge. It is estimated that up to eighty per cent of the horses the stewards were paid not to test over an eighteen-month period came home first. Great for those in the know, and terrible for everyone else who was following form and trusting in the integrity of the sport. The horses were given the lot: cocaine, speed, Viagra, caffeine and elephant juice. The cheats also used the banned equine painkiller phenylbutazone, commonly called 'bute', and the diuretic Lasix, which stopped horses bleeding during a race.

The primary drug of choice, however, was good old-fashioned baking soda. There's no need to be too clever if the people responsible for policing the game are bent and on the payroll. When the stewards turned a blind eye to a certain horse, its trainer was able to push a hose through its nostril and into its stomach, in order to pump in the bicarbonate of soda mixture.

The scam was worth an awful lot of money, and people did not want to see the rivers of gold dry up. Within weeks of his appointment in August 2011, the new chief steward of Harness

Racing NSW, Bill Cable, had his car firebombed outside his home on the outskirts of southern Sydney. That was on a Friday night. The next Monday morning, the two stewards, Bentley and O'Toole, were confronted with evidence of their bribe-taking and immediately resigned.

Things were just starting to hot up. Harness Racing NSW put regulatory boss Reid Sanders in charge of investigating the allegations covering multiple races. He later reported that he had been the subject of a number of verbal threats since taking the job.

A three-man panel was appointed to hear the cases: Justice Wayne Haylen, Racing NSW's chief steward, Ray Murrihy, and former Racing Victoria chief steward Des Gleeson. They held their meetings away from the racing body's Bankstown headquarters for fear that critical information about the inquiry might be leaked to people in the industry. Instead, they met in the secure confines of the main Sydney court precinct in Phillip Street.

Two filing cabinets were filled with information during the first month, and around fifty letters were sent out demanding participants' phone records. One owner, Mark Vallender, was warned off after refusing to hand over his phone records. He was not accused of any other wrongdoing. However, he also had an interest in a thoroughbred called Bag Of Nickels in partnership with Peter Michael Bentley, the father of disgraced steward Matthew Bentley. Nor was Bentley senior accused of any wrongdoing. The *Daily Telegraph* published a photograph of the owner and the steward at the Goulburn and District Race Club under the headline 'Liaison of intrigue as trot scandal widens.'[5]

Successful driver Robbie Byrnes was also warned off for refusing to hand over his phone records, as was trainer Michael Siejka the following March. There was plenty more to come.

Racing regulator Sanders said the investigation was 'unprecedented' in racing: 'In my knowledge, there has never been an investigation of this nature and scale in any racing code in Australia and the world.'[6] An infinite number of people might be involved, and a huge number of races – he had no idea at that stage if it was one or 500. But Sanders would soon find out. NSW Police also began investigating with a special team, Strike Force Tairora, looking into the ever-widening scandal. They swooped in November.

On Thursday, 24 November 2011, O'Toole's twenty-year association with the sport ended when he was arrested and charged with corruption. The police action came just two days before Harness Racing NSW's biggest event, the Miracle Mile, at Menangle on the Saturday night. Also arrested was the state's premier driver, Greg Bennett. The 45-year-old had been slated to drive Karloo Mick in the big race but was stood down indefinitely by Harness Racing NSW. He was replaced for the $500,000 premier race by a twenty-year-old, Robbie Morris. Young trainer Michael Russo, aged twenty-four, was also charged after properties were searched. Sanders said his team had been about to lay charges but would hold off while the police case was underway.

In court, O'Toole was accused of taking up to $400,000 in corrupt payments in the race-fixing rort. The money was paid into his wife's bank account. The police case listed thirty-seven different races in which they alleged corrupt behaviour had occurred. The races were spread over the eighteen months before O'Toole's resignation, with ten run between 30 June and 20 July 2011. In several cases there were multiple fixed races at the same meeting.

The fixing covered six New South Wales racetracks: the three Sydney tracks of Penrith, Menangle and Bankstown, plus

Goulburn, in the Southern Highlands, Parkes and Bathurst, in the central west of the state. The majority of the crooked activity occurred at Penrith, Menangle (during the midweek meetings) and Bankstown. The big-money meetings on Saturday nights at Menangle did not feature because, there, every horse in every race was mandatorily drug-tested. O'Toole did not enter a plea and was arrested on bail.

The next day, police arrested young trainer/driver Cameron Fitzpatrick (son of premier trainer Paul) and trainer Dean Atkinson. 'This is just scraping the tip of the iceberg,' said Sanders amid warnings that the money trail might lead interstate.[7]

All this cast a pall over proceedings at the Miracle Mile on Saturday night. Harness racing legend Brian Hancock said: 'It was hard to look a few different people in the eye and know whether or not they have been involved.' He told the *Daily Telegraph* racing writer Brent Zerafa that he would have no sympathy for anyone found guilty of corrupting the sport to which he had dedicated forty-five years of his life. Even if they were friends. 'I noticed a few people looking down at their toes and you start to wonder, are they the next who will go? There was something uneasy about the night, I enjoyed the racing and the Miracle Mile is always a tremendous race with plenty of action – but it was just a little different.'[8]

Goulburn-based Dean Atkinson was the first to be sanctioned by Harness Racing NSW. He had already pleaded guilty to three charges laid by the police at Picton Local Court in December. In January the 47-year-old appeared before the investigatory panel and said he had received threatening phone calls since his guilty plea. A horse owner he had worked for had called him and accused him of 'being a snitch.' He asked for the hearing to be closed to the public because 'there are some things in the brief [of evidence] which leads me to fear for my family'.[9]

This struck a chord with Sanders, who had received similar threats himself. Sanders requested that a transcript of an earlier interview with Atkinson not be released for reasons of public safety. 'Some of these people play for keeps,' he said.[10] Atkinson was found to have paid steward Matthew Bentley three times to stop his horses being drug-tested at two separate race meetings. At Penrith on 12 May 2011, he bribed him to turn a blind eye to horses The Reluctant Dancer and The Open, and five days later at Menangle to again avoid swabbing The Reluctant Dancer. He was disqualified for ten years, ordered to pay back the $6584 in prize money and had the wins disqualified.

The Atkinson case represented the first real effort to clean up an industry that had been making a right pig's ear of its reputation up until then. When the scandal broke, the head of harness racing in New South Wales, Sam Nati, met with a leading young driver who admitted he had been involved in a couple of hot races. Despite this, the driver, who had taken his parents along to the meeting, was allowed to keep racing and went on to win a number of races across the state. Nati told the *Sydney Morning Herald* that, despite the admission, he was adopting an innocent-until-proven-guilty approach. And proving guilt was not something at which the harness racing honchos were too adept.

In January, trainer Greg Sarina and his son, driver Ben Sarina, were called before a special inquiry to face allegations that they had given false evidence to Harness Racing NSW. Chief investigator Sanders tendered phone records showing that the trainer had made a string of calls to crooked steward O'Toole. Both the Sarina men said they had no idea who the number belonged to. The phone was actually registered to a man called Nathan

Milne. Unfortunately, Sanders had never heard of him, saying he was relying on police statements that this was O'Toole's phone, although it was registered in a different name.

The chairman of the panel, Justice Haylen, felt that this was unsatisfactory. Not only did it pre-empt the police case, it offered no concrete evidence that the phone was O'Toole's. That brought into question a number of other matters they were considering. If they could not prove that this was O'Toole's phone, how could they prove that the fix was in with everyone else they were investigating? 'You have to actually establish the case against Mr Sarina – it is not up to him to prove he is not guilty,' Justice Haylen helpfully explained.[11] And this was when Harness Racing NSW were stepping up the fight – no wonder the races were called the red hots for so long.

Racing minister George Souris was on hand to announce the appointment of a new five-member board for Harness Racing NSW. He said the first board appointed under the new independent model represented a new era for the sport. Existing board members Chris Edwards and Graeme Campbell were joined by owner, sponsor and breeder Rod Smith and the former deputy director general of the New South Wales department of premier and cabinet, Alexander Smith. The most significant appointment was the first inspector of the Independent Commission Against Corruption, Graham Kelly. Crucially, he was an outsider to the sport. He said: 'I see probity as a very important part of corporate governance ... that has been my field for the past 15 years.'[12]

Phew! At last, someone not afraid to kick the crooks out of the industry.

In 2003, people were talking about harness trainers in Mildura, Victoria, giving their horses a little something extra to pep them up. In October that year an unfancied twelve-year-old horse called Our Equal Opportunity tottered onto the track at Moonee Valley. In 142 starts, he had never ever won a city meeting, so the odds were heavily against him. The horse bolted home.

It was a performance so unlikely that it could only be put down to magic – blue magic. Its trainer was Rod Weightman, a 37-year-old Ballarat horseman with an undistinguished track record. Even given his father's lifelong history in harness racing, it would be hard to explain how just a few weeks in Weightman's stables had turned an old battler like Our Equal Opportunity from a zero to a hero. Weightman's success rate had been nothing to write home about – he had clocked up an average over the previous ten years of just two winners for every ten starters.

In 2003 that all changed. Over the first eight months of the season, Weightman fielded sixty-nine broken-down old horses, bought for a few thousand bucks each, and had thirty-one winners. That was a success rate of almost fifty per cent! Some of those horses, whose form was previously thought to have been long gone, backed up to win again and again. The best of them – an old nag called Angus Puddleduck – clocked up four straight wins. It couldn't last, and it didn't.

Weightman's luck was running out. Ballarat police were investigating a number of people suspected of handling drugs and stolen property, and his property was one of the sites under surveillance. Unfortunately for him, one of the police officers on the case had previously been on the racing squad; he tipped Harness Racing Victoria's stewards to be on hand when the police conducted their dawn raid.

Andrew Rule pieced together the full story in *The Age*. The foggy morning raid of armed police and dogs culminated in

Weightman being handcuffed and led, unprotesting, into the backyard. He saw the waiting stewards and grimaced: 'That really tops off the morning.'[13]

There were sixty-two unlabelled vials of blue liquid in Weightman's refrigerator, which the police already had a fair idea would test positive for propantheline bromide – a drug that enhanced stamina in horses by opening their airways and veins, increasing the flow of oxygen. It works better in old horses that have lost form rather than in young horses struggling to find their form in the first place. Urine samples previously taken from Weightman's horses were retested for the 'blue magic'. Seven turned up positive, and he was disqualified for five years. The police had also turned up a few items of stolen property, including a motorcycle, a ride-on lawnmower and six kilograms of cannabis, which eventually resulted in a $4400 fine.

Did any of that actually teach him a lesson? Midway through his disqualification, Weightman was named as the sender of an Express Post parcel containing eight syringes of banned drug EPO to a leading Western Australian trainer, Clinton Hall. Weightman did not bother to attend the Victorian stewards' inquiry and was warned off until he did show up, while Hall was given a five-year worldwide disqualification for receiving the parcel containing the synthetic EPO darbepoetin alfa. Unrepentant, Weightman sold his property, bought a townhouse with a pool and spa and said he was enjoying the holiday.

The man who supplied Weightman with the blue magic that led to his downfall was Robert Asquith. He was a chain-smoking, coffee-swilling conman who claimed to be related to the First World War British prime minister Herbert Asquith. He had arrived in Ballarat at the end of the 1990s from Queensland in an old car with wife Jill, claiming to have been a big deal in harness racing in New Zealand. He did not publicise the fact that he had handed in his licence there after being caught importing hormonal drugs.

The couple took cheap digs – a loft above a stables – near Dowling Forest racecourse, in return for looking after the owner's horses. Jill started training gallopers at Ballarat. In 2003 she was suspended when one of her horses returned a high bicarbonate reading, thanks to a 'milkshake' she gave it to improve performance. She needed to do something – she had only managed three winners out of fifty-four starters.

Robert Asquith, meanwhile, was getting around the traps as a 'horse manipulator'; trots trainers often use chiropractors to relieve spinal problems caused by the unnatural gait used for harness racing. Once through the stable door, he would offer extra help from drugs that he claimed were unswabbable. According to Andrew Rule in *The Age*: 'Some suspected the chemicals came from Mexico via Sydney and that Asquith mixed the solutions himself, using various food dyes to provide different colours before settling on blue.'[14] In the 1990s it had been known as 'Canadian pink'.

Weightman paid $150 a pop for the blue magic. Asquith was offering big discounts to trainers who would tell him which horses had been injected with the drug in each race so that he could cash in on the punt.

At the end of 2003, Asquith returned to New Zealand. There were rumours of an affair with a younger woman. He and the amazingly tolerant and long-suffering Jill set up home in a farmhouse outside Oxford, an hour's drive north-west of Christchurch. Asquith might have changed location, but soon he was again peddling the same old magic.

A sample fell into the hands of New Zealand harness racing

officials, who began an investigation that again pointed to the 47-year-old Asquith as the supplier. Independently, the police in New Zealand were investigating fraud allegations involving doping and betting in harness racing.

A week after Weightman's arrest in Australia, harness racing officials in New Zealand teamed up with the local police to mount a series of raids on prominent harness racing identities. Harness Racing NZ's general manager, Edward Rennell, said: 'We knew with the profile of the people we approached it would generate quite a bit of media interest, but we have taken the approach of being open and transparent.'[15]

Trainer Mark Purdon was astonished to see police cars rolling up the driveway of his prestigious training centre in Russley Road, near Christchurch. Only a week earlier, the same driveway had seen New Zealand racing minister Damien O'Connor arriving to seek Purdon's views on the state of harness racing in New Zealand. At the same time, police cars were pulling into the properties of trainers Nigel McGrath, David and Catherine Butt, David's cousin Tim and thoroughbred trainer Paul Harris.

The Butts and Harris were quickly cleared, but the spotlight fell squarely on McGrath and Purdon. With Purdon, the authorities were looking closely at the alleged doping of a horse called Light And Sound at meetings in March and April 2004. Also under the microscope was Light And Sound's owner, John Seaton. Together, they were harness racing royalty. Seaton was a self-made man, a former truck driver worth over $35 million, and one of the biggest sponsors of harness racing in New Zealand. He was also the man who had introduced Purdon to a new acquaintance of his from Club Aspinall, the high-rollers' room at Christchurch Casino: Robert Asquith.

The heat on Asquith was increasing. Three further trainers had been charged with using blue magic in Australia. The authorities were keen to talk to him; they suspected he was the supplier. The New Zealand police had charged him under the Medicines Act with supplying a prescription medicine, a seemingly minor offence that was punishable with a $1000 fine. It did not seem much, but the scam was unravelling.

It emerged that Asquith was a fraud and a failure who no more deserved to be in the high-rollers' room than Harry the one-legged hobo. Not only that, but a lot of people who had accepted blue magic from Asquith were looking at him as a possible snitch. So were the police.

Two days before he was due in court, Asquith left a note for his wife at their brick farmhouse at the foot of the snow-capped New Zealand alps, went to an outbuilding and hanged himself. He took with him to the grave his secrets about blue magic, who bought it and who used it.

Asquith might have been dead but the blue magic case was not. A month later, in August, Nigel McGrath was found guilty of administering the concoction to his horses on three occasions. He said he was doing it to treat their ulcers. Vets were expensive, he said, and he had not talked about it because he wanted to keep his edge. He was banned for three years.

In November 2004, in the middle of Cup Week, the highlight of the Canterbury social and racing calendar, the authorities publicly announced that John Seaton would be charged in relation to the doping of Light And Sound. Seaton was the man whose investment had turned harness racing around in New Zealand; he had won two New Zealand Cups, three Derbies and NZ$1.58 million in stakes. He went absolutely mental.

Seaton abused harness racing officials at the New Zealand

Trotting Cup meeting at Addington Raceway in Christchurch, calling chief executive Edward Rennell 'a low prick'.[16] The charge Purdon faced came from a statement he had given to police early on that he had given Light And Sound a substance on two occasions. He had not thought the substance was banned. Seaton had suggested it, he said, and Asquith had provided it. Light And Sound won the races but never tested positive for blue magic.

Purdon initially pleaded guilty to the charge but in fact was never found guilty. He went on to leave all this behind and carry on his stellar career as one of New Zealand's most successful trainers.

But the charges weighed enormously on Seaton. He was furious about media coverage that suggested he had tried to boost the horse to sell it at a higher price. Seaton, fifty-five years old and a bombastic larrikin, told anyone who would listen that he and Purdon were innocent, and that he had hired a Queen's counsel to fight his case. Privately, he was also dealing with another stress: his wife, Ann, had been in remission from a grave illness but had relapsed. It was a lot to handle – too much.

On 15 November 2004, Seaton took a gun into the bathroom of his luxury farmhouse and shot himself. Another casualty for blue magic, and for the world of racing.

RACE 11

A NEW THREAD

On Saturday, 31 March 1984, trainer George Brown came home from the races in Brisbane in a highly distressed state. 'He was very, very agitated, I have never seen him that agitated,' said his partner, Pat Goodwin.[1]

Brown's horse Risley, which was running in the last race at Doomben, had been backed down from 14/1 to as low as 4/1 at Wollongong, and from 12/1 to 8/1 at city meetings; these were the days when you had to be at a track to bet. Despite the excited betting, the horse had trailed home second from last. 'He was upset with the ride of the jockey and said he was disgusted with the whole run,' said Pat.[2]

He had good reason to be troubled by that ride. Two weeks earlier, Brown had told his estranged wife that he had agreed to switch the slow-running Risley for a much faster horse that looked just like her. It was a classic ring-in.

There was an awful lot of money at stake on fixed races in Queensland. Bookies in Sydney and Melbourne were leery of taking bets on races in Brisbane because they were so crooked. In the months before Risley's run, two other horses, Wishane Myth and Aquitane, were widely known to have been nobbled. But that just wasn't Brown's way. His brother Allan said: 'Nobody ever saw George talking to hooligans or gangsters.'[3]

On the day of the race at Doomben, Brown was late handing in Risley's papers and was fined $50. He had got cold feet and did not go through with the last-minute substitution. Some very serious people lost a lot of money when the real Risley slowly trailed home; her ring-in was meant to charge over the finishing line first. No wonder Brown was agitated.

He was not much better when he left his home in Kensington near Randwick Racecourse to go to work the next Monday morning. Pat would never see him alive again. One professional punter, Arthur Harris, said later that a 'couple of men' were dispatched to teach George a lesson.[4] The men were Tongan, high on drugs and went too far.

The trainer was systematically tortured. His left arm was twisted until it popped from its socket and the bones snapped. His legs were hit with a heavy blunt instrument, probably an iron bar, and both were broken above the knee. He eventually died from two massive blows to the head that fractured his skull.

George's broken body was then piled into a Ford Falcon and torched on the F6 near Bulli south of Sydney. 'George Brown was a horseman,' racing journalist Max Presnell told the ABC. 'He was never going to make the annals of the all-time greats. But he knew what he was doing and … he was a kind man, a pleasant man. Nobody deserved to die the way that George Brown died.'[5]

Four months after George Brown's broken and burnt body was discovered, trainer Hayden Haitana, a big-drinking part-Maori, was approached to facilitate another ring-in. He was left in no doubt about what would happen to him if he didn't play ball. 'Oh, they just told me I'd end up like George Brown, you know. Um, there's always those threats involved; there's guys walking around the stables carrying guns and stuff, pistols,' he later said.[6] Haitana's jockey brother Pat had finished a six-month sentence in Brisbane's Wacol Prison for drink-driving. His cellmate had been a conman called John Gillespie. He was looking for a trainer to help with a ring-in, and Pat suggested his brother.

Gillespie had tried a similar trick at Doomben two years earlier, substituting the horse Apparent Heir for Mannasong. The plunge failed when Mannasong, supposedly the fast horse, nevertheless trailed home hopelessly slow. It still earned Gold Coast trainer Bill Steer a lifetime ban.

At the time, Gillespie had been working for SP bookmaker Michael Sayers, a violent underworld character who covered his gambling losses by running drugs. Gillespie was in hock to Sayers for around $5000. Sayers himself was in debt to other SP operators, including the Sydney organised-crime tsar George Freeman. That was a big debt and not a good one to have. It was possibly this that persuaded Sayers to bankroll the ring-in.

Gillespie got to work and found the good horse first. In May 1984 he bought Dashing Solitaire, an eight-year-old gelding with great breeding. His owners included breeder Jack Ingham, Sydney Turf Club director Don Storey and the Hollywood actor James Mason. He cost $10,000. Gillespie then had to find a horse that looked just like him. He eventually settled on a moderately successful picnic racer called Fine Cotton. He was a dark-brown horse with two white socks on his back legs and a white star on the left side of his forehead. A dead ringer for Dashing Solitaire. Gillespie offered $2000 cash in hand for the horse, and the owners jumped at the chance.

Both horses were sent to Haitana's modest training facility in Coffs Harbour. Fine Cotton was entered into a string of races to push his odds down as low as possible. The seventy-race veteran gave the conspirators a shock when he sprinted down the straight at Bundamba on 1 August. He tired, however, and finished close to the back, which showed Haitana that he must make sure the old fella was properly exhausted before he got on the track again. At Doomben on 8 August Fine Cotton started at 20/1 and finished tenth in a field of twelve.

Things were looking good for the Saturday, 11 August 1984, but then disaster struck – Dashing Solitaire crashed into a barbed-wire fence while being unloaded from his horse float. He couldn't race. The conspirators needed a new horse – and fast.

They scratched Fine Cotton and instead put him down for a race the following Saturday. Haitana said that Fine Cotton, the supposed dud, was flying and could in fact win on his own merits. The conspirators did not believe him, and when he offered to fire Fine Cotton up with elephant juice the idea was rejected.

Haitana wanted to walk away but there was no way out. 'I tried to walk out, but they were going to shoot my brother Pat. They said "You can hide, but he can't. We will shoot him on a racetrack."'[7] Haitana turned to the bottle, while Gillespie turned to a horse he had been looking at previously called Bold Personality. It had been trained by Tommy Smith and was going for $20,000. Gillespie paid the owner, Bill Naoum, with a rubber cheque just a few days before the big race on 18 August.

But there were a couple of problems with the plan. Firstly, Bold Personality was a successful and easily recognisable Group 2 horse. Secondly, he did not look anything like Fine Cotton.

By now, Haitana had fled home to Coffs Harbour, but he was found and escorted back to Brisbane for the race. Meanwhile, the conspirators had been hard at work. One of the scammers, Tomaso di Luzio, brought Bold Personality up from Coffs Harbour. Unfortunately, he knew nothing about horses and had put a heavy winter blanket on the gelding for the long road journey. By the time he arrived, Bold Personality was dehydrated and in distress.

Haitana attempted to give the horse a drench by inserting a tube into its nose to flush its stomach, an operation he botched so badly that the horse started to bleed and had to have its head lashed to the rafters of the barn to stop hurting itself as it thrashed around in distress. The crooks then used women's hair dye to darken Bold Personality's coat, and Taubman's white gloss enamel to replicate Fine Cotton's socks. Neither worked; the dye turned red and had to be washed off on the lawn of another conspirator, Robert North, the next morning. The paint ran on to the horse's hooves, and eventually they had to bandage his legs to cover the markings.

Finally, the Marx Brothers of Australian racing set out for Brisbane's Eagle Farm on 18 August 1984, with Fine Cotton in another float just in case they needed to switch the horses after the race. It was the worst-kept secret in racing.

Down in Sydney, bookmaking giants Bill and Robbie Waterhouse were driving out to the races at Warwick Farm. 'Rob had told me on the way to the races that there was a strong tip for a horse in Brisbane and to be careful,' Bill wrote many years later. 'He didn't tell me the name but said he would send someone to my stand to let me know before the race. I didn't take much notice, but once betting had opened for the fourth race, Robbie sent a runner to tell me the horse to watch in Brisbane was Fine Cotton.'[8]

Bill was working the interstate ring and, as the betting plunge began, he blinked, turning the price off the board to make sure he did not get caught until the price settled. The word was already out that Sayers was betting heavily with SP bookmakers on the race.

Years later, it emerged through an Administrative Appeals Tribunal confidential tax assessment that Robbie had been given $40,000 by Sayers to put on the horse four days before the race. He was not told the name until the Saturday morning. The approach came through his trusted clerk, Garry Clarke, and Robbie said he simply put the money on as a commission agent for Sayers – although he did add $10,000 of his own.

As investigators later discovered, Robbie had in fact spread the Waterhouse bank around. Among the people betting for him around the country that day were Clarke's pregnant wife, Glenis, in Southport in south-east Queensland, young employee Gregory Ford at Tamworth, another employee, Bobby Hines, at Kempsey, business associate Peter McCoy in Canberra, Catholic priest and family friend Father Edwin O'Dwyer at the Appin Dogs, and merchant banker Ian Murray at Warwick Farm.

Across Australia, it was a $1-million plunge. The opening price on Fine Cotton was 33/1, then it was cut to 20/1, and most Sydney bookmakers opened it at 8/1. The punters went crazy.

Bookmaker Mark Read, the author of some famous plunges of his own, was stunned at the betting on a horse that had lost its last three starts. Ian Murray approached him with a bet of $120,000 to $20,000 but Read only took a quarter of that. As Read slashed his odds, Murray kept coming back for more. He also approached Bill Waterhouse, who cut his bet for a $40,000 win to $14,000 for $1000. Waterhouse said Murray warned him: 'Be careful of this one, Bill.' He added ruefully: 'It would only be much later that I found out Murray's betting included a commission arranged through Rob.'[9] Most of the big betting was happening in Sydney, and even as the horse firmed to 2/1, the punters were still splashing cash in a frenzy. None of the betting made sense.

Unless, of course, you happened to be in Queensland and knew what was going on. In the mounting yard before the Second Commerce Novice Handicap, eighteen-year-old apprentice jockey Gus Philpot, who was riding Fine Cotton in the race, wondered why everyone else was looking at him so knowingly. Haitana told him to give it his best shot and then snuck away to put $50 on the second favourite, Harbour Gold. No one checked Philpot's horse or noticed that Fine Cotton no longer had a small white star on the left of his head but a great big one in the middle of its forehead. 'I reckon you could have put a rhinoceros in the race and no-one would have noticed,' he later joked.[10]

One man who would have noticed was Bold Personality's most recent owner, Bill Naoum, who had turned up for a day at the races. The conspirator Gillespie was ordered to ply Naoum with drinks and keep him in the bar – with his back to the screen – while the race was run.

As the barrier opened, Philpot was immediately struck by the pull of a horse that he thought was a tired old picnic racer. Despite his terrible treatment in the lead-up to the race, Bold Personality was still a quality racehorse, and out on the track he knew what to do.

Across Australia, punters listened breathlessly to the commentary: 'Fine Cotton's still the leader, he's about a neck in front. Harbour Gold's coming at him solidly now. Fine Cotton and Harbour Gold, they're going to fight it out. Harbour Gold's just about got his nose in front, Fine Cotton's kicking again on the inside. Fine Cotton and Harbour Gold. Fine Cotton's in front. They're drawing to the line. He's just in front – Fine Cotton and Harbour Gold lunge right on the line. They hit it. Pretty tight this one. Fine Cotton or Harbour Gold – it could go either way, then Cabaret Kingdom.'[11]

Fine Cotton had won by a nose. As the horse was being led back to the mounting yard, a man started the chant: 'Ring in!'

A happy but agitated Hayden Haitana was waiting in the winners' stall and began talking up his training regime. That was until someone pointed out that the horse was actually Bold Personality. The stewards were called, the crowd wanted their money, the bookmakers were holding the tickets and no one knew what was happening.

The stewards refused to release the correct weight, which gives the green light for bets to be paid, and asked for Fine Cotton's owners to come forward. Brisbane racing figure Mal McGregor-Lowndes had bought a half-share in the horse from Gillespie. In the past, he had been convicted of painting sparrows yellow and selling them as canaries. On raceday he turned up and explained he had paid $1500 for the horse on 31 July, saying he knew the horse was a hopeless picnic racer and so had not even put a bet on him.

The real conspirators were nowhere to be seen. Fine Cotton was disqualified and Harbour Gold was awarded the race. Most bookies did not hand back the bets. There was a lot of anger that the horse was disqualified, which prevented the punters from getting their money back. Others felt that it was poetic justice that those who knew and were prepared to gamble on a crooked race should do their dough.

As the Brisbane Consorting Squad got to work locating the conspirators, Channel Nine's premier current affairs show, *60 Minutes*, was hot on the heels of the only person known publically to be involved: Hayden Haitana. He had cashed in his $50 bet on Harbour Gold and was negotiating a $10,000 fee through an intermediary for his story.

When the interview with Jana Wendt appeared on Sunday night the following week, it caused a sensation. A nervy Haitana, sitting in a Sydney hotel room, told Wendt he had been approached by a man called Terry Malouf to set up the ring-in. He said Malouf showed him a gun and said: 'Do you want to end up like trainer Brown?'[12] And then, Haitana added, Malouf told him a man called 'Bob Waterhouse' was behind the crooked race. That allegation was repeated the next day in the Queensland parliament. Robbie Waterhouse was in the cross-hairs. He denied everything.

The AJC in Sydney was concerned about the plunge there and launched an investigation; John Schreck was appointed to head up the inquiry. Almost sixty witnesses were called to attend. During his evidence, Robbie Waterhouse was asked if he had heard anything about Fine Cotton. 'Not at all,' he said. 'It would appear to me to be, for a start smacking completely of complete amateurism. Obviously the tip has spread like oil on water.'[13] His reply damned him for years; had he accepted some responsibility for the events that day, it's likely he would have got off rather more lightly. Instead, the stewards recommended that Robbie Waterhouse should show cause why his bookmaker's licence should not be revoked and why he should not be warned off.

Everyone else was going down with the ship too. The stewards recommended that Father O'Dwyer, Bobbie Hines, John Gough, Peter McCoy, Ian Murray, Glenis and Garry Clarke and Bill Waterhouse should also show cause why they should not be warned off. Additionally, Hines, Glenis Clarke, McCoy and Bill Waterhouse should show cause why they should not have their licences revoked. The AJC heard submissions over three days, and on 30 November 1984 confirmed all of the findings. Robbie and Bill Waterhouse immediately appealed to the New South Wales Racing Appeals Tribunal, before Judge Alf Goran.

The truth was out there, and Schreck was determined to find it. He rode out on the trail of merchant banker Ian Murray, who was on a trout-fishing expedition in the wilds of Tasmania. 'We proceeded to madly dive around all the tracks we could find around the central parts, lakes of Tasmania. And as it would happen we, we eventually went across over this ridge, and there before us, like the charge of the cavalry coming, was Mr Murray and his people,' Schreck told ABC television years later. 'It was freezing cold, a big raging fire going, and he and I went a bit away from the rest of the group and chatted with a couple of big thick scotches trying to keep warm in this Tasmanian mountain weather. And he decided that it was in his interests, his family's interests, and racing's interests generally to come back and give evidence.'[14]

That evidence was damning: Murray said he had put the money on for Robbie. Later, Robbie would say that he had not disclosed the full extent of his dealings with Murray because the banker had emphatically stressed that his name could not be mentioned in relation to Fine Cotton. 'If I'd told the truth from the start I wouldn't have been in any trouble,' said Robbie. 'I regret not having done that. It's hard once you get on a roller-coaster it's hard to get off the roller-coaster and you know, I was untruthful about it, which was very wrong and I regret it I wouldn't do it ever again. But it's hard once you get on that roller-coaster to get off and it perhaps required more strength of character than I had at that time.'[15]

Once Judge Goran heard Murray's new version of events, he blasted Robbie, taking particular exception to the way Robbie had presented himself as a scientific bookmaker who studied form, rather than as someone who had a network of dodgy people around him. Goran claimed that the family business of W. S. Waterhouse shared the profits because they operated from a common pool, and upheld the judgement. He could not, however, find any direct evidence linking the Waterhouses to the ring-in in Queensland.

Bill Waterhouse was shocked by the decision and denied any involvement or prior knowledge. 'To this day, I still wonder how anyone in their right mind could ever think that Rob and I would have been mixed up with such fools,' he later wrote.[16]

The warning-off also had a devastating effect on Robbie's wife, Gai. They owned ten horses together. Robbie could not go to the stables to see the horses. But when Gai attempted to become a trainer in her own right, the warning-off was used by the AJC as a reason to deny her application. 'An Australian rule of racing at that time prevented ah, the spouse or partner of a disqualified person from being a licensed person … that was the rules. It wasn't the AJC's decision – they had no choice,' said Schreck.[17]

Gai had already nailed her colours to the mast. She was working as a foreperson under her maiden name, and when the Fine Cotton affair broke, she changed her name to Waterhouse to support Robbie. When she applied for a trainer's licence in 1989, the AJC rejected her application. She went to the New South Wales Equal Opportunity Tribunal the next year, claiming that the AJC was playing dirty, turning the case into a rerun of the Fine Cotton affair. They argued that she was under the influence of a deceitful and corrupting husband.

Clearly, that was discrimination. Gai appealed, and the Court of Appeal asked the Equal Opportunity Tribunal to rehear the matter. The AJC immediately took it to the High Court. As the lawyers worked on the case, AJC chairman Jim Bell realised that the committee had lost public support and appeared completely out of touch. The racing public was questioning why the AJC wanted to deny this woman a chance to follow in her legendary father's footsteps.

The AJC committee caved in and granted her licence in 1992. 'They were wrong, and they were proven wrong ... by the ruling that has since been passed that, and it was really I suppose a landmark victory for working women in Australia,' Gai said. 'Because you can't be judged on your spouse you know, you have to be judged on your own merits. And that's where the AJC made their big boo-boo.'[18]

She went on to prove them wrong again and again. Gai Waterhouse has since become one of the most successful people in Australian racing. In the 2012 Sydney Autumn Carnival she claimed her fifth Group 1 win and fourth treble in successive Saturdays, when the John Singleton-owned super-mare More Joyous won the Doncaster Mile. It was her seventh Doncaster win, equalling her father's long-standing record in the famous race at Royal Randwick. 'It is a very special moment,' Gai said. It also helped to bring her prize-money tally for the first five weeks of the carnival to $5 million. 'I hope Dad is up there smiling. The Doncaster is one of the great races and we have been trying for a few years now to get our seventh win.'[19]

Tommy Smith would indeed have been proud. Gai had fought a long battle against a staid and conservative racing establishment. 'Dad was a hard act to follow. It's lovely that we can have one part of the dream come true,' she said.[20]

For Robbie, it was going to be a long and lonely road to get his own dream back on track. In Queensland, Hayden Haitana, Robert North and John Gillespie were all jailed for their part in the Fine Cotton ring-in. Gillespie had flitted out after two 'policemen' who looked like Islanders had called at his home to see him. He wasn't there and didn't go back, eventually being found cowering in a cupboard in Victoria. A lot of stewards were also booted out of Queensland racing, which had a lot of ground to make up if it was to repair its reputation.

As did Robbie. In 1986 he was charged with trying to defraud bookmakers, but the case was dismissed in 1988. The following year, he was served with a summons alleging he had committed perjury before Judge Goran at the Racing Appeals Tribunal. That one ended up with him serving eight months in periodic detention.

In 1995 Robbie finally got a chance to try to clear his name. It did not go well. His estranged brother, David, came out of the woodwork with explosive new claims. They were locked in a bitter family feud over money. David said his brother was indeed the mastermind behind the Fine Cotton affair. He could not substantiate the claim, however, and Robbie continued to categorically deny it. Needless to say, the AJC rejected his application to regain his licence. Robbie tried again in 1997, and David came back and submitted an affidavit to back up his original claim.

Robbie pulled out of that application and the affidavit was not aired publicly until 2010. But it was a touchy subject. Almost three weeks after his 1997 attempt to get his licence back, the *Sunday Age* and the *Sun-Herald* ran a story by Andrew Rule that told the story of George Brown's torture. It did not mention David's affidavit but Robbie sued, claiming the article implied he was a torturer and a murderer. He lost, but as a part of the court case Robbie attached David's affidavit to the paperwork. The *Sydney Morning Herald*'s Rick Feneley got hold of it in 2010.

In the affidavit, David recalled a conversation Robbie had had with him and their father, Bill, in St James Court in 1986, while facing the ultimately doomed charges of trying to defraud bookmakers. The *Daily Mirror* that afternoon ran with the front-page headline: 'Racehorse trainer murder: bookie link – fresh lead.' David claimed that Robbie told them: 'They're going to arrest me over the George Brown murder.' David said he attempted to reassure his brother that he did not have a bookmaker's licence so it couldn't be him. But Robbie said he'd had one when George Brown was murdered. Pressed on what he had to do with the murdered trainer, Robbie allegedly said: 'He was involved in a couple of ring-ins for me but don't ask me any more questions – I don't want to talk about it.'[21]

There has never been any evidence produced to back up this hugely damaging claim, which Robbie has always denied. David's reliability as a witness was questionable. In the Supreme Court in Melbourne, Justice Bill Ormiston had presided over a case between David and an art dealer named Brian Pearce. The judge dismissed Pearce's claim that David had defrauded him of $1.8 million in the purchases of oil paintings and racehorses. He also threw out David's counterclaim over an unpaid $25,500 cheque, saying that David was a 'devious and unreliable witness' and 'a person whose commercial morality was of the lowest order'.[22]

If Robbie did not mastermind the Fine Cotton ring-in, who did? It has never been proved that Robbie did anything more than jump on the same tip on which thousands of other people were attempting to cash in. A controversial book on Bill Waterhouse's life, published in 1990 by journalist Kevin Perkins and titled *The Gambling Man*, dug deep into the story, but it was extremely favourable to the Waterhouse family and became mired in legal action with several parties, including David. It was a biased sensation, digging dirt, including personal allegations against Sheriff Schreck.

Bill Waterhouse denied claims he was behind the book, even though it was published in Tonga, which had Bill as its honorary consul in Sydney. But in 2009 he wrote that it explained a lot: 'Among the most amazing disclosures by Perkins was that the gangster George Freeman had caused serious trouble to Robbie and me over Fine Cotton by influencing or manipulating people of authority in the background. These included Freeman's contacts in the media, the police, politics and even at the AJC. Perkins revealed that Freeman, with his hatred for us, took advantage of the situation to make sure Robbie and I were the fall guys.'[23]

This view is backed up by a former satchel-swinger who was around at the time. Speaking quietly over a beer at the Bowlers Club in the middle of Sydney, he says: 'There is no doubt Robbie was set up. He was cocky, a couple of other bookmakers were cheesed off with him. There had been other ring-ins that had been pulled off without any problem. They knew Robbie would follow the money and they were happy to let him take the fall.'[24]

According to this man, Robbie has borne the brunt of the Fine Cotton scandal while the real masterminds have been quietly chuckling behind their form guides for years.

That view reached a whole new level in 2010, when Adam Shand of the *Sunday Mail* in Queensland tracked down John Gillespie. Now seventy, the crook with a rap sheet 350 offences long – including stealing, armed robbery and false pretences – said he wanted to put the record straight. He had been found guilty of staging the ring-in and had been sentenced to four years in jail, of which he had served five months behind bars and two years of home detention. A much longer sentence, it had been thought, came in the form of the public humiliation and ridicule he suffered for organising such a botched fix.

Not so, said Gillespie. 'I don't mind if people think it was a joke or whatever because I walked away with $1.8 million,' he said.[25] Fine Cotton was never supposed to win. The trick was to get the horse disqualified and clean up on the original favourite, Harbour Gold. As the plunge on Fine Cotton brought his odds in from 33/1 to 7/2, so the odds on Harbour Gold drifted out to 5/1.

According to Gillespie, the mastermind had been SP bookmaker Mick Sayers. He had summoned Gillespie to his Bronte home at the start of the year and shown him $1 million in cash spread out on the kitchen table. It was money he owed to George Freeman, and Sayers was not happy about it. He told Gillespie that Freeman had won the money by fixing a race the previous month. There had been only one trier in the race – Freeman had paid all the other jockeys to pull up their horses and let his rider take the winning post first. Sayers wanted his revenge and needed a race-fixer. He had been told by armed robber Bertram Douglas Kidd that his old Boggo Road jail-mate John Gillespie was his man.

Gillespie claims he persuaded Sayers that by 'failing' in the sting, they could do even better. It would be sweet revenge on Freeman, who would lose money by plunging on Fine Cotton. Sayers agreed and coughed up the cash to bankroll the fix. Gillespie leaked information about the sting to people in Freeman's camp. Trainer Hayden Haitana was kept in the dark about the double sting, however. 'Hayden had a big mouth, particularly when he was on the drink, so we expected him to tell people of the ring-in,' Gillespie said.[26]

News spread far and wide. On the day of the race, Gillespie was busy. Not only was he keeping Fine Cotton's former owner's glass topped up, he was also entertaining two Queensland police officers in the bar. As he watched Fine Cotton's double squeeze home in front of Harbour Gold, he had to put a carefully orchestrated plan into action. He had his people strategically placed. On his signal from the grandstand, they started chanting: 'Ring-in, ring-in!' As the inquiry began, Gillespie met Haitana in the Eagle Farm bar and told him to scram. Unfortunately for Gillespie, Haitana scrammed straight into the arms of *60 Minutes*, and Gillespie's involvement became public knowledge.

Gillespie was meeting with a fellow conspirator, the Brisbane socialite Robert North, to discuss the matter when the telephone rang. It was George Freeman. 'Bob handed the telephone to me and Freeman said to me: "We know what you have done and I am sending two men to Brisbane to fix you up". I replied that they had better be your best blokes otherwise they wouldn't be coming back. Then I hung up on Freeman,' Gillespie said, with all the bravado of hindsight. 'I looked around and Bob, who had the heart of a split pea, had fainted and fallen to the ground.'[27]

Gillespie fled. He said he put $1.8 million – his share of the winnings – in an offshore bank account. The ring-in's author and bankroller, Sayers, deposited $12 million in a Swiss bank account. Not that it did him much good – he was murdered the next year. Gunned down in his driveway. That killing has long been believed to be because he had stolen heroin from a Sydney drug dealer, Barry McCann. Gillespie now suggested it was revenge for Fine Cotton.

He left Australia for the United States just before his fraud trial for Fine Cotton, after Queensland's then racing minister, Russ Hinze, called and warned him that Freeman's associate, Christopher Dale 'Rent-a-kill' Flannery, was going to shoot him when he fronted for court. Gillespie eventually did his time and then moved to Thailand and Malaysia, where he invested his money from the sting in bars, restaurants and racing.

The man who pursued Robbie Waterhouse so doggedly in New South Wales, chief steward John Schreck, dismissed this new version of events. 'With great respect to Mr Gillespie, anything he says you would have to take with a great big pinch of salt,' he said. 'Truly, Dick Francis could not think up something like that.'[28]

Did the stewards really get it so wrong? The odds are certainly against it. One observer close to those involved at the time scoffed at suggestions of Robbie's innocence. 'Just follow the money – Robbie was the only one who had people scattered around to make money on Fine Cotton. The problem is that he showed no contrition,' he said.[29]

After seventeen years in exile, Robbie Waterhouse was finally allowed back on the track in 2001, with his father following five months later. Bill went on to train Robbie's son, Tom, who since emerged as one of Australia's biggest bookies.

Robbie did not immediately cover himself in glory, however. Six months after he was allowed back at the track, he was embroiled in what became known as the 'extravagant odds affair'. At a midweek race in Canterbury, Robbie had given his old Canberra mate Peter McCoy odds of 500/1 on thirteen horses that were only paying between $1.70 and $3.80. Robbie said it was to allow his friend to clear an outstanding debt.

The extravagant odds affair went through five different levels of judicial process, from a stewards' inquiry to the courts. Robbie's penalty went from a two-year disqualification for giving misleading evidence to, finally, a nine-month suspension. After the Thoroughbred Racing Board's first hearing, when the media attention was at its height, the organisation's chief executive, Merv Hill, was asked whether Robbie would ever get his licence back. 'I wouldn't be giving you 500 to 1, that's for sure,' he quipped.[30] It was a flip comment that a judge would later decide showed the board had prejudged the issue.

The charge of having given misleading evidence related to Robbie's claim that McCoy had gone home to Braidwood with his settling bag. McCoy was actually working for the Waterhouses in their betting shop in Fiji at the time, and Robbie's staff on the day were really waiting for him in the car. It was the lie that got Robbie into trouble, not the bets. His staff – his daughter, Kate, and son, Tom – were hauled before the stewards, and many speculated that this would cause trouble in the home of the racing dynasty. Even as Hill was making his ill-judged comments, Gai sent out an email from Tulloch Lodge: 'I have remained silent to allow the hearing to take place. However, my silence on this matter should not be misinterpreted. I love Rob and stand by him.'[31]

The Waterhouses were rock-solid, and Robbie was quickly back in action. It is in the blood. After all the ordeals, he said, it was great to be back on track and doing business. In 2012

Robbie lost a bundle when punters backed More Joyous in from $4.40 to $3.70 as the wet Randwick track dried out. He had spent the week listening to his wife browbeating owner John Singleton into letting the horse race. 'She was the only one they wanted to back as the track got better,' he said. 'I lost on the race, like I do on all Doncasters when Gai wins it. I was trying to avoid it, and it was still a disaster.'[32]

But after seventeen years on the outer, it was the kind of disaster he could happily live with.

RACE 12

TRACKSIDE TANTRUM

'I own the fucking horse, Gai!'

In the Parade Ring at Sydney's Royal Randwick Racecourse, one of Australia's most famous horseracing partnerships and a lifelong friendship were imploding live on national television. Ad man, philanthropist and horse lover John Singleton had finally had enough. Fingers pointing and head bobbing, he vented his fury at trainer and racing royalty Gai Waterhouse.

At stake was Singleton's pride and joy, More Joyous, a six-year-old mare he had bred and loved. More Joyous had 21 wins from 32 starts and had earned nearly $4.6 million in prize money. More to the point, she was the best horse Singleton had ever produced. She was part of a fine family, bred out of his dam Sunday Joy, who had won the Group 1 AJC Australian Oaks in 2003. He had also bred Sunday Joy's half-sister Tuesday

Joy, and she too had delivered him a hatful of Group 1 wins. So More Joyous was the pick of a fabulous crop, with a fantastic racing pedigree.

When not training at Waterhouse's Tulloch Lodge, the mare holidayed at Singleton's Strawberry Hills Farm at Mount White on the New South Wales Central Coast, two hours north of Sydney. That April 2013 race day at Randwick was the much-anticipated showdown between More Joyous and All Too Hard in the 1400 metre All Aged Stakes. So when her price started to drop off, easing from $3 to $2.50, Singleton became increasingly agitated. An ultimatum was issued: More Joyous needed to win or be highly placed. If not, Singleton's horses would be pulled from Gai's stables.

But things were about to get a lot worse.

Singleton was already displeased with his trainer. Their relationship had been fractured by an incident some months before, in October 2012 at the Cox Plate, which had betrayed the mare's incredible racing pedigree: More Joyous stormed out of her first-ever race to win by five lengths and her career had seen her win eight Group 1 races. Singleton had long been eyeing the elusive Cox Plate. Before the 2012 spring classic at Moonee Valley, Singleton said he had told his racing manager, Duncan Grimley, to instruct Gai to choose barrier four to six if possible. The distance, 2040 metres, was always going to be tough, but with the right barrier Singleton thought his horse had a chance.

At the barrier draw luck was shining on him and More Joyous's name came out first, giving Gai the choice of any barrier she wanted. She picked barrier eleven. Singleton was stunned. He called News Limited racing writer Ray Thomas to vent his feelings: 'I love Gai but this is bloody madness,' he fumed.

'If this was a normal race and not the Cox Plate, the horse would be scratched and the trainer sacked!'[1] He was angry and on the record. 'This isn't death, it is suicide,' he said. 'It will be almost impossible for her to win now. The bookies aren't idiots – she is out to $13 and will probably end up $20 on race day. I'm absolutely gutted.'[2]

For her part, Gai argued that the barrier draw would give More Joyous's regular jockey, Nash Rawiller, more options in the long race and prevent him from being trapped on the inside rail. She dismissed the row with Singleton as 'a lovers tiff'. 'My job is to win the race and I think she has a terrific barrier,' she said.[3]

It didn't work quite as she planned. More Joyous was trapped wide at the first turn and eventually passed the post in a very lacklustre eleventh place. The friendship that had begun almost forty years before when Gai had visited Singleton at his home for career advice about show business, on the advice of her legendary horse trainer father Tommy Smith, was teetering on the brink. What happened at the All Aged Stakes at Royal Randwick would push it over the edge.

Singleton had been unhappy even before the race. He was interviewed by racing channel TVN with his mate and Magic Millions owner Gerry Harvey. Asked if he was confident about More Joyous's chances in the race Singleton replied: 'Absolutely no confidence because the trainer's son has been spruiking to all his mates, very good mates of mine, that it has got no chance, it has got problems and I don't know what the problems are and I don't know what the no chance is.' And then he added, damningly: 'But, anyway, there is no conflict of interest.'[4]

The trainer's son was, of course, the ubiquitous bookmaker Tom Waterhouse, a bookmaker Singleton had been happy to praise to the *Sydney Morning Herald* a few months before as a risk-taking, hard-working, IT and media-savvy genius who was 'unbelievably good at what he does.' 'It's a long time since we've had bookies like Tom,' he enthused. 'Most of them have become very beige, but he just seems to have the flair.'[5]

Tom had certainly taken the Waterhouse family name in bookmaking to new heights. His grandfather, Bill Waterhouse, and father, Robbie, were of course already well known, after both being warned off over the Fine Cotton affair and returning successfully to the bookmaking business. And now Tom was the smiling, clean face of new-look gambling, regularly appearing on television sports shows to talk through the odds.

Singo, a family friend whose daughter Sally had grown up with 'young Tom', had clearly had a change of heart since shovelling on that effusive praise.[6] Had Tom Waterhouse, son of his lifelong friend and trainer Gai, really known more than him about the chances of his champion mare in the All Aged Stakes that day?

The race had already been hyped up as a showdown between Singleton's champion More Joyous and All Too Hard, the half-brother of legendary Black Caviar. Gerry Harvey had bought the three-year-old from Nathan Tinkler for $20 million. Harvey was in the stands with Singleton to watch the race. It was a cracker. All Too Hard certainly did not disappoint his new owner, easily tracking More Joyous from fourth place before sweeping down the centre to win the race. More Joyous trailed home second last in seventh place.

Singleton was incandescent. 'It's too much. It's a conflict of interest,' he exploded on Channel Seven.[7] 'Tom has been saying she has got problems, and I don't know about them.' Singleton said he was going to bet $100,000 on his favourite horse, instead he was sacking her trainer. 'When Gai's son knows last night exactly the result today, the conflict of interest becomes personal.'[8] Boy was he sore. 'I just don't enjoy her association. We've had a great ride, Gai and I. I was one of the people who went to the licensing [hearing] to help but I think everything comes to an end and this has definitely come to an end. It's over,' he fumed.[9] 'I just don't like being treated like that by her or her lackeys.'[10]

Adding fuel to the fire, he said it was the third time he had heard that one of his horses had no chance. The feud escalated with Singleton and Gai's husband Robbie reportedly having a full and frank exchange of views of the 'fuck off' variety when their paths next crossed.

Meanwhile, the stewards were circling. An inquiry was opened. Millions of dollars had been invested in the race and allegations were flying. Racing NSW chief steward Ray Murrihy spoke to Gai after the race and reminded her she needed to report any problems to the stewards. 'No setbacks at all, sir,' she said. 'She worked unbelievably well on Thursday morning, but had some heat on her neck and she was monitored by the vets. We could find nothing wrong with her [on race morning]. If I thought there was something wrong I would have told you. There was nothing that would affect her performance.'[11]

Just not racing very well, apparently. And there was no substance to the suggestion of family secrets, with husband Robbie putting the horse down as a good chance. 'Rob had More Joyous at 2–1 and I called Tom when I was told about [Singo's] assertions, [and] he denied them,' she said.[12]

Singleton stuck to his guns but refused to name his sources, saying only that they included a Group 1 jockey and others who were internationally respected. 'I'm not prepared to give them up, unless legally required,' he said.[13] Fuel was added to the fire when Tom Waterhouse's online rival Sportsbet offered punters a 'Justice Refund' on the race. 'From comments post-race, it appears the mare should never have taken her place in the field,' proclaimed Sportsbet's Head of Communications Haydn Lane from his position on the bandwagon. 'In our opinion More Joyous never stood a chance, and as such we're more than happy to refund punters' bets as they would have been dealt an injustice otherwise. More than $150,000 has been refunded.'[14]

Singleton's horses were moved from Gai's stables the next morning. But now Tom was in the crosshairs. What had he known? He used his commercial links with Channel Nine to put his side of events, and followed that up with a string of other media interviews. 'I never told anyone that More Joyous couldn't win and I'm very disappointed at what John said on Saturday,' he told Fairfax Media.[15] 'He and Mum have been friends for a long time and he knows how hard she works and she would never run any horse when it was injured.'[16] And he told TVN's *Racing Review* that More Joyous's poor run had cost him a packet. 'All Too Hard was backed off the map. I laid All Too Hard till the cows came home,' Tom said. 'More Joyous is a 300-and-something-thousand-dollar better result than All Too Hard.'[17]

On Twitter he told his followers that he was upping the stakes. 'Stunned and upset by Singo's comments regarding Gai Waterhouse and me. They are completely false and wrong. I'm meeting with lawyers today,' he tweeted. Even his grandad joined in. Bill Waterhouse, who retired from bookmaking in 2010 after mentoring his grandson, rallied strongly to the Waterhouse flag. 'Singo and I go back a long way,' he told Ray Thomas.[18] 'I was touched last year when he especially chartered a jet so he could make my ninetieth birthday celebration. However,

I was gobsmacked to watch on live television last Saturday how he seemed to deliberately set out to destroy the reputation of my daughter-in-law and grandson – based solely on Chinese whispers that were plain wrong. As a former barrister, I am sure this will end up being the greatest show about nothing. The long and short is people making unfounded and public statements with allegations against licensed people, rather than informing the stewards, can only be to the detriment and harm of our beloved industry of racing. Singo should know better.'[19]

The heat was on. Just who the hell were these trusted friends of Singo's?

One of them turned up on the doorstep of Singo's Central Coast farm the morning after the race. Andrew Johns, rugby immortal and Australian football legend, was looking anything but. He was 'agitated, dishevelled and hadn't slept . . . I have never seen anyone more worried,' said Singleton later.[20] For a man who was so sure-footed and confident on the football field, he was a far cry from that off it.

Over the course of two stewards' inquiries over the next fortnight, Johns's crucial role in what turned out to be a very Sin City Sydney racing saga finally came to light. His actions and choice of words would have far-reaching consequences and would pull in a familiar cast of racing characters, including colourful jockey Allan Robinson and brothel owner and punter Eddie Hayson.

Before Johns turned up at Singleton's farm, he had already bowed to pressure from a Sunday *Footy Show* producer and gone on air to explain the blow-up – telling Channel Nine viewers that Tom Waterhouse had told him More Joyous was 'off'. It was only listening on the car radio on the way home that he realised what he had said. By the time he tried to clarify it, the hare was running and the dogs were in hot pursuit. Johns was worried that if push came to shove, Channel Nine would choose to back advertiser Tom Waterhouse, who spent millions of dollars a year in advertising, over a football caller. He backpedalled, twice clarifying that young Tom hadn't discussed the horse's health.

So what really had happened?

On the Wednesday before the race, Waterhouse stable foreman Dave Meijer had noticed the horse was off her food. It seems More Joyous had a stiff neck, and on Thursday morning the vet injected her with the anti-arthritic drug Cartrophen. That afternoon, Johns and Tom Waterhouse met at the Anzac Day NRL match. 'As is the usual practice before matches, Tom and I engaged in some light-hearted discussions concerning rugby league and racing,' explained Johns.[21] But he insisted there was no discussion of the health of More Joyous.

For his part, Waterhouse denied telling the retired footballer that the horse was 'off'. Johns went on to say in a statement to the first inquiry that he had embellished what Tom had told him. Singo was stunned at that, doubting the use of the term. 'He'd eaten a dictionary or someone at Channel Nine had improved his vocabulary. I've known him since he was fourteen or fifteen – he's never used a word like that,' said Singleton.[22]

The night after meeting with Tom, warmly ensconced in the corporate suite following the Manly game, Johns related a version of his conversation with Tom to Eddie Hayson. Like all punters, Hayson loves the inside line. In 2005 he organised the Lucy's Light greyhound sting and in 2006 he was reprimanded by Racing NSW for illegally betting on his horse Flying Song. He also made a motza betting that the Newcastle Knights would lose to the struggling Warriors after he heard Knights' star Johns had a neck injury and would not be playing.

It seems Hayson passed on his conversation with Johns to jockey Allan Robinson, who himself has a colourful relationship with the stipes. In fact, it was Hayson and Robinson who were called up for bringing racing into disrepute in 2006 by sponsoring a race at Rosehill called 'The Hat Doesn't Fit Handicap', a direct dig at Racing NSW Chief Steward Ray Murrihy's trademark porkpie hat.

On Friday morning More Joyous had been injected with antibiotics, after the Waterhouse stable vet, Leanne Begg, took receipt of test results showing the horse had inflammation. Both Singleton's racing manager and vet were informed, but neither passed on the information to Singleton. He was finally put in the loop when Robinson called him on Saturday afternoon to tell him the word on the street was that his horse was not right. Singo went off, stormed up to Gai in the parade ring and the saga became public.

With the allegations swirling and a sense of impropriety behind the scenes, the situation had to be cleared up. The first inquiry was adjourned after the three key witnesses – Johns, Hayson and Robinson – failed to show up. Instead, a packed public gallery was treated to Gai Waterhouse telling Singleton: 'It's an absolute disgrace . . . You're an absolute sham, John, you really are.'[23] Not to mention a drunk. And, for good measure, she added that the seven-year-old mare was too old to win races, 'like you, John.'[24] Oh dear.

After the inquiry, Singleton gave an interview to his nephew, Ben Damon, on Channel 7 telling Johns to 'man up' and attend the inquiry the following week. 'If I found out that Andrew Johns, who I have a high regard for, as has the whole Australian sporting community, has rung up and told me a lot of nonsense and has done damage not only to Gai and myself but to Tom and Robbie, I'll apologise to anyone who was hurt by it,' said Singleton. 'He owes me an apology. He needs to front up and man up. How can you be so strong on the field and so weak off it? If he embellished it he owes me an apology and I owe them [the Waterhouses] an apology. My respect for Andrew Johns has diminished massively.'[25] So the scene was set.

At the heart of the issue lay Tom Waterhouse's relationship with his mother, Gai. It's not the first time having trainers and bookmakers in the same family has proved a problem. In 1989 the Australian Jockey Club blocked Gai's licence because of her marriage to Robbie. It took three years of legal battles to show that was discriminatory. But now Australia had been treated to regular high-profile advertising for tomwaterhouse.com and its tagline 'I know what punters want'. Was he leveraging his mother's brand, and if so, was that acceptable? There had been an outcry when he signed an advertising deal with Channel Nine that saw him join the panel for the National Rugby League Coverage. He was moved to a separate segment as Senator Nick Xenophon led the protest that Tom was forcing gambling onto children who were watching sport.

Yet an investigation by John Stensholt in the *Australian Financial Review* showed that Waterhouse, the highest-profile player in Australia's gambling market, was in reality quite a small fish. Tomwaterhouse.com was estimated to have just 3.5 per cent of the Australian online gambling market, with an estimated turnover of around $300 million. His marketing and advertising was believed to be costing around $20 million, with profit on turnover only believed to be around eight or nine per cent. Just as the Singleton saga blew up, Tom was in negotiations with oversees players who were considering buying the business. It was certainly a bad look.

Hotelier and horse owner Ross Visalli, who has several horses trained by Waterhouse, told the *Sydney Morning Herald*, 'The publicity would definitely not be helping the Waterhouse brand, which Gai relies on to lure customers and owners.' 'With Tom being a bookie, there is what could appear to be a conflict of interest, and this would not help her sell her services. It is not doing Tommy's brand any good either.'[26] So on Monday morning, as the players turned up with their lawyers at the stewards' inquiry, it would be good to finally clear the air.

Ray Murrihy, on guard after the previous week's display, opened proceedings with the warning, 'Egos are to be left outside – there's not to be any name calling.'[27] First up was Johns. The *Daily Telegraph*'s sports editor, Phil Rothfield, was not alone in noticing that Johns's exemplary memory for every play and player on a football field appeared to have abandoned him in the inquiry room. 'I can't recall,' Johns said repeatedly, and 'I fumbled my words,' as Murrihy produced logs of phone calls and text messages.[28]

Then came Hayson. He could not recall the exact words uttered about More Joyous, but remembered they were very negative. Murrihy asked him if he had become involved because of his legal wrangles with Tom Waterhouse over his gambling debts. 'That's a silly question,' said Hayson. 'All debts were settled months ago and they've always been polite and courteous to me.'[29]

Next up was jockey Allan Robinson, whose colourful lawyer, Chris Murphy, had said the Waterhouse's styling as racing royalty 'turns him sick.'[30] Robinson repeated his involvement in passing on the news about More Joyous to Singleton, and then threatened to throw a spanner in the works, saying he would come back after lunch with fresh evidence. But Johns and Hayson had already left and Robinson refused to spill the new beans without them present, despite Murphy urging him to do so. That left the stewards to draw their conclusions.

Singleton was fined $20,000 for bringing racing into disrepute by blowing up before and after the race, but the fine was reduced to $15,000 because of his early guilty plea and good character. For her part, Gai denied two charges of failing to inform the stewards about the horse's health. More importantly, Murrihy told Tom Waterhouse, 'There's simply no evidence . . . that between when Mrs Waterhouse found out at midday on Thursday [that the horse was not in peak condition] and you spoke to Andrew Johns at about 4 pm, [that] directly or indirectly, there was communications from Mrs Waterhouse to you.'[31]

But he warned Tom he needed to isolate his business from his mother's and hinted that Racing NSW may help him to do that. 'You must take care, and we say to you in the form of a direction, you must not in your advertising and commentary, get too close to the bone in using the Waterhouse name and using your mother's name,' he said.[32]

Outside the inquiry, Murrihy told the *Sydney Morning Herald* that he hoped Tom had come away with 'the very strong thought that he should ensure public perception doesn't join Gai Waterhouse Stables with his bookmaking operation.'[33] And, he added, there 'needs to be a clear line between what he's doing and what his mother is doing being a very successful trainer.'[34]

Afterwards, others were keen to weigh in even more strongly. New South Wales Sports Minister Graham Annesley told the *Herald* there needed to be 'a clear delineation between sport and sports betting. The proliferation of betting advertising in sports broadcasting recently has definitely blurred that line.'[35]

Outspoken Independent federal senator Nick Xenophon said the inquiry had shot the messenger by fining Singleton. 'If there was ever a case for reform of the racing industry to strengthen integrity, this is it,' he said.[36] Former Labor leader, horse breeder and racegoer Mark Latham wrote in his *Australian Financial Review* column: 'Arising from the More Joyous affair, legislation should be passed to prevent conflicts of interest. The time has come to say to the Waterhouses: you can be a family of trainers or a family of bookmakers, but not both.'[37]

The More Joyous affair dragged on, with Gai Waterhouse unsuccessfully defending the two charges that she had failed to inform stewards of the horse's condition. 'Every TV station, every newspaper in the whole world . . . even the Queen said to her racing manager, "What's going on with Gai Waterhouse in Australia?" ' she fumed at the stewards.[38] 'I have been treated like a third-rate person and my family has been dragged through the mud, through the mire,' she went on. 'All these people who have been to the inquiry have had to sit next to the major player and have been inhibited by Mr Singleton. It is shoddy and embarrassing to racing.'[39] She was fined $5500 and vowed to appeal.

Meanwhile, the stewards put on notice that they intended to look into whether More Joyous had a condition they should have been notified about in the lead-up to the running of the Group 1 Queen of the Turf Stakes at Rosehill Gardens on 6 April 2013, in which More Joyous had finished fifth.

That inquiry ended with Waterhouse receiving a $2000 fine for failing to inform stewards that More Joyous had been lame in the lead-up to the race. The horse had an abscess in her near front foot, and instead of running her on the track Waterhouse had chosen to swim the horse in 'boisterous conditions' at Botany Bay.

So what exactly did the stewards and punting public have a right to know? Dave Meijer, who had since left the stables, gave evidence that Waterhouse had been trying to hide More Joyous's lameness before the race. Murrihy asked her why she'd wanted to hide that. Wasn't she entitled to tell the stewards the horse was lame? 'It's not a matter for the public,' Waterhouse replied.[40]

Afterwards, the stewards received a stinging rebuke from Waterhouse, who was again considering an appeal. Reading from a prepared statement she said: 'I'm disappointed with the stewards' decision. I've acknowledged I take great care of all my horses, and I wouldn't have raced a horse if it wasn't fit or healthy.'[41] More to the point, she said this was a rule that every trainer thought was wrong. 'The trainers believe the interpretation of this rule is untenable, and the meaning of the rule is already the subject of an appeal that will affect all trainers.'

In the aftermath of the More Joyous farrago, young Tom penned a story for the *Daily Telegraph* saying he was sorry about his high profile on TV and the message it sent. He had listened to the Australian public, not to mention the then prime minister, Julia Gillard, who had said families were sick of gambling getting in the way of live sport. So he was toning down his advertising. 'Because I stand up as the bookmaker, and do not present as a faceless corporation, I also have, somehow, become the public face of the entire Australian gambling industry. If people have an issue with gambling, it seems to become an issue with me personally and I have to cop it on the chin,' he wrote.[42]

The controversy died down. Elsewhere, Black Caviar began the next stage of her lucrative career with the $88,000-a-pop stallion Exceed and Excel named as the first to serve the wonder mare. Damien Oliver returned to trackwork after his eight-month ban for betting on Miss Octopussy. He conceded his reputation had 'copped a bit of a whack. But it's up to me to try and win back that respect by doing my best and working hard.'[43] And the Office of Public Prosecutions decided there was insufficient evidence to lay charges against champion jockey Danny Nikolic and his brother John over allegations that a race at Cranbourne in 2011 – which Nikolic won on Smoking Aces – was fixed. John Nikolic said his brother's reputation had been trashed. 'We're vindicated, but you have to be annoyed that your reputation can be totally trashed.'[44]

It seems a lot of reputations had been trashed – but in Australia, the races go on.

EPILOGUE

'Going around the corner for the first time, only 200 metres after the start, I was positioned well and running a strong second. I let the rider in front cross me. In a split second I lost control of the horse. He faltered underneath me, his action lost and his legs wildly flaying.'

Melbourne Cup-winning jockey Darren Beadman was on the favourite and taking the sharp first corner at Happy Valley in Hong Kong when his horse, trained by fellow Australian John Moore, started to struggle. 'I tried everything I knew to hold him together so that the other jockey could cross in front of me. I have never been so terrified in my life. Because of my horse's travelling speed, his weight drew him outwards and then he simply crashed dead underneath me, throwing me up in the air like a rag doll. I fell spine-jarringly on my head and was knocked out cold.'[1]

By the time the other horses in the race had come around for the second time, Beadman was only just coming round after his 70-kilometres-per-hour fall. The horse had been bleeding internally. In his 1998 biography, *Daylight Ahead*, Beadman said he had never had a horse drop dead on him like that. 'I will never be sure about this incident, but someone once told me that cyanide can kill a horse that way.'[2]

It was particularly worrying because exactly the same thing happened on his second ride back. Beadman was on the favourite, trained by Australian David Oughton, and 200 metres from the start the horse crashed beneath him. The fall was spectacular, although this time Beadman walked away with just a bruised foot. Once again, the horse had been bleeding internally. 'Doubly suspicious. Was organised crime responsible? I will never know, but the coincidences were certainly mystifying.'[3]

Trainer John Moore and some of the owners urged Beadman to go home. There are big players in Hong Kong. Beadman went, but he came back for another season and ended up with a ban after the horse he was riding at Sha Tin, Better Choice, came in fifth, two lengths behind a horse ridden by Australian Darren Gauci. Beadman insisted he had not pulled the horse, but a huge offshore betting plunge on Gauci's winner swayed the stewards against him. He was given a nine-month ban and came home to Australia. The authorities were convinced he was part of a bigger ring; Hong Kong's head of security even offered him an all-expenses-paid trip to return and spill the beans. 'The authorities had cracked something and they thought I was part of it, but they were wrong,' Beadman said. 'I did not pull the horse. There was no conspiracy; it was just a lousy ride.'[4]

Beadman went on to rebuild his career and then quit sensationally to preach at the Hillsong Church. He did return to racing in Hong Kong, only to have another horror fall during a barrier trial at Sha Tin in 2012. He was left with a brain injury that affected his balance, speech and memory. In hospital, the psychologist asked him to put on the skull cap that saved his life. It had a three- or four-inch mark in the back where it was hit by the horse's hoof.

Beadman put it on and started crying. He knew what that injury meant. 'I Googled it, when you read it you say, "Shit the bloke should be dead,"' he told the *Sydney Morning Herald* journalist Craig Young. 'I don't like saying I'm lucky, but I'm blessed to be alive. Most of the cases end up vegetables or stay in a coma. I'm not trying to dramatise it; I'm saying how it is.'[5]

But just how lucky was Beadman? When Young called the jockey back a few days later, it became clear that Beadman had no recollection of their earlier conversation. Recovering at home, the star jockey could not watch the Formula One motor racing on television: 'The cameras, in the cars, I couldn't watch the TV because the speed they were going into the corners was making my head spin.' His emotions were up and down, and there was no guarantee he would get back into the saddle. 'Mate, my last ride [in a race] was a winner, that was where I was at. I'm just glad I've had my day in the sun.'[6]

Beadman's time in the sun deservedly cemented his place in racing's Hall of Fame. But as we've seen, racing is tough on jockeys. And the toll continues. Jockey Hari Singh was placed in an induced coma following a nasty fall at Tamworth in August 2012. The effect was keenly felt by the 28-year-old jockey's wife and daughter, who were frantically trying to get out from their home in India to be by his bedside.

In his early days, Nash Rawiller, who has ridden winners worth more than $40 million in prize money, was ready to quit.

'My body was screaming for me to give it away,' he said.[7] At breaking point from the years of fasting, he took a six-week campervan tour of New Zealand with his younger brother, Todd, to look at his life. He came back because he feels racing is his calling. Just as it is for so many hard-working people involved in the industry. Their lives dramatically improved after Racing NSW had their race-fields legislation victory in the High Court over the wagering operators. Racing NSW chief executive Peter V'Landys explained why that was so important: 'If prize money is low, trainers cannot charge owners a proper fee for their services ... owners could not invest in racing if they could not get a reasonable return. This cascades all the way down to the strappers and to all other people who work in the industry. No money in the industry, no income to the participants.'[8]

As that money flowed into racing, the future looked brighter. Black Caviar was making Australian racing look good – swooping to win her photo finish at Royal Ascot. Of course, the great mare's twenty-second straight win should never have been a photo finish. Jockey Luke Nolen took the flak for his rookie mistake of easing up in the final straight: 'I let her idle through the last 200 [metres] and I underestimated just how stiff a track this straight six furlongs is, and also the opposition. And I shit myself duly. And I'm afraid my brain fade might be talked about more than this mare's fantastic effort,' the shaken jockey said afterwards.[9] But even as Nolen started hissing at reporters who badgered him about the mistake, it turned out that Black Caviar's drop in performance was down to an undetected injury.

However, things in racing are not quite as rosy as the officials and powerbrokers would like us to believe. Lawyer David Landa quit within months of being given the job of Integrity Auditor for Greyhound and Harness Racing in NSW in 2012. He said he was unable to meet the public's expectation that he would be someone who could police integrity, honesty and fair dealing in the sport: 'I felt that apart from the role being ineffective and not capable of performing what I felt the legislators may have intended, it was a fiction and it was a fraud really on the public,' he told ABC's *Four Corners* program.[10] This was the same *Four Corners* investigation that had revealed that the police officers investigating Les Samba's murder were also looking at race-fixing and Danny Nikolic's ride on Smoking Aces. During the program, Racing Victoria integrity chief Sal Perna called for other states to follow Victoria's crackdown on racing crooks by cooperating with the police. Even better, he said, would be a national racing integrity body. 'So that we can work together on it and address issues not only nationally but internationally,' he said. 'It's about bringing in specialists that are specialist investigators, specialist analysts and wagering analysts, and bringing in all the bodies together so they can share information and work out how to do it in a concerted way.'[11]

At the moment someone in the industry who is under surveillance in one state can swan into another and carry on as he or she pleases. But John Schreck disagrees with Perna and believes stewards should be left to get on with their jobs, using expertise and circumstantial evidence to put together a case against cheats. He does not believe the police are much chop at sorting out racing rorts. 'My experience of having worked with the police is that they haven't been of very much assistance to me and I have been disappointed with their lack of understanding and knowledge of the sport. They usually start with the perception that everyone is a crook but when I go to the racetrack I believe everyone is doing the right thing unless proven otherwise. I have nothing but admiration for jockeys and what they do – it's a dangerous business and they put their lives on the line. What other job do you do where two ambulances follow you as you work?'[12]

No one is saying that policing racing is straightforward. Certainly, it was good work by Harness Racing NSW to pick up Narrandera driver Jackson Painting's $500 bet on his own mount, My Caracal, five minutes before the Leeton harness races on Sunday, 15 July 2012. The winning punt paid $2 on the NSW tote and was picked up by an automated alert monitoring participants' accounts. It was a good spot and a clear step in the right direction for harness racing after its shocking recent record. Not so good was the $200 fine he received, which still left him $800 in the black. Harness Racing NSW's head of integrity services, Reid Sanders, explained: 'Drivers are not allowed to place bets on harness racing. Backing a horse apart from their own would be a much more serious charge, this is still a serious matter, but from the evidence thus far it does not appear that any bets have been placed on other runners.'[13]

Everyone wants a slice of the action and if they can't get it fairly then, as we have seen, they will often resort to other means. But picking up attempts at race-fixing is not always easy. The Sydney *Daily Telegraph*'s fearless race commentator Ken Callander earned the wrath of the queen of the track Gai Waterhouse in the first half of 2012. He had had the temerity to question why some of her hotly performing favourites were suddenly running so badly. 'It is not they are losing. It is by how far and how they are losing,' he wrote.[14] That was after her in-form favourites Battant, Charing Cross and Samui Lad trailed in second last, last and last at Rosehill. The previous week at Warwick Farm, Betrayal had come up short as though it 'had run into a brick wall'.[15] Why? asked Callender. When Masahiko came home 22 lengths behind the leader at Rosehill the following week, Callander spelled it out: 'If Gai frequented the betting ring she would know when a horse eases from $3.50 to $6.50, punters start asking questions and jumping to conclusions. With Gai married to leading bookie Robbie Waterhouse the innuendo and suggestion ran riot.'[16]

Waterhouse made it clear she was unimpressed with the stories when NSW chief steward Ray Murrihy quizzed her in the stewards' room following the Masahiko disappointment. Afterwards the stewards agreed with her argument that it was a very heavy track. Murrihy said: 'Some of those horses pulled up sore. I took the trouble to pull out the statistics and over a six-month period anyone betting on Gai Waterhouse favourites would have come out with a profit.'[17] Schreck observed that it's the punters who make a favourite – and perhaps the fact that these horses were trained by Gai Waterhouse gave them an undeserved boost in the popularity stakes. 'But make no mistake,' he said, 'drugs in horse-racing are the biggest problem the sport has faced in a long, long time. The dopers are always one step ahead because the analysts don't know what they are looking for until they have found it. That's why the sport needs to spend a lot of money on detection.'[18]

There is no suggestion that Gai Waterhouse is anything other than a straight shooter and an asset to racing in Australia. But she is a clean swimmer in a dirty pool. At the same time as those baseless rumours were flying, the *Sun-Herald* reported that elsewhere an unrelated drugs drama was engulfing the sport. A veterinarian in Queensland wasn't answering questions and Murrihy's deputy, Greg Rudolph, confirmed that a number of horses had returned elevated testosterone levels. All very fishy.

The bottom line in racing is exactly that – money. The stewards do their level best to police the sport but, as Schreck says, the dopers and cheats are always one step ahead. While the majority of people involved are honest, hard-working and love the sport, there are always greedy, unscrupulous sharks involved in racing who are out to make a killing. And that's why you can never be sure that the race you are watching hasn't been fixed.

NOTES

Introduction

1. Chris Roots, 'Black Caviar gets bookies' stamp of approval before Goodwood gallop', *Sydney Morning Herald*, 9 May 2012.
2. Patrick Bartley, 'A royal send-off for Caviar', *Sun-Herald*, 13 May 2012.
3. Scott Walsh, 'Black flash', *Sunday Telegraph*, 13 May 2012.
4. Patrick Bartley, 'A royal send-off for Caviar', *Sun-Herald*, 13 May 2012.
5. Scott Walsh, 'Black flash', *Sunday Telegraph*, 13 May 2012.
6. Ray Thomas, 'Caviar a global celebrity', *Telegraph*, 10 May 2012.

Race 1: Murder

1. Rod Nicholson and Jon Kaila, 'I'm meeting a bloke: victim Les Samba's last hours', *Sunday Herald Sun*, 6 March 2011.
2. Ibid.
3. Ibid.
4. Ibid.
5. 'Of bullets and blood: murder haunts daughter', *Telegraph*, 15 October 2011.
6. Ruth Lamperd, 'Victoria Samba still haunted by her father's murder', *Herald Sun*, 15 October 2011.
7. Ibid.
8. Paul Millar, 'Police mull Samba theories', *Age*, 29 March 2011.
9. Jon Kaila, 'Les Samba's final fatal steps', *Sunday Herald Sun*, 26 February 2012.
10. Ibid.
11. Kate McClymont and Tom Reilly, 'Heavy hitter much preferred the shadows' *Sydney Morning Herald*, 5 March 2011.
12. Rod Nicholson and Jon Kaila, 'I'm meeting a bloke: victim Les Samba's last hours', *Sunday Herald Sun*, 6 March 2006.
13. Nick McKenzie, 'On the wrong track', *Age*, 7 August 2012.
14. Anthony Dowsley, 'Gavin and Travis Eades suspects in Les Samba murder' *Herald Sun*, 31 March 2011.
15. Ibid.
16. John Silvester, 'When your name was Les Samba, you were always riding your luck with the dance of death', *Age*, 2 April 2011.
17. Max Presnell, 'Colourful identity Samba latest to join a select club', *Sun-Herald*, 6 March 2011.
18. Ibid.

19. Yoni Bashan, 'Cannabis found on slain trainer Les Samba's farms', *Sunday Herald Sun*, 17 April 2011.
20. Yoni Bashan, 'Drugs, FBI, McGurk: Racehorse owner Les Samba's Mafia connections', *Sunday Telegraph*, 17 April 2011.
21. Ibid.
22. Max Presnell, 'Colourful identity Samba latest to join a select club', *Sun-Herald*, 6 March 2011.

Race 2: Lucky Breeders

1. Alex Steedman, 'Sidereus almost gets bowled in Pago Pago Stakes', www.racingandsports.com.au, 12 April 2008.
2. Angus Grigg, 'Tinkler bets on revenge', *Australian Financial Review*, 16 October 2010.
3. Ibid.
4. Ibid.
5. Ibid.
6. Ray Thomas, 'Keeping a stiff upper lip', *Daily Telegraph*, 23 September 2011.
7. Staff writers, 'Fast lane not fast enough', *Sydney Morning Herald*, 29 February 2012.
8. Tom Reilly, 'Horse trading over pasta, wine and legal agreement', *Sydney Morning Herald*, 14 October 2011.
9. Ibid.
10. Tom Reilly, 'Billionaire Tinkler facing "mutiny" over failure to pay employee super contributions', *Sydney Morning Herald*, 20 August 2012.
11. Tom Reilly and Paddy Manning, 'Has Nathan Tinkler's luck run out?', *Sydney Morning Herald*, 17 August 2012.
12. Angus Grigg and Colleen Ryan, 'They're off: Tinkler takes on the sport of kings', *Australian Financial Review*, 9 September 2011.

13. Angus Grigg, '"Buyback" keeps filly at stud', *Australian Financial Review*, 28 September 2011.
14. Thoroughbred Breeders Australia, 'New Thoroughbred Code of Conduct', press release, 20 July 2011.
15. Angus Grigg and Colleen Ryan, 'They're off: Tinkler takes on the sport of kings', *Australian Financial Review*, 9 September 2011.
16. Angus Grigg, 'Horse breeder runs close to the rails', *Australian Financial Review*, 1 November 2011.
17. Timothy McDonald, 'Challenge to artificial insemination ban for thoroughbreds', *AM*, ABC Radio, 5 September 2011.
18. Joe Schneider, 'Thoroughbred sex rules opponents seen free to compete in racing', Bloomberg, 19 December 2011.
19. Ray Thomas, 'Nikolic produces Randwick's ride of the decade', *Daily Telegraph*, 18 March 2012.
20. Ibid.
21. Interview with author, Friday, 13 July 2012.
22. Brent Zerafa, 'War of attrition', *Daily Telegraph*, 3 April 2012.
23. Productivity Commission (2010), *Gambling*, Report No. 50, Canberra, page 16.15.
24. Matthew Benns, 'Highest of stakes', *Sun-Herald*, 5 July 2009.
25. Ibid.
26. Ibid.
27. Ibid.
28. Letsgohorseracing, 'Victorian Racing Minister calls for national race field legislation', www.letsgohorseracing.com.au, 16 April 2010.
29. Craig Young, 'Racing boss hails $100m tax decision as huge win', *Sydney Morning Herald*, weekend edition, 31 March–1 April 2012.
30. Ibid.

31. Craig Young, 'Victorians follow NSW on tax but reckon they had it right', *Sydney Morning Herald*, 13 April 2012.
32. Ibid.
33. Productivity Commission (2010), *Gambling*, Report No. 50, Canberra, page 16.17.
34. Patrick Smith, 'More than meets the eye in days of intrigue', *Australian*, 27 February 2012.
35. Ibid.
36. Ibid.
37. Ibid.
38. Ibid.
39. Productivity Commission (2010), *Gambling*, Report No. 50, Canberra, page 16.17.
40. Ken Callander, 'Sourisly Barry, is chairman's job an old mate's act of parliament', *Daily Telegraph*, 19 December 2011.
41. Ibid.
42. Ken Callander, 'Messara can be the punters' pal', *Daily Telegraph*, 26 December 2011.
43. Vanda Carson, 'Randwick trainer John O'Shea's tip was a bad bed, court hears', *Daily Telegraph*, 6 March 2012.
44. Chris Roots, 'O'Shea to consider future after lost appeal', *Sydney Morning Herald*, 6 March 2012.
45. Craig Young, 'Court ruling spells change ahead for those who deal in bloodstock', *Sydney Morning Herald*, 12 March 2012.
46. Ibid.

Race 3: Hoop or Dupe?

1. apnonline.com.au; 'The Track'; Munce's commentary.
2. Ibid.

3. Ibid.
4. Ibid.
5. Ibid.
6. Ray Thomas, 'Chris Munce relives hell in Hong Kong', *Daily Telegraph*, 5 December 2008.
7. Alan Aitken, 'Wins and losses for Hong Kong watchdog', *Age*, 7 July 2006.
8. Jailed Munce given 2 1/2 years for betting conspiracy', *Illawarra Mercury*, 2 March 2007.
9. Ibid.
10. Ibid.
11. Ibid.
12. Ibid.
13. Ray Thomas, 'Chris Munce relives hell in Hong Kong', *Daily Telegraph*, 5 December 2008.
14. Ibid.
15. Craig Young, 'Munce back in saddle as Racing NSW snubs ban', *Sydney Morning Herald*, 4 December 2008.
16. Ibid.
17. Peter Kogoy, 'Decision to allow Chris Munce to ride angers Hong Kong', *Australian*, 4 December 2008.
18. Brent Zerafa, 'Blake Shinn and Peter Robl admit betting on races', *Herald Sun*, 19 November 2010.
19. Brent Zerafa, 'Blake Shinn's $800-a-day gambling habit', *Daily Telegraph*, 24 May 2011.
20. Craig Young, 'Spicy entree to autumn's racing banquet as jockeys, trainers feel the pressure', *Sydney Morning Herald*, 26 March 2012.
21. Ibid.
22. Ray Thomas, 'Stupid greedy jockeys banned', *Daily Telegraph*, 27 November 2010.

23. Racing NSW, 'Appeal by WILLIAM PEARSON (10 December 2004)', notice, www.racingnsw.com.au, 17 December 2004.
24. Ibid.
25. Ibid.
26. Ibid.
27. Letsgohorseracing, 'Jockey El-Issa disqualified for two years – punter friend charged at Bold Glance inquiry', www.letsgohorseracing.com.au, 1 April 2011.
28. Racing Queensland, 'Stewards Report on Bold Glance inquiry', www.racingqueensland.com.au, 20 April 2011.
29. Ibid.
30. Kate McClymont, 'Revealed: how Sydney races are fixed', *Sydney Morning Herald*, 7 April 1995.
31. Kate McClymont, 'Horse talk', *Sydney Morning Herald*, 18 November 2000.
32. Kate McClymont, 'Revealed: how Sydney races are fixed', *Sydney Morning Herald*, 7 April 1995.
33. Kate McClymont, 'Horse talk', *Sydney Morning Herald*, 18 November 2000.
34. Ibid.
35. Ibid.
36. Ibid.
37. Ibid.
38. Kate McClymont, 'Revealed: how Sydney races are fixed', *Sydney Morning Herald*, 7 April 1995.
39. Ibid.
40. Ibid.
41. Kate McClymont, 'Horse talk', *Sydney Morning Herald*, 18 November 2000.

42. Ibid.
43. Kate McClymont and Steve Mooney, 'Drugs probe uncovers race-fixing "by accident"', *Sydney Morning Herald*, 3 March 1995.
44. Ibid.

Race 4: Wasted

1. Brad Thompson, 'Katsidis had big plans for Shoot Out', *Brisbane Times*, 20 October 2010.
2. Adrian Dunn, 'Tributes for "A1 bloke" Stathi Katsidis', *Herald Sun*, 20 October 2010.
3. Brad Thompson, 'Katsidis had big plans for Shoot Out', *Brisbane Times*, 20 October 2010.
4. David Murray, 'Fiancée tells how party led to fight with jockey Stathi Katsidis just before his death', *Sunday Mail*, 8 May 2011.
5. Sophie Elsworth, 'Drugs, booze bender killed leading jockey Stathi Katsidis', *Courier-Mail*, 7 May 2011.
6. David Murray, 'Jockey drug binges rife, says insider who partied regularly with Katsidis', *Sunday Mail*, 28 August 2011.
7. Craig Young, 'Roller-coaster drug ride of a jockey who blew everything but survived', *Sydney Morning Herald*, 27 June 2011.
8. Ibid.
9. Jessica Halloran, 'Too many apprentice jockeys are cast adrift in a world of drugs and corruption', *Sunday Telegraph*, 12 June 2011.
10. Ibid.
11. Ibid.
12. Ibid.
13. Jessica Halloran, 'Inside the life of Mitch Beadman', *Sunday Telegraph*, 7 November 2009.
14. Jessica Halloran, 'Too many apprentice jockeys are cast

adrift in a world of drugs and corruption', *Sunday Telegraph*, 12 June 2011.
15. Ibid.
16. AAP, 'Former hoops honoured in Melbourne, Sydney', 31 August 2012: www.2ky.com.au/news/article.php?id=14101
17. Australian Jockeys' Association (2008), *Racing For Our Lives: A Plan to Protect Australian Jockeys*, brochure.
18. Interview with the author, 22 February 2012.
19. Australian Jockeys' Association, 'Programme 5 – Safety', www.australianjockeys.org.
20. Nathan Exelby, 'Young jockey Corey Gilby dies after track fall at Julia Creek', *Courier-Mail*, 15 November 2011.
21. 'Race of their lives', *60 Minutes*, 30 October 2005.
22. National Jockeys' Trust, 'Ray Silburn talks about the National Jockeys' Trust', video, www.australianjockeys.org, 25 October 2008.
23. Craig Young, 'Silburn keeps smiling in face of misfortune', *Sydney Morning Herald*, 2 June 2005.
24. Australian Jockeys' Association (2008), *Racing For Our Lives: A Plan to Protect Australian Jockeys*, brochure.
25. Ibid.
26. Australian Jockeys' Association (2008), *Racing For Our Lives: A Plan to Protect Australian Jockeys*, brochure.
27. Ibid.
28. Ibid.
29. Interview with the author, 22 February 2012.
30. Ibid.
31. Ibid.
32. Interview with the author, 22 February 2012.
33. Richard Guilliatt, 'Dark side of the track', *Weekend Australian Magazine*, 27 January 2011.

34. Ibid.
35. Ibid.
36. 'Race of their lives', *60 Minutes*, 30 October 2005.
37. Ibid.
38. Interview with the author, 22 February 2012.
39. Interview with the author, 17 February 2012. I offer my thanks to Dr Sullivan for her permission for me to use her thesis in this book.
40. Ibid.
41. Vivienne Sullivan (2009), *Wasting Away: the Influences of Weight Management on Jockeys' Physical, Psychological and Social Wellbeing*, PhD thesis, Victoria University.
42. Tony McMahon, 'Jockeys suspended', *Morning Bulletin*, 8 February 2012.
43. Ibid.
44. Vivienne Sullivan (2009), *Wasting Away: the Influences of Weight Management on Jockeys' Physical, Psychological and Social Wellbeing*, PhD thesis, Victoria University.
45. Ibid.
46. Ibid.
47. Ibid.
48. Victoria University, 'Jockeys sweat over reigning in weight', media release, 8 October 2009.
49. Gai Waterhouse, 'Gai's Blog Thursday (5/1)', www.gaiwaterhouse.com.au, 5 January 2012.
50. Interview with the author, 22 February 2012.
51. Racing NSW, 'Letter to the Editor', *Racing NSW Official Monthly Publication*, February 2012.
52. Interview with the author, 28 February 2012.
53. Ibid.
54. Ibid.

55. Tony White (and wires), 'Two jockeys rushed to hospital after four-horse fall', *Sydney Morning Herald*, 15 June 2008.
56. Ibid.
57. Ibid.
58. Grantlee Kieza, 'Long ride home', *Sunday Telegraph*, 22 April 2012.
59. Ibid.
60. Interview with the author, 28 February 2012.

Race 5: Rape

1. Amanda Keenan, 'Sex a racing tradition: rapists' father', *Australian*, 19 August 2000.
2. Ibid.
3. Ibid.
4. David Reardon, 'Teenage jockeys jailed over sex attack', *Age*, 19 August 2000.
5. Ibid.
6. Amanda Keenan, 'Sex a racing tradition: rapists' father', *Australian*, 19 August 2000.
7. Ibid.
8. Philippa McDonald, 'Bittersweet honour for abused jockey', *Lateline*, ABC TV, 1 February 2001.
9. Rebecca Baillie, 'Female jockey speaks out against sexual abuse', *7.30 Report*, ABC TV, 8 February 2001.
10. Leisa Scott and Trudy Harris, 'Silent suffering of women jockeys', *Australian*, 3 March 2001.
11. Trudy Harris, 'Abuse inquiry must go national: female jockeys', *Australian*, 15 March 2001.
12. Report by Judge Barrie Thorley reviewing policies, procedures and practices in the NSW Racing Industry, 18 July 2001, page 24.

13. Ibid., page 22.
14. Ibid.
15. Ibid., page 25.
16. Scott Tucker, 'National inquiry rejected', *Newcastle Herald*, 20 July 2001.
17. Report by Judge Barrie Thorley reviewing policies, procedures and practices in the NSW Racing Industry, 18 July 2001, page 26.
18. Johanna Leggatt, 'Racing and rape: the terror of the stables. Women tell of threats, abuse and sexual harassment', *Sun-Herald*, 24 June 2001.
19. Ibid.
20. Interview with the author, 29 February 2012.
21. Ibid.
22. Ibid.
23. Ibid.
24. John Ellicott, 'Turf chiefs sideline sex investigator', *Australian*, 16 August 2001.
25. Leisa Scott and Trudy Harris, 'Silent suffering of women jockeys', *Australian*, 3 March 2001.
26. Ibid.
27. Ibid.
28. Interview with the author, 22 February 2012.
29. Ibid.
30. Essential Research (2010), Member Research 2010: Australian Jockeys' Association. Final Report, Sydney.
31. Vivienne Sullivan (2009), *Wasting Away: The Influences of Weight Management on Jockeys' Physical, Psychological and Social Wellbeing*, PhD thesis, Victoria University, p. 261
32. Essential Research (2010), Member Research 2010. Australian Jockeys' Association. Final Report. Sydney.

33. Ibid.
34. Ibid.
35. Ibid.
36. Interview with the author, 22 February 2012.
37. Interview with the author, 28 February 2012.
38. Ibid.
39. Lowell Cohn, 'Woman jockey Stra beats the odds in bid to race', *Press Democrat*, 26 February 2010.
40. Interview with the author, 29 February 2012.
41. Ibid.
42. Clay Lucas, 'Hore-Lacy fined over indecent assault', *Sydney Morning Herald*, 26 March 2012.
43. Brendan Cormick, 'Trainer Rick Hore-Lacy fined for sexual harassment', *Australian*, 27 March 2012.
44. Ibid.
45. Ibid.

Race 6: The Big Plunge

1. Adam Shand, 'The Passionate Punter', *Sunday*, GTV 9, 3 September 2006.
2. Max Presnell, 'How Hong Kong keeps its riders on a much tighter rein', *Sydney Morning Herald*, 16 June 2006.
3. Ibid.
4. Josh Massoud, 'I'll keep going', *Daily Telegraph*, 8 July 2006.
5. Adam Shand, 'The Passionate Punter', *Sunday*, GTV 9, 3 September 2006.
6. Racing NSW, 'Unhealthy contact finding in Interfere inquiry', www.thoroughbrednews.com.au, 28 July 2006.
7. Adam Shand, 'The Passionate Punter', *Sunday*, GTV 9, 3 September 2006.
8. Ibid.

9. Matt Stewart, 'Jockeys' boss fears new bet types could lead to corruption', *Herald Sun*, 9 November 2011.
10. AAP, 'Hayson reprimanded over Betfair wager', www.racingandsports.com.au, 22 March 2006.
11. Hayson and Andrew Johns owned six racehorses together. They also owned a $620,000 horse called Regreagon, named after Andrew's brother Matthew Johns' *Footy Show* alter ego, in partnership with Matthew Johns and Melanie Martin, the wife of Hayson's trainer, Tim Martin. Matthew Johns said he received five per cent of the horse's winnings and that it had only just been brought to his attention that his partner also ran a brothel. 'As long as he doesn't take the horse there, I don't have a problem with it,' he said. (Greg Bearup and Kate McClymont, 'The brothel, league stars and a betting plunge', *Sydney Morning Herald*, 10 June 2006.)
12. Greg Bearup and Kate McClymont, 'The brothel, league stars and a betting plunge', *Sydney Morning Herald*, 10 June 2006.
13. Ibid.
14. 'Martin horses at centre of new Allan Robinson inquiry', www.racingandsports.com.au, 13 July 2006.
15. AAP, 'Robinson blows up, inquiry adjourned', www.racingandsports.com.au, 3 July 2006.
16. Adam Shand, 'The Passionate Punter', *Sunday*, GTV 9, 3 September 2006.
17. Adam Shand, 'The Passionate Punter', *Sunday*, GTV 9, 3 September 2006.
18. John Schell, 'Robbo offended, Purton banned', *Sydney Morning Herald*, 4 July 2006.
19. AAP, 'Purton's sentence halved', www.racingandsports.com.au, 14 July 2006.
20. Ibid.

21. AAP, 'Jockey Zac Purton to fight two month ban', www.racingandsports.com.au, 3 July 2006.
22. Ibid.
23. John Schell, 'Robbo offended, Purton banned', *Sydney Morning Herald*, 4 July 2006.
24. Ibid.
25. Racing NSW, 'RNSW stewards conclude inquiry into betting activities', www.thoroughbrednews.com.au, 14 August 2009.
26. Racing Appeals Tribunal of New South Wales, 'Appeal by Allan Robinson (1 October 2009)', 13 October 2009.
27. Ibid.
28. Ibid.
29. Geoff Wilson, 'Allan Robinson facing end of the road', *Newcastle Herald*, 9 August 2010.
30. Kate McClymont, 'Hayson's luck runs out as bad debts and love gone wrong lead to court', *Sydney Morning Herald*, 16 April 2012.
31. Andrew Webster, 'In the blood for fearless Tom', *Daily Telegraph*, 10 June 2011.
32. Bill Waterhouse, *What Are The Odds?*, Sydney: Vintage, 2009, page 374.
33. *What Are The Odds?*, page 375.
34. *What Are The Odds?*, page 377.
35. *What Are The Odds?*, page 378.
36. Patrick Bartley, 'Bookie recalls millions of reasons Packer went racing', *Age*, 28 October 2010.
37. Michael Harvey, 'Did Sydney bookmaker Bruce McHugh win $55m in three days off media mogul Kerry Packer?', *Daily Telegraph*, 12 September 2011.
38. Paul Millar, 'Beasley couldn't say no to his mate's $1.8m punt', *Age*, 3 April 2009.

39. Ibid.
40. Ibid.
41. Racing Victoria Limited, 'Hearing result – licensed bookmaker Simon Beasley', www.racingvictoria.net.au, 3 April 2009.
42. Ibid.
43. Duncan Hughes, 'CBA sues bookmaker for $17m', *Age*, 1 June 2004.
44. Craig Young, 'So you think he'll win? Mark Read doesn't', *Age*, 26 October 2010.
45. Ian Manning, '$1 million plunge gets bookies', *Sun-Herald*, 10 January 1982.
46. Phil Purser, 'The best $65 I ever spent', www.justracing.com.au, 16 March 2006.
47. Ibid.
48. Ian Manning, '$1 million plunge gets bookies', *Sun-Herald*, 10 January 1982.
49. Nick Tabakoff, 'The world's biggest punter is Zeljko Ranogajec, and he's an Australian', *Daily Telegraph*, 13 February 2010.
50. Gabriella Coslovich, 'Hobart's infamous son plays to the gallery', *Age*, 22 January 2011.
51. Angus Grigg and Hannah Low, 'The gambler', *Australian Financial Review*, 11 February 2012.
52. Ibid.
53. Ibid.
54. Ibid.
55. Ibid.
56. Ibid.
57. Brent Zerafa, 'Our $17m Cup win', *Daily Telegraph*, 25 July 2012.

58. Max Presnell, 'Banjo, Fred and Alan came at the game from different angles', *Sydney Morning Herald*, 20 May 2012.
59. Letsgohorseracing, 'Big punters question whether action will be taken over suspicious plunge', www.letsgohorseracing.com.au, 16 May 2010; Craig Cook, 'Jockeys questioned after Australia-wide betting plunge', *Courier-Mail*, 17 May 2010.

Race 7: The Fix

1. AAP, 'Crystal Lily wins Golden Slipper', *Sydney Morning Herald*, 3 April 2010.
2. Ibid.
3. Rod Nicholson, 'Golden Slipper winner Crystal Lily dies during trackwork', *Herald Sun*, 23 September 2011.
4. Ibid.
5. AAP, 'Hunter loses Zendi to heart attack', www.virtualform guide.com.au, 13 May 2011.
6. AAP, 'Melbourne Cup contender Cedarberg drops dead', *Sydney Morning Herald*, 16 August 2011.
7. 'Spate of deaths baffle RVL', *Herald Sun*, 26 September 2011.
8. Ibid.
9. Ibid.
10. Matt Stewart, 'Shock jock Alan Jones claims there is a drugs link to horse deaths', *Herald Sun*, 29 September 2011.
11. Ibid.
12. Brent Zerara, 'Queen of turf sets record straight', *Daily Telegraph*, 20 February 2012.
13. Craig Young, 'Moody gets warning for drug-link incident', *Sydney Morning Herald*, 19 October 2011
14. Tony Arrold, 'Takeover Target a victim of drug slur', *Australian*, 24 May 2008.

15. Mark Jeffreys, 'Trainer Mark Johnson riles Royal Ascot-bound Aussies', *Daily Mail*, 10 June 2008.
16. Greg Wood, 'Poisonous steroids should be flushed from our system', *Guardian*, 10 June 2008.
17. Andrew Webster, 'Cup runneth over with money, not glory', *Daily Telegraph*, 31 October 2011.
18. Walt Bogdanich, Joe Drape, Dara L. Miles and Griffin Palmer, 'Mangled horses, maimed jockeys', *New York Times*, 24 March 2012.
19. Ibid.
20. Ernie Manning, 'Trainer of Oliver horse suspended for two years', *Age*, 6 December 2002.
21. Ibid.
22. AAP, 'Wolfe cleared of blame in jockey's death', 1 December 2003.
23. Damien Murphy, 'Phar Lap poisoning theory down the drain', *Sydney Morning Herald*, 31 October 2011.
24. Andrew Eddy, 'The drugs challenge', *Age*, 28 December 2004.
25. Ibid.
26. Greg Hoy, 'History of horse doping questions sports reputation', *7.30*, ABC TV, 27 December 2011.
27. Ibid.
28. John Schell, 'Even a Waterhouse horse snorts, of course, of course', *Sydney Morning Herald*, 26 July 2005.
29. Kate McClymont, 'The buck stops here: Gai cops cocaine fine', *Sydney Morning Herald*, 30 July 2005.
30. Racing NSW, 'Appeal by Gai Waterhouse (2 September 2005)', www.racingnsw.com.au, 13 September 2005.
31. Tony Arrold, 'Trainer Gai Waterhouse fined $10,000 after filly's drug saga', *Australian*, 16 May 2008.

32. Andrew Eddy, 'The drugs challenge', *Age*, 28 December 2004.
33. AAP, 'Samples from Laming horses positive to EPO', www.abc.net.au, 14 August 2009.
34. Brendan Cormick, 'Trainer Richard Laming banned for three years over EPO', *Australian*, 11 November 2010.
35. 'Episode Five: Follow the Money', *The Track*, ABC TV, August 2000.
36. Ibid.
37. Andrew Eddy, 'The drugs challenge', *Age*, 28 December 2004.
38. Max Presnell and Tony Bourke, 'Police get names in nobbling scandal', *Sydney Morning Herald*, 20 February 1990.
39. Max Presnell, 'Trainers warned to watch for nobblers', *Sydney Morning Herald*, 14 February 1991.
40. Ibid.

Race 8: Rampant

1. Brendan Cormick, 'Disgraced racing boss quits', *Australian*, 15 February 2008.
2. Brendan Cormick, 'Board in dark over Allanson's bets', *Australian*, 16 February 2008.
3. Rod Nicholson, 'I've paid a big penalty: shamed ex-racing chief regrets "foolish" bets', *Sunday Herald Sun*, 19 October 2008.
4. Brendan Cormick, 'Officials still chasing tails after Allanson report finalised', *Australian*, 7 March 2008.
5. Judge G. D. Lewis AM (2008), *A Report on Integrity Assurance in the Victorian Racing Industry*, Melbourne: Department of Justice (Victoria).
6. Ibid.

7. Ibid.
8. Ibid.
9. Nick McKenzie, 'Bad form', *Age*, 14 June 2008.
10. Judge G. D. Lewis AM (2008), *A Report on Integrity Assurance in the Victorian Racing Industry*, Melbourne: Department of Justice (Victoria).
11. AAP, 'Racehorse trainer denies Mokbel links', www.racingandsports.com.au, 24 October 2007.
12. Judge G. D. Lewis AM (2008), *A Report on Integrity Assurance in the Victorian Racing Industry*, Melbourne: Department of Justice (Victoria).
13. Nick McKenzie, 'Bad form', *Age*, 14 June 2008.
14. Ibid.
15. Nick McKenzie, 'No action on race tips', *Age*, 23 April 2009.
16. Nick McKenzie, 'Top jockey took Mokbel cash in return for tips', *Brisbane Times*, 14 June 2008.
17. Judge G. D. Lewis AM (2008), *A Report on Integrity Assurance in the Victorian Racing Industry*, Melbourne: Department of Justice (Victoria).
18. Ibid.
19. Nick McKenzie, 'Bad form', *Age*, 14 June 2008.
20. Judge G. D. Lewis AM (2008), *A Report on Integrity Assurance in the Victorian Racing Industry*, Melbourne: Department of Justice (Victoria).
21. Racing NSW, 'Appeal by Frank Hudson (11 January 2005)', 15 February 2005.
22. Ibid.
23. Judge G. D. Lewis AM (2008), *A Report on Integrity Assurance in the Victorian Racing Industry*, Melbourne: Department of Justice (Victoria).
24. Ibid.

25. Aneeka Simonis, 'The Baillieu Dump: Racing Victoria looks at new ways of charging jockeys', www.crikey.com.au, 31 October 2011.
26. Patrick Smith, 'Danny Nikolic caught in betting probe', *Australian*, 13 February 2010.
27. Adam Hamilton, 'Stipes' bet probe after Finishing Card loses to New Venture', *Herald Sun*, 10 February 2010.
28. Racing Victoria Limited, 'Reasons for Decision in the matter of jockey Mr Danny Nikolic as heard on Monday 21 June to Wednesday 23 June 2010', www.racingvictoria.net.au, 29 June 2010.
29. Nick Tabakoff, 'Neville Clements speaks out', *Herald Sun*, 12 March 2010.
30. Patrick Bartley, '"Outsider" with a lifelong passion for racing: the new RVL chief', *Age*, 23 July 2008.
31. Mark Ryan, 'Inquiry finds organised crime links to Victorian racing', *Daily Telegraph*, 14 August 2008.

Race 9: Big Hurdles

1. Robert Windmill, 'From hospital bed to winners circle', *Sunday Telegraph*, 4 March 2012.
2. AAP, 'O'Brien cops warning for tweet', www.virtualformguide.com.au, 24 May 2012.
3. Michael Manley, 'Horse deaths at Flemington raise queries over track conditions', *Herald Sun*, 20 May 2012.
4. RSPCA, 'What is the RSPCA position on racing two-year-old horses?', www.rspca.org.au, 1 December 2009.
5. HorseRacingKills, 'Two-year-old racing', www.horseracingkills.org.
6. Interview with the author, 23 March 2012.
7. Adam Hamilton, 'Horse put down at Warrnambool jumps race after breaking its leg', *Herald Sun*, 5 May 2010.

8. RSPCA Victoria, 'RSPCA Victoria withdraws from horse cruelty prosecution', www.rspcavic.org, 2 March 2012.
9. Interview with the author, 22 March 2012.
10. Patrick Bartley, 'Relief at last for horseman at centre of jumps storm', *Age*, 1 March 2012.
11. Ibid.
12. Interview with the author, 22 March 2012.
13. Tim Habel and Matt Stewart, 'Elderly woman, toddler injured by runaway horse still in hospital', *Herald Sun*, 6 May 2011.
14. 'Woman from Snowy River', *Australian Story*, ABC TV, 19 March 2012.
15. Ibid.
16. Ibid.
17. Ibid.
18. Ibid.
19. John Stewart, 'RSPCA study finds violation of whip rules', *Lateline*, ABC TV, 20 March 2012.
20. Ibid.
21. 'Academic's anti-whip report given the flick', *Daily Telegraph*, 22 March 2012.
22. Max Presnell, 'Whip wailers need a dose of thoroughbred reality', *Sydney Morning Herald*, 26 March 2012.
23. Max Presnell, 'The jig's up this time but battery power will live on', *Sydney Morning Herald*, 19 January 2007.
24. Mark Ryan, 'Just blatant cruelty', *Daily Telegraph*, 17 January 2007.
25. Brendan Cormick, 'Never question love and pride in jumps racing', *Australian*, 8 May 2010.
26. Ibid.
27. Ariella Hayek (2004), Epidemiology of Horses Leaving the Racing and Breeding Industries. A thesis submitted

in partial fulfilment of the requirements for the degree of Bachelor of Science, University of Sydney.

28. Ibid.
29. Amanda Doughty, 'An epidemiological survey of the dentition and foot condition of slaughtered horses in Australia', School of Animal Studies and The Centre for Animal Welfare and Ethics, the University of Queensland, Gatton, June 2008.
30. Sally Webster, 'NZ horses dead meat in Europe', *Herald on Sunday*, 29 April 2012.
31. Sally Webster, 'From stable to table', *Herald on Sunday*, 29 April 2012.
32. Ibid.
33. Interview with the author, 22 March 2012.
34. Interview with the author, 23 March 2012.
35. Ibid.
36. Ray Thomas, 'Diva Queen of the Decade', *Daily Telegraph*, 1 January 2010.
37. Lissa Christopher, 'Leading slow horses to slaughter', *Sydney Morning Herald*, 3 January 2010.
38. Adrian Dunn, 'Disaster at first hurdles', *Daily Telegraph*, 29 March 2012.

Race 10: Red Hots

1. Tom Reilly and Chris Roots, 'Insider blew whistle on corruption in trotting', *Sydney Morning Herald*, 3 September 2011.
2. Chris Roots, 'Harness industry clean-out not before time says frustrated owner', *Sydney Morning Herald*, 28 November 2011.
3. Ibid.
4. Tom Reilly and Chris Roots, 'Insider blew whistle on corruption in trotting', *Sydney Morning Herald*, 3 September 2011.

5. Brent Zerafa, 'Liaison of intrigue as trot scandal widens', *Daily Telegraph*, 24 August 2011.
6. Nick Tabakoff, 'Corruption probe to dwarf Fine Cotton', *Daily Telegraph*, 13 October 2011.
7. Brent Zerafa, 'Net widens', *Daily Telegraph*, 27 November 2011.
8. Brent Zerafa, 'Dark cloud hangs over red hots', *Daily Telegraph*, 28 November 2011.
9. Paul Bibby, 'Trainer fears for family's safety, inquiry told', *Sydney Morning Herald*, 13 January 2012.
10. Ibid.
11. Ibid.
12. Chris Roots, 'Probity to the fore as Kelly begins the rebuild', *Sun-Herald*, 5 February 2012.
13. Andrew Rule, 'A crooked mile', *Good Weekend*, 29 January 2005.
14. Ibid.
15. Geoff Cumming and Phil Taylor, 'Racing: Blue Magic and the trail of death', *New Zealand Herald*, 20 November 2004.
16. Andrew Rule, 'A crooked mile', *Good Weekend*, 29 January 2005.

Race 11: A New Thread

1. John Ellicott, 'Police reopen 1984 murder case', *Illawarra Mercury*, 8 December 2007.
2. Ibid.
3. Ibid.
4. Rick Feneley, 'Racing family at odds over brother's amazing claim', *Age*, 30 November 2010.
5. 'Episode Five: Follow the Money', *The Track*, ABC TV, August 2000.

6. Ibid.
7. Robert Craddock, 'They said they'd shoot my brother', *Courier-Mail*, 13 August 2001 (quoted on page 105 of *Waterhouse and Smith* by John Ellicott, Hardie Grant Books, 2008).
8. *What Are the Odds?*, page 410.
9. Ibid.
10. John Ellicott (2008), *Waterhouse and Smith*, Melbourne, Hardie Grant Books, page 112.
11. Ross Solly, 'Robbie Waterhouse book-making licence?', *The World Today*, ABC Radio, 18 June 2001.
12. John Ellicott (2008), *Waterhouse and Smith*, Melbourne, Hardie Grant Books, page 120.
13. Ibid., page 122.
14. 'Episode Five: Follow the Money', *The Track*, ABC TV, August 2000.
15. Ibid.
16. *What Are the Odds?*, page 407.
17. 'Episode Five: Follow the Money', *The Track*, ABC TV, August 2000.
18. Ibid.
19. Ray Thomas, 'Gai and Singo's heavenly Joy', *Sunday Telegraph*, 22 April 2012.
20. Ibid.
21. Rick Feneley, 'Racing family at odds over brother's amazing claim', *Sydney Morning Herald*, 30 November 2010.
22. Ibid.
23. *What Are the Odds?*, page 447.
24. Interview with the author, July 2011.
25. Adam Shand, 'John Gillespie says he won $1.8 million on Fine Cotton's race', *Sunday Mail*, 23 May 2010.

26. Ibid.
27. Ibid.
28. Ibid.
29. Interview with the author, 11 May 2012.
30. John Ellicott (2008), *Waterhouse and Smith*, Melbourne, Hardie Grant Books, page 150.
31. Ibid.
32. Chris Roots, 'Gai joyous but hubby feels pain after mile', *Sun-Herald*, 22 April 2012.

Race 12: Trackside Tantrum

1. Ray Thomas, 'Inquiry looms into circumstances surrounding John Singleton, Gai Waterhouse and the More Joyous feud', News Limited Network, 28 April 2013.
2. Ibid.
3. Ben Broad, 'John Singleton's frustration with Gai Waterhouse may have been building since 2012 Cox Plate barrier draw', News Limited Network, 28 April 2013.
4. TVN broadcast, 27 April 2013: http://www.youtube.com/watch?v=Nx6htI086ic&NR=1&feature=endscreen
5. Tim Elliott, 'The inside running on a racing bust-up', *Sydney Morning Herald*, 4 May 2013.
6. Ibid.
7. Caryl Williamson, 'Waterhouse fires back', *Newcastle Herald*, 29 April 2013.
8. Tim Elliott, 'The inside running on a racing bust-up', *Sydney Morning Herald*, 4 May 2013.
9. Chris Roots, 'No more joy, Singo splits with lady Gai', *Sun Herald*, 28 April 2013.
10. Ibid.
11. Ibid.

12. Max Presnell, 'No winners as racing's odd couple call it quits', *Sun-Herald*, 28 April 2013.
13. Ibid.
14. Ibid.
15. Caryl Williamson, 'Waterhouse fires back', *Newcastle Herald*, 29 April 2013.
16. Ibid.
17. Ibid.
18. Ray Thomas, 'Knives out as feud keeps coming', *Herald Sun*, 5 May 2013.
19. Ibid.
20. Kate McClymont, 'Gai cracks the whip', *Sydney Morning Herald*, 7 May 2013.
21. Ray Thomas, 'Knives out as feud keeps coming', *Herald Sun*, 5 May 2013.
22. Neil Chenoweth, 'He was drunk and she was very stroppy', *Australian Financial Review*, 7 May 2013.
23. Fiona Carruthers, 'Horseplay rebounds on racing royalty', *Australian Financial Review*, 7 May 2013.
24. Ibid.
25. 'Man up Singleton tells Andrew Johns', *Australian Financial Review*, 7 May 2012: http://www.afr.com/p/national/man_up_singleton_tells_andrew_johns_aWrGuhuyPsK2zuIqE6LP4I
26. Tim Elliott, 'The inside running on a racing bust-up', *Sydney Morning Herald*, 4 May 2013.
27. Phil Rothfield, 'Joey's recall shows he is merely mortal', *Daily Telegraph*, 14 May 2013.
28. Roy Masters, 'Off and running. How three-letter-word started saga that transfixed Sydney', *Sydney Morning Herald*, 14 May 2013.

29. Phil Rothfield, 'Joey's recall shows he is merely mortal', *Daily Telegraph*, 14 May 2013.
30. Richard Zachariah, 'Privilege stoking fires of a bitter conflict', *Daily Telegraph*, 13 May 2013.
31. Lisa Davies and Kate McClymont, 'Racing tells Tom: grow up', *Sydney Morning Herald*, 14 May 2013.
32. Ibid.
33. Ibid.
34. Ibid.
35. Ibid.
36. Ibid.
37. Mark Latham, 'Horse racing on the wrong track', *Australian Financial Review*, 18 May 2013.
38. Damien Murphy, 'Gai fined $5500 but takes whip to stewards', *Sydney Morning Herald*, 28 May 2013.
39. Ibid.
40. Caryl Williamson and Nic Ashman, 'Waterhouse takes swipe at lame rule after Joyous fine', *Sydney Morning Herald*, 24 July 2013.
41. Christian Nicolussi, 'No joy but it's finished', *Daily Telegraph*, 24 July 2013.
42. Tom Waterhouse, 'I'm sorry and I have listened to your message', *Daily Telegraph*, 31 May 2013.
43. Matt Stewart and AAP, 'Back on track', *Daily Telegraph*, 16 July 2013.
44. Mark Buttler, 'No charges for Nikolic over race-fixing claims', *Daily Telegraph*, 16 July 2013.

Epilogue

1. Darren Beadman and Craig Heilmann (1998), *Daylight Ahead: the Darren Beadman Story*, K.E.G Publishing, page 22.

2. Ibid.
3. Ibid.
4. Ibid.
5. Craig Young, 'Beadman in tears as gravity of fall sinks in', *Sydney Morning Herald*, 26 March 2012.
6. Ibid.
7. Ray Thomas, 'The day I gave racing away', Daily Telegraph, 13 April 2012.
8. Craig Young, 'V'Landys bullish about the future of the state's game', *Sydney Morning Herald*, 2 July 2012.
9. Karen Kissane, 'Home in a fretful finish, heart-stopping Caviar may have raced her last', *Sydney Morning Herald*, 25 June 2012.
10. Nick McKenzie, *Four Corners*, ABC, 6 August 2012.
11. Ibid.
12. Interview with the author, 10 August 2012.
13. Brent Zerafa, 'Too hot to trot,' *Daily Telegraph*, 18 July 2012.
14. Ken Callander, 'Stewards owe it to the punters to find out why Gai's horses are hitting brick walls', *Daily Telegraph*, 11 June 2012.
15. Ibid.
16. Ken Callender, 'Memo Gai: stewards are there to uphold the integrity of racing', *Daily Telegraph*, 18 June 2012.
17. Interview with the author, 10 August 2012.
18. Ibid.

ACKNOWLEDGEMENTS

And they're off! First out of the gate for thanks in a book of this kind is my publisher at Random House, Alison Urquhart, who gently persuaded me that a book which looked at the seedy underbelly of Australia's racing industry would be a worthwhile publication. She was, as always, absolutely right.

Producing a book, like fielding a racehorse, is a team effort. It could not have been done without the support of the team at Random House, led by publishing director Nikki Christer. Special mention has to go to the most diligent and eagle-eyed of editors, Catherine Hill, who has lived and breathed every word. Anything you have subsequently heard about it can be attributed to the efforts of publicist Jessica Malpass. The fact that we all slept at night was because lawyer Richard Potter once again cast his careful eye over everything.

A huge amount of research went into this book. My former Fairfax colleagues Helen Bayliss, Jim O'Rourke, Heath Gilmore, Richard Coleman and Craig Young deserve special mention. Frank Walker and David Hickie provided reassurance and guidance by reading an early draft of the manuscript. There are many others closely involved in the racing industry who care greatly for its future and spoke to me on condition of anonymity. I thank them for their trust and hope I have conveyed their fears and concerns accurately.

My office colleagues Nigel Wright and Robbie Graham displayed enormous tolerance as the stress mounted and the piles of paper and documents spread inexorably across the floor. They have my eternal gratitude for providing a sounding board when I needed one and for not once complaining. Moral support was also provided by my good friends Sean Berry, Miranda Wood and Sarah Price. Last, in what should be a photo finish of thanks, are the three people who lived this book every day with me: my daughters, Emma and Jane, and my partner, Therese. Thank you for putting up with me.

INDEX

Matthew Benns is a freelance journalist and is the author of the bestselling *The Men Who Killed Qantas* and *Dirty Money*, published by Random House. He has previously worked as a journalist for numerous British newspapers including the *Daily Mail*, *The Times*, the *Guardian*, *Today* and the *Sun*, and also as an investigative journalist for the Australian *Sun-Herald*. He lives in Sydney.

Also by Matthew Benns

When the Bough Breaks
The Men Who Killed Qantas
Dirty Money